THE LIFE AND THOUGHT OF YEH SHIH

Winston Wan Lo

The Life
and Thought
of Yeh Shih

UNIVERSITY PRESSES OF FLORIDA

THE CHINESE UNIVERSITY OF HONG KONG

Library of Congress Catalog Card Number 73-92410

University Presses of Florida, Gainesville, Florida 32306
The Chinese University of Hong Kong, Shatin N.T., Hong Kong

For permissions and other rights under this Copyright, please contact:

Publications Office
The Chinese University of Hong Kong
677 Nathan Road, 12th Floor
Kowloon, Hong Kong

Printed in Hong Kong
in 11 on 12 pt Imprint type
by Dai Nippon Printing Co. (H.K.) Ltd.

To my father
who exemplifies the best of Chinese scholarship

Contents

Acknowledgement

THE PRESENT book is based on the dissertation which I submitted to Harvard University in 1970 in partial fulfilment for the requirement of the Ph.D. degree in the Joint History and Far Eastern Languages program. Through the years in which the project grew from an idea to a doctoral dissertation and then to a book, I have been deeply in the debt of many people. My thanks are due first of all to Professor Lien-sheng Yang who initiated me into this rewarding subject and has provided me with unfailing guidance ever since; to Professor James T.C. Liu whose thorough review of the entire manuscript spared me of many unnecessary mistakes and enabled me to recast the subject-matter in a more coherent form; to Professors John K. Fairbank and Benjamin I. Schwartz for their valuable suggestions.

I am also greatly indebted to Professor George A. Lensen for his generous encouragement of my research efforts. I also take this opportunity to thank the History Department of Florida State University for granting me a leave of absence during the academic year 1972–73 to expedite the revisions of my manuscript for publication. Financial support during the leave of absence came partly from the University of Hong Kong, my *alma mater*, for which I am indebted to my former mentor, Dr. L.K. Young, Professor and Head of the Department of History, for making the arrangements.

A word of appreciation is also due Mr. T.C. Lai, Mr. Adrian Teng and Mr. C.C. Ho and others of the staff of the Publications Office of The Chinese University of Hong Kong for undertaking the editing and printing of the book. With methodical thoroughness they weeded out typographical errors and imposed a consistency of style. I am also indebted to Mr. Philip L. Martin, Director of the Florida State University Press for consenting to be co-publisher of the book.

Among others who have in various manners contributed to the readability of the text, I must mention my good friend Professor Andrew J. Nathan of Columbia University who went through a considerable portion of the manuscript meticulously and lastly my wife, Ann Lee-on, who has struggled with me through all the stages that the manuscript went through, serving as my faithfull research assistant, typist, editor and critic simultaneously.

I am, of course, responsible for all the imperfections of the book.

WINSTON WAN LO

Introduction

THE SUBJECT of this study, Yeh Shih (1150–1223), was not a byword for wisdom in China. He was merely a scholar, although to be recognized as a scholar in a land where almost every one of the thousands of mandarins in government service had scholarly pretensions was no mean accomplishment.[1]

His scholarly activities contributed to the rise of the Neo-Confucian ideology which held sway in China as the state orthodoxy during the Yüan (1260–1367), Ming (1368–1643) and Ch'ing (1644–1911) dynasties; but he was also its most uncompromising critic. He wrote extensively on every aspect of the sinological universe; but the most influential of his writings do not bear on academic matters at all — they were addressed to the realities of the regime under which he lived. In his attempt to mould the attitudes of his contemporaries, he may be considered a publicist. Blessed with a lucid and powerful style, his success as a publicist was due, moreover, to the coherence and scope of his writings. Encompassing every aspect of state and society, they provided a penetrating commentary on his times, a transitional period in the development of Chinese society.

Nowadays, after the radical transformation of Chinese society brought about by the communists, it is unlikely that anybody takes the once prevalent myth of the "unchanging China" seriously.[2] Chinese society before the coming of the communists was not entirely static although the tempo of change was imperceptibly slow. There were, however, times in the long life of this civilization when the pace of change quickened so that the cumulative result of change became perceptible to the discerning mind. The two or three hundred years preceding the birth of Yeh Shih were a good example. The process of change had been carried so far in this case that renowned scholars have

---

[1] His biography in the official history of the Sung dynasty (*Sung-shih*, to be cited subsequently as SS) was assigned to the *ju-lin* (Confucian Scholars) section. See SS 434. This official biography is reproduced in the Chung-hua ed. of the collected works of Yeh Shih and will be cited subsequently as YSC, "Pen-chuan".

[2] The great metahistorians, Hegel, Sprengler, Arnold Toynbee, each produced a slightly different version of this myth. For a handy reference to their ideas, see John Meskill, ed., *The Patterns of Chinese History* (D.C. Heath: 1965), ch. 2, "World History from the West", pp. 12–24.

referred to these years as a watershed or "Great Divide" in the evolution of Chinese culture.[3]

The quickening of pace started during the seventh or eighth century when the T'ang dynasty ruled in China. Despite the splendor of the imperial court and the proud record of the dynasty in military conquests and civil administration, the T'ang dynasty was in many respects a medieval empire. Society was dominated by a hereditary aristocracy (men-fa) who owned much wealth and to a great extent controlled the government.[4] Urbanization and inter-regional trade were at a low level. The economy was subsistence-oriented and most of the peasants could be regarded as serfs owned either by the state or by the aristocratic families.

This T'ang pattern was being gradually eroded by changes that were going on in the various facets of Chinese society. By the time of the Sung dynasty (960–1276), a new patterning of the institutions was emerging. The subsistence economy of serf cultivators was increasingly giving way to a market-oriented agriculture, flourishing cities of commerce and industry, and considerable inter-regional trade.[5] Serfs became landowning or tenant peasants. The hereditary men-fa aristocracy was replaced by an elite based on personal achievements. China was acquiring the traits characteristic of modern societies: private ownership of land as opposed to communal ownership, status based on achievements rather than heredity, considerable social mobility, etc. In fact it is the fashion among many scholars under the influence of the Kyōto School of sinologists to regard the Sung period as the beginning of modern times in Chinese history.[6]

However, the process of change seemed to have slowed down by the last century of the Sung period. The momentum was lost and when the alien dynasties, viz. Jürchen Chin (1115–1234) and Mongol Yüan (1260–1367) were established in China, with their indifference to

[3] For a critical evaluation of the modern schemes of periodization which recognized the Sung period as a turning point in Chinese history, see James T.C. Liu, "The Neo-Traditional Period", in Changes in Sung China (D.C. Heath), ed. by James T.C. Liu and Peter Golas.

[4] The original impetus for systematic study of T'ang history and society among Chinese and Japanese scholars probably came from the theorizing of the great Japanese Sinologist, Naitō Torajiro. The most well-known Chinese authorities on the T'ang is Ch'en Yin-ko. Among Japanese scholars, Niida Tōru on legal institutions, Sudō Yoshiyuki on land and economic issues may be mentioned. In recent years, Denis Twitchett, E.G. Pulleyblank and Edward Shafer have made valuable contributions to our knowledge of the T'ang period.

[5] For a convenient account of this societal change, see Edward Kracke, Jr., "Change within Tradition", in Far Eastern Quarterly 14 (1954–55), pp. 479–488. For more bibliographic information with regard to economic development, see ch. 6, note 1.

[6] See James T.C. Liu, "The Neo-Traditional Period".

culture, there was evidence of regression. By the middle of the fourteenth century, China had in fact reverted to an earlier, more primitive form of socio-political organization.[7] Therefore, the beginning of modern times in China, if we accept the Sung period as the beginning, did not lead to the sustained economic development and greatly improved standards of living that we customarily associate with the modern age.

The failure to achieve sustained development in China was not due to the paucity of natural resources or the lethargy of the Chinese people. China under the Sung dynasty, even with the Northern provinces cut off by the Jürchen invasion, was bigger and more prosperous than Western Europe of the late Middle Ages. Technologically, Sung China was also well ahead of its Western counterparts as the medieval travellers from Europe testified. One of the most convincing arguments that has been adduced by Western sinologists to explain the stagnation of traditional China was the inhibiting effect of the bureaucratic tradition.[8] No areas of life were immune to the probing scrutiny of a theoretically omnipotent state which appropriated all vital resources for its own purpose. Private initiative was either stifled or directed into channels that posed no threat to the security of the state. There was nothing in Chinese civilization comparable to the Western bourgeoisie, historically the source of dynamic growth of Europe in modern times. This is because the charters and immunities, which, as a sort of institutional greenhouse, nurtured the tender plant of European bourgeoisie, were entirely lacking in China.

Political and social institutions are not altogether autonomous entities: they owe their staying power to the legitimation provided by widely accepted ideologies. The capitalistic institutions which had been developing for a long time in medieval Europe, for example, required the rationalizing doctrines of the Reformed Churches of the sixteenth century to overcome deep-seated ideological and institutional barriers before they could usher in the commercial and industrial revolutions.[9] By the same token, it may be argued, the bureaucratic tradition in China

---

[7] Evidences of regression in social structure and economic organization are easy to document. In both areas, China under Mongol rule showed an increase of the element of coersion, e.g., slaves increasing at the expense of free men, forced requisition of goods at the expense of free trade. For a systematic account of Chinese society under the Mongols, see Meng Ssu-ming, *Yüan-tai she-hui chieh-chi chih-tu* (Peiping: 1938) and Franz Shurmann, *Economic Structure of the Yüan Dynasty* (Harvard University Press: 1956).

[8] The most eloquent exponent of this view was Etienne Balazs; see his *Chinese Civilization and Bureaucracy* (Yale University Press: 1964), particularly chs. 1, 2, 4.

[9] This is the celebrated Max Weber's thesis "The Protestant Ethic and the Rise of Capitalism".

required the sanction of Confucian teaching to maintain its sway in China.

To a greater extent than the powerful bureaucratic tradition, Confucius and his teaching have been accused of holding back progress in China. This was the line of attack of the iconoclasts of the May Fourth movement.[10] The implication was that Confucianism was a conservative creed and as such inhibited change. From the point of view of the impartial student of history, this accusation is unwarranted because Confucius, who lived and died during the feudal age of China, could not prevent the exploitation of his teaching by the imperial rulers of China hundreds of years after his death. What came to be known as Confucianism during the imperial age of China, therefore, did not correspond exactly to the original teaching of Confucius. It was a synthetic product drawing its content from the teaching of Confucius and from other sources in accordance with what may be called "the principle of elective affinity"—ideas purporting to come from Confucius which promoted the interests of rulers were emphasized, unfavorable ideas were suppressed.[11] There is no logical reason why this imperial Confucianism should always be a conservative or inhibiting force. Professor DeBary, for instance, has drawn our attention to the fact that a recognizable form of Confucianism was an important ingredient in the thinking of the leading statesmen who presided over the transformation of Japan during the Meiji period.[12] The Chinese reform movement of the late nineteenth century also indicates that, given sufficient provocation, Confucian-minded statesmen were capable of abandoning time-honored methods of government and entertaining thoughts of reform. It is therefore unwise to regard conservatism as the given datum of Confucianism; rather, it should be viewed as a problem to be explained.

Confucianism, the major factor in the evolution of Chinese culture, was caught up in the process of change and development that characterized China of the T'ang and Sung period. This was inevitable as it could not remain unchanged when the socio-economic structure of Chinese society changed. The Sung version of Confucianism was so

---

[10] See the classic account of this subject, Chow Tse-tsung, *May-fourth Movement* (Harvard University Press: 1960), particularly ch. 12.

[11] For a comprehensive account of the ingredients incorporated into imperial Confucianism of the Han period, see Tjan Tjoe Som, *Po Hu T'ung* (E. J. Brill: 1949). The term "elective affinity", originally coined by Max Weber, is now part of the professional vocabulary of the sociologists. See J. Milton Yinger, *Religion and the Individual*, pp. 140, 215, 217–218, 299.

[12] William DeBary, "Some Common Tendencies in Neo-Confucianism", in Arthur Wright, ed., *Confucianism in Action* (Stanford University Press: 1959).

different from the classical Confucianism of the Han period (B.C. 206 –
A.D. 220) that it is customary to refer to it as Neo-Confucianism. The
new pattern of classical exegesis, ethics, social and political organization
that characterized Neo-Confucianism did not emerge overnight; it took
years to evolve. Before the intellectual trends crystallized into the
Neo-Confucian pattern, we may assume that there was considerable
fluidity in the ideological basis of Chinese culture. It is not inconceivable
that Neo-Confucianism could have evolved in such a manner as to
reinforce and sanction the process of change and development that
was transforming China from a medieval society to one possessing many
attributes of a modern society. The implication of this line of reasoning
is worth pursuing.

We have indicated that under certain conditions Confucian statesmen
were capable of responding to external stimuli in a positive manner.
During the Sung period, there were two sets of circumstances which,
by challenging the ruling elite to exert themselves, could conceivably
have generated the required dynamics to sustain the long-term process
of change.

If Sung Confucianists were unconcerned about the slowing down of
the long-term development process, they were or should have been
highly sensitive to the cyclical process of dynastic rise and decline.
Hitherto no dynasty had been able to stay in power permanently.
Successive dynasties that ruled in China seemed to have followed a
recognizable sequence of development, viz. a period of consolidation
following the seizure of power by the founder of the dynasty, peace
and prosperity brought by the energy and administrative ability of
his immediate successors, a long period of decline due to deterioration
of the administrative machinery, inept rulers and mounting fiscal
difficulties, and then the end with the eruption of rebellions or foreign
invasions dealing the *coup de grace*.[13]

Sung scholar-officials were proud of the achievements of their dynasty
in civil administration and justly so. The dynasty seemed to have
solved many of the problems that plagued its predeccessors, such as
arrogant army generals, semi-independent military governors, powerful
consort families and eunuchs seeking to play kingmakers. It had an
efficient system of provincial administration which enabled it to exercise
unprecedented control over the territories of the empire. Humane and
generous in dealing with both officials and commoners alike, the
dynasty could count upon their loyalty to an extent rivaling that

[13] Most modern historians recognize a cyclical pattern in Chinese history. For a
concise account, see Edwin O. Reischauer, "The Dynastic Cycle", in *East Asia:
The Great Tradition* (Houghton Mifflin Co.: 1960), pp. 114–118.

received by the Han and the T'ang, the mightiest dynasties of the past.[14]

In view of the impressive credentials of the Sung ruling elite in coping with major political problems, it is perhaps reasonable to assume that in their most optimistic moments they took the permanence of their regime for granted. Under the illusion of permanence, they probably thought that they could be spared the fate of all previous dynasties, namely, decline and fall; the process of dynastic decline which inexorably took hold of all previous dynasties would be suspended for them. We may also assume that when unmistakable signs of the process of dynastic decline were revealed, despite their vain hopes of permanence, they would make strenuous efforts to combat the process.

However, it is not always easy for people closely identified with the regime in power to recognize and acknowledge the signs of decay. Prolonged success breeds complacency, with the result that warnings of danger are habitually ignored. The social and political critic in China who drew attention to unsavory aspects of reality was normally as coldly received by the authorities as the prophet of doom, Jeremiah, was treated by the elders and high priests of Jerusalem. Can we assume that the critics of the Sung dynasty fared better?

Unlike the Han and the T'ang dynasties, the Sung dynasty was never known for its martial prowess. Even before the dynasty came into existence, the area around modern Peking had been incorporated into the semi-barbarian Liao empire founded by the Khitan people. By the beginning of the eleventh century, the Tangghut kingdom of Hsi-hsia gained independence from Sung China, annexing some territories in the North-west. The Jürchens of Manchuria came to power in the beginning of the twelve century, toppled the Liao empire and marched down into the North China Plain.[15] Sung defences crumbled all along the line. The capital K'ai-feng fell, the emperor and his clan were taken prisoner. For a moment, it appeared that the Sung dynasty was finished. A younger brother of the captured emperor, however, evaded capture, rallied the loyalist forces and managed to perpetuate Sung rule in South China, conceding the North to the Jürchen conquerors. The capital of the Sung empire was moved to Hangchow and,

---

[14] For a comprehensive account of the Sung dynasty, see Edward Kracke, Jr., *Civil Service in Sung China* (Harvard University Press: 1953), ch. 2.

[15] For the origin of the Jürchen, see *Chih-shih* 1 (History of the Chin Dynasty), compiled by T'o T'o *et al*. Notable contributions to the study of the Jürchen and the Chin period have been made by Mikami Tsungio, Toyama Gunji, Jing-shen Tao and Ts'ung-wu Yao. For the Jürchen invasion and its aftermath, the convenient work by Chang P'u, *Sung-shih chi-shih pen-mo* (The Complete Story of Important Episodes in Sung History), may be consulted. To be cited as SSCSPM.

in recognition of this move, historians refer to the dynasty after the Jürchen invasion as the Southern Sung (1126–1276) and that before the invasion as the Northern Sung (960–1125). The Southern Sung co-existed with the Chin empire of the Jürchens for about a hundred years until both were annihilated by the rise of a more virile people along China's inner Asian frontier, the Mongols.

Thus by stages, China passed under barbarian domination. Ruling China by the right of conquest, the foreign conquerors had little regard for Confucian values. The Mongols in fact went out of their way to humble the Confucian literati assigning them a legal status just a shade above that of the prostitutes. Considering that under the Sung regime, the literati were closely related to the ruling elite, their downfall was precipitous. Faced with such bleak prospects, did they make any effort to avert the approaching fate?

Historically, as far as the Sung scholar-officials were concerned, the event that produced the greatest trauma was the Jürchen invasion and conquest. By comparison, the loss of territories to the Khitan and Tangghut states was of marginal importance. The total conquest of China by the Mongols lay in the future and could not be easily anticipated. The Jürchen invasion which necessitated the transfer of the capital to Hangchow and the loss of territories North of the Huai River was a shattering blow. The territories lost to the invaders probably represented one third of the area of the Sung empire at its height, but due to their political and historic significance, the loss was more grievously felt.[16] North China was the homeland of the great dynasties of the past from which they exercised rule and hegemony over the entire Chinese world.

For reasons of expediency, the Southern Sung acceded to the Chin claim of paramountcy at the time a peace treaty was signed in 1142, putting an end to the hostilities between the two powers. This formal acknowledgement of Chin paramountcy, coupled with a loss of territories, put a severe strain on the prestige of the Sung ruling elite. The long-accepted doctrine of the Mandate of Heaven which furnished legitimacy to the dynasty in power recognized only one legitimate holder of the mandate, who should be the paramount lord of China.

[16] In pre-modern times when provinces and kingdoms were regarded as the patrimonies of kings and princes, a ruler usually did not receive uniform support from all the lands he claimed proprietory rights. The territorial possessions therefore had varying significance for the regime in power, depending on the amount of material and sentimental support received. For a treatment of this subject in Chinese history, see Joseph B.R. Whitney, *China, Area, Administration and Nation Building* (University of Chicago, Dept. of Geography, Research Paper No. 123: 1970), ch. 2. "China's Space-polity".

Since the Southern Sung did not fulfill these conditions, it was difficult to sustain the claim of legitimacy.

To bridge the gap between theory and reality, the ruling elite of the Southern Sung fostered the ideology of *hui-fu* (recovery of lost territories and lost grandeur). The current humiliation of the dynasty was, according to this ideology, but a temporary aberration which would eventually pass away. In line with this way of thinking, Hangchow was not referred to as *ching-shih* (imperial capital) but only as *hsing-chai* (halting place of the imperial carriage). Maps were prepared and inscribed on stone tablets in schools and colleges to affirm the claim of the dynasty to the lost territories.[17]

Before the Sung-Chin relationship stabilized into a pattern of peaceful co-existence with the conclusion of the peace treaty in 1142, *hui-fu* could be regarded as the avowed objective of the dynasty; after that, little more than a convenient rationalization. However, as a piece of rationalization it could also be a source of embarrassment to the dynasty.

The existence of the officially sanctioned myth of *hui-fu* dramatized the inadequacy of the dynasty. As the years went by and no visible progress towards the goal was made, a sceptical frame of mind developed. The commitment of the rulers to the goal was questioned and pressure for a reappraisal of the basic policies and institutions of the dynasty increased. Can we assume that this pressure to live up to the claim of the dynasty to be the legitimate ruler of China generated sufficient pressure to counteract the process of dynastic decline?

In considering this question, we may find it expedient to deal with the Southern Sung period first as the process of dynastic decline reached a more serious stage at that time than during the period of the Northern Sung. The myth of *hui-fu* was essentially a Southern Sung phenomenon. The traumatic effects of the Northern Sung debacle and Jürchen invasion were also crucial to the crystallization of the Neo-Confucianist ideology.

The life of Yeh Shih spanned the crucial middle years of the Southern Sung dynasty. He witnessed two abortive attempts by the dynasty to implement the *hui-fu* objective through military conquest. He also saw the Neo-Confucian ideology rise to a position of undisputed dominance in the academic and intellectual life of the country. He was naturally no mere observer of these developments, but an active participant. His celebrated political commentary was in fact written to promote the *hui-fu* ideology, and as a statesman, he worked untiringly

---

[17] Masuda Tadao, "Sōdai no chizu to minzoku undō", *Shirin* 27 (1942).

for the regeneration of the dynasty. As a scholar, he not only contributed to the rise of Neo-Confucianism but sought to direct its development into desirable channels.

I have not attempted to cover every aspect of his life and thought. While there is no question that as a person and thinker, he was interesting in his own right,[18] it cannot be denied that his significance lies primarily in his historic position: he provided a frame of reference in the (as yet little explored) ideological landscape of the Southern Sung period. The main body of this study is in two parts. The first part, essentially biographical in nature, follows Yeh Shih's career. The second part seeks to analyse his approaches to the many problems confronting the dynasty in a series of topical studies.

[18] As an indication of Yeh Shih's intellectual stature, it may be observed that Huang Tsung-hsi (1610–1695), who pioneered in the systematic study of the history of Neo-Confucianism, endorsed Sun Chih-hung's (Yeh Shih's disciple) evaluation of Yeh Shih, "Shui-hsin (Yeh Shih's courtesy name) was a man of rare, transcending insight, treading not the steps of ordinary men." See *Sung-Yüan hsüeh-an* (to be cited subsequently as SYHA) 54. The unconventionality of Yeh Shih's thought on some subjects has intrigued a number of modern scholars. Lü Chen-yu, for instance, sees in him a forerunner of philosophic materialism in China. See his essay, "Lun Yeh Shih ssu-hsiang" (An Evaluation of Yeh Shih's Thought), in *Yeh Shih chi* (Chung-hua shu-chü, Peking: 1961), 3 vols. The foregoing edition of Yeh Shih's writings will be used for subsequent citations. The abbreviation YSC applies to the first two of the three volume set, and YSC PC (*Yeh Shih chi Pieh-chi*) refers to the third Volume. The abbreviation HHCYHM will be used to refer to Yeh Shih's bibliographical survey of Chinese literature, *Hsi-hsüeh chi-yen hsü-mu* (Ching-hsiang lou ts'ung-shu ed., 50 *chüan*).

CHAPTER ONE

The Changing Intellectual Climate

I

IN VIEW of the problematical nature of Neo-Confucianism, it may be desirable to reconsider the issue raised in the Introduction. The hypothetical question is: could Neo-Confucianism have evolved in such a manner as to lend sanction to the process of development that was evident in Chinese society of the T'ang and Sung period?

Before we can presume to answer the question, it is necessary to know what actually happened. To know what actually happened is no easy matter. The object of our investigation, the evolution of Neo-Confucianism, is not a tangible, disparate reality, but the ethos of a civilization in transition as expressed in the subtle changes men felt and thought of themselves, their institutions and their universe. To gauge the extent of change, I will make use of a simple descriptive model. Our model will focus on two successive stages in the evolution of the Neo-Confucian ethos, corresponding roughly to the two historiographical sub-divisions of the Sung dynasty, the Northern Sung and the Southern Sung.

The period of the Northern Sung was a time of optimism and of faith in the efficacy of human efforts. In almost every area of endeavor, there was an upsurge of activity, making it one of the most creative phases in Chinese history.

The creativity of the age was no historic accident. Thanks to rising agricultural productivity and vigorous commercial-industrial growth, China under the Sung was far more prosperous and affluent than under the preceding dynasties.[1] Sung China was also more tranquil. The founders

---

[1] There is an extensive body of monographic literature on Sung economic development in both Western and Oriental languages. For agricultural development, see the various works by Sudō Yoshiyuki. For land tenure, see Denis Twitchett, *Land Tenure and the Social Order in T'ang and Sung China* (Luzac and Company: 1963). For industrial development, see Robert Hartwell, particularly his studies on coal and iron. For commercial development, see Shiba Yoshinobu, *Commerce and Society in Sung China*, trans. by Mark Elvin, Center for Chinese Studies, University of Michigan: 1970. Also, Shiba Yoshinobu and Yamane Yukio, *Markets in China during the Sung, Ming and Ch'ing Periods*, trans. by Hawaii University, Center for Cultural and Technical Interchange, Translation Series 23.

of the dynasty seemed to have been able to rest the spectre that haunted China since the T'ang period, namely, insubordinate army commanders and provincial governors. Since the conclusion of the Khitan wars with the Treaty of Shan-yüan in 1004, there were no major threats of foreign invasions or internal rebellions for a hundred years.[2] The conjunction of material affluence and political security produced a climate of hope and expectations, spurring development in art, literature and philosophy.

In the cultural milieu of China, progress often assumed the paradoxical form of going backward. This was no doubt due to the strong historical sense of Chinese thinkers which required utopian thought to be firmly anchored in a historic context. From the time of Confucius, all original teachers sought to justify their innovations by claiming the sanction of history. To the Chinese, utopias were not imaginary commonwealths suspended somewhere in space. They were "historic realities", representing the Golden Age in remote antiquity. The striving for higher ideals therefore often found expression in efforts to restore the pristine perfection of the lost golden age. This interest in restoration (fu-ku) was a prominent motif in the intellectual and moral fermentation of the Northern Sung period.[3] The pattern of presenting innovations as returning to a desirable tradition was so well established that the great men of the Northern Sung period, for all their originality, did not deviate.

Idealistic statesmen desirous of political reform, such as Fan Chung-yen (989–1052), Ou-yang Hsiu (1007–1072), Wang An-shih (1021–1086), turned to the model institutions of the Three Dynasties for inspiration.[4] Classical scholars, such as Hu Yüan (993–1059), Sun Fu (992–1057), Hu An-kuo (1074–1138), convinced that the traditional commentaries had distorted the message of the classics, went back directly to the text of the Confucian classics, and ushered in a new period of classical study.[5] Historians, such as Ou-yang Hsiu, Sung Ch'i

[2] The rise of the Tangghut kingdom of Hsi-hsia caused considerable anxiety in the 1040's. A combination of adroit diplomacy and effective military actions of the Sung army commanders, however, quickly brought the situation under control. See Tao Jing-shen, "Yü Ching and Sung Policies Towards Liao and Hsia, 1042–1044", in Journal of Asian History 6:2 (1972), pp. 114–122.

[3] For the significance of the theme of fu-ku restorationism in Neo-Confucian thought, see William DeBary, "A Reappraisal of Neo-Confucianism", in Arthur F. Wright, ed., Studies in Chinese Thought (Chicago University Press: 1953).

[4] For Fan Chung-yen and Ou-yang Hsiu, see the excellent studies by James T.C. Liu. Of the proliferation of monographic literature on Wang An-shih, the studies by K'e Chang-i, H.R. Williamson and James T.C. Liu are well-known. Of more recent studies, that of Higashi Kazuo is probably the most significant.

[5] James T.C. Liu, in his study of Ou-yang Hsiu, ch. 7, "The Classicist", gives a concise account of the characteristics of Sung classical scholarship. For more detailed

(998–1061), Liu Shu (1032–1078), Ssu-ma Kuang (1019–1086), chagrined by the faults of traditional historiography, went back to the paragon of historical writings, the *Ch'un-ch'iu* (Spring and Autumn Annals) for example, and proceeded to re-write the histories.[6] Men of letters, such as Su Hsün (1009–1066), Su Shih (1036–1101), and Su Che (1039–1112), dissatisfied with the ornate *pien-wen* (double harness) style currently in vogue, went back to the free prose style of the Warring States and the Han period for models, and produced a new literature.[7] In all these areas of accomplishments, the great men of Northern Sung, while professing to return to the lofty standards of the past, were actually breaking new ground, blazing bright trails for succeeding generations to follow.

This Northern Sung syndrome was perhaps best exemplified in the strain of thought popularly referred to in Western literature as Neo-Confucianism, although it denotes but one dimension of it. The origin of this strain may be traced to the mid-T'ang period when the celebrated essayist Han Yü (768–824) ushered in a militant form of Confucianism.[8] To combat the stifling influence of Buddhism in Chinese society, he sought to establish a criterion whereby the orthodox in Chinese culture could be distinguished from the heterodox. Thus came into existence the idea of *tao-t'ung* (the legitimate transmission of the teaching of the sages). Whatever lay beyond this *tao-t'ung* tradition was heterodox. In his formulation, the sage-ruler Yao transmitted the *tao* to Shun, Shun to Yü, Yü to T'ang, T'ang to King Wen and King Wu, King Wen and King Wu to the Duke of Chou, the Duke of Chou to Confucius, Confucius to Mencius. After Mencius, there was no one worthy enough for *tao* to be transmitted to.

This doctrine of *tao-t'ung* was a potentially explosive one. Although

information of individual scholars, see their respective records in SYHA: Hu Yüan (993–1059) SYHA 1 "An-ting hsüeh-an", Sun Fu (992–1057) SYHA 2 "T'ai-shan hsüeh-an", Hu An-kuo (1073–1137) SYHA 33 "Wu-i hsüeh-an".

[6] For the vision of Sung historians, see James T.C. Liu, *Ou-yang Hsiu, an Eleventh Century Neo-Confucianist* (Stanford University Press: 1957), ch. 8, "Historian"; also, Edwin G. Pulleyblank, "Chinese Historical Criticism, Liu Chih-chi and Ssu-ma Kuang", in Beaseley and Pulleyblank, eds., *Historians of China and Japan* (London: 1961). For more information on the less known historians: Sung Chi (998–1061), see his biography in SS 284; Liu Shu (1032–1078), see his biolgraphy in SS 444.

[7] There is a lively account of the life and literary significance of Su Shih by Lin Yutang, *The Gay Genius: the Life and Times of Su Tung-po* (John Day: 1947). There is a good, solid account of the *ku-wen* literary movement of the Sung period by Lo Ken-che, *Chung-kuo wen-hsüeh p'i-p'ing shih* (A History of Chinese Literary Criticism), vol. 3, Shanghai, Ku-tien wen-hsüeh ch'u-pan she: 1961.

[8] For the significance of Han Yü in the Sung Neo-Confucianist or *tao-hsüeh* movement, see Carson Chang, *The Development of Neo-Confucian Thought* (Bookman Associates, New York: 1957), ch. 4, "Han Yü, the Pioneer".

after the death of Mencius, no one was worthy to be entrusted with the
tao, the logic of *tao-t'ung* did not preclude the possibility that some man
then living or yet to be born might prove to be worthy of the trust.
The man who received the mantle of the ancient sage-rulers and of
Confucius and Mencius, could indeed speak with an authority denied
to other mortals. Han Yü did not specifically claim that he had received
it — he merely hinted at it. A number of Northern Sung scholars, reflecting the prevailing optimism of the times, were less modest. In
unequivocable terms, they claimed to have recovered the *tao* which had
been eclipsed for a thousand years since the death of Mencius.[9]

Aspirants to the mantle of the sages, of course, had to make themselves
acceptable. The sages had died long ago. How then could anyone
living at the time of the Northern Sung enter into a special relationship
with them and receive the *tao*? It is unlikely that Han Yü faced the
implication of this problem which was in fact involved in his doctrine
of *tao-t'ung*. It was believed that emperors Yao, Shun and Yü ruled
in succession so that *tao* could be transmitted by personal contact. However, the rulers Yü and T'ang were separated by an interval of about
five hundred years. How was *tao* transmitted across this barrier of time?

The Northern Sung scholars recognized the importance of this issue
and grappled with it successfully. They examined the nature of *tao-t'ung*
and came to the conclusion that what was passed on from sage to sage
was not any articulate doctrine but the mind (*ch'uan-hsin*). This message

---

[9] Liu K'ai, the pioneer of Northern Sung *ku-wen* movement, set the pace in this
regard. Claiming to be the master of the Sung dynasty, he consciously set himself the
task which Confucius was known to have undertaken, namely, editing and emending
the text of the classics. See his self-portrayal, "Tung-chaio Yeh-fu chuan" (Biography
of the Hermit from the Eastern Suburb) and "Pu-wang hsien-shen chuan" (Biography
of the Man who Retrieves and Mends) in his collected work, *Ho-tung hsien-shen chi* 2.

Among the outstanding scholars of the Northern Sung, the most unequivocal in
claiming the *tao-t'ung* succession is Ch'eng I. For a solid study of his philosophic ideas,
see A.C. Graham, *Two Chinese Philosophers, Ch'eng Ming-tao and Ch'eng I-ch'uan*
(L. Lund Humphries: 1958). In his memorial to the Dowager Empress Hsüan-jen
(Shang T'ai-huang T'ai-hou shu), Ch'eng I wrote, "I am inclined to believe that the
learning of the sages has not been propagated for a long time. Fortunately, I recovered
it (i.e. the teaching of the sages) from the surviving classical writings, and not minding
my own [limitations], have taken upon myself the responsibility of propagating it."
See *Erh-Ch'eng ch'üan-shu*, I-ch'uan section, 2:28a. Ch'eng I's claim of having recovered the *tao* was accepted by some of his contemporaries, e.g., Wen Yen-po (1006–
1097). See the tombstone inscription Wen wrote for Ch'eng I's elder brother, Ch'eng
Hao, in *Erh-Ch'eng ch'üan-shu*, I-ch'uan section, 7:7b. By the time of the Southern
Sung, Ch'eng I's accession to the *tao-t'ung* line of sages seems to have gained wide
acceptance. See Yang Wan-li's reference to it in his *Ch'eng-chai chi* 79, Preface for
The Collected Works of Me-t'ang Hsien-shen.

Among the friends of Ch'eng I, Chang Tsai's claim to the *tao-t'ung* succession is
indisputable though less explicit. See his celebrated quatrain setting forth the purpose
or self-image of the *tao-hsüeh* movement (*Chang-tzu ch'üan-shu yü-lu* 2:6b).

of the mind, like electric sparks leaping across the barrier of time and space, enabled sages to understand and communicate with one another.[10]

We may label scholars committed to this line of thought the *tao-hsüeh* scholars, although the term *tao-hsüeh* was not popularly used to designate a distinct academic trend until early in the Southern Sung period.[11] On the premise that only a sage can understand a sage, *tao-hsüeh* scholars bent their efforts towards attaining sagehood themselves.

The *tao-hsüeh* scholars' search for sagehood was analogous to, and probably also patterned after, the devout Buddhist's search for salvation. Although the type of Buddhism they had contact with was considerably sinicized, it nevertheless retained much of its Indian heritage.[12] Edgarton, the eminent Indologist, postulates a dichotomy between what he labels the extraordinary norm and the ordinary norm governing the behavioral patterns of Indians.[13] For the majority of men, coming under the domain of the ordinary norm, the routine of life was governed by three main ends or purposes: (*a*) *dharma*, the observance of religious, ethical or legal obligations; (*b*) *kama*, gratification of sexual desires and (*c*) *artha*, making a living in an honorable way. The extraordinary norm was for the few, the moral or spiritual elite who sought salvation of the higher sense, *moksha*. Salvation in the higher sense could not be attained in the course of ordinary life, no matter how scrupulous one was in the observance of the prescriptions of *dharma*. The seekers of *moksha* had to renounce the world, lead the life of an ascetic and commit themselves totally to the goal of salvation. Buddhism preached a way of salvation in the Indian sense. The main bearers of Buddhist values were the *sangha*, the monks who avowedly severed relations with the mundane world and sought salvation in an undistracted environment, the monasteries.

Chinese cultural tradition did not admit of this dichotomy between

[10] The doctrine of the transmission of the *tao* via the communion of the mind (*hsin-ch'uan*) was probably inspired by the Ch'an example of the transmission of the dharma outside of the sutras. See Carson Chang, *op. cit.*, ch. 6, "Buddhism as Stimulus to Neo-Confucianism". Specific reference to the doctrine of *hsin-ch'uan* may be found in Chang Chiu-ch'eng's use of the term to designate his memoirs (*Heng-pu hsin-ch'uan*). See SYHA 40; also, *Chang-tzu ch'üan-shu* 12:4a. (See note 22 for translation of Chang Tsai's use of the term.)

[11] In its narrow connotation, the term *tao-hsüeh*, designating the learning of the Ch'eng brothers, Chang Tsai, Chou Tun-i was first employed as a word of reproach. See SSCSPM 80 (On the Elevation and Suppression of *tao-hsüeh*). With the compilation of the *Sung-shih* in the Yüan period which set up the category of *tao-hsüeh* among Confucian scholars, the term *tao-hsüeh* henceforth was usually taken in its narrow sense.

[12] For an account of Sung Buddhism, see Kenneth Ch'en, *Buddhism in China: A Historical Survey* (Princeton University Press: 1964).

[13] Franklin Edgerton, "Dominant Ideas in the Formation of Indian Culture", *Journal of American Oriental Society*, vol. 62 (1942), pp. 151–156.

the ordinary norm and the extraordinary norm. The sage was not someone who turned his back on civil society but one who fulfilled to the highest degree the same ethical injunctions incumbent on ordinary men and women. In fact, Confucius, who, more than anybody else, shaped China's ethics, did not talk much about the sage. The ideal that he wanted to promote was that of *chün-tzu*, the gentleman with moral sensibility, fortitude, and knowledge.[14] It is indeed necessary for the man who aspired to be a *chün-tzu* to be instructed, but the emphasis was not so much on learning as on action. One became a *chün-tzu* not by talking about it but by being one, in his dealings with other men.

The *tao-hsüeh* search for sagehood clearly displayed the mentality of the extraordinary norm.[15] Being Confucianists, they naturally could not turn their backs on civil society. However, unlike conventional Confucianists who sought self-fulfilment by active involvement in the mundane world, they gave the impression that exertions along the line of the normal career of a scholar-official, viz., studying for the civil service examination, seeking office and promotion, doing what one could for emperor and people, were irrelevant to their desired goal, that of becoming a sage. This goal had to be sought in a special way, outside of the routine life of a scholar-official.[16] The intensity of this quest varied with individuals. For some, the quest for sagehood was such an absorbing preoccupation that office-holding was felt to be a serious impediment. Shao Yung (1011–1077), for instance, led the life of a recluse.[17]

Tao-hsüeh scholars raised the question "What is it that makes a sage?" Studying the Confucian classics, they extracted those portions that had a bearing on their quest, such as the following passage from the *Chung-yung* (Doctrine of the Mean) chapter of *Li-chi* (Book of Rites) which purports to show the transforming power of the sage:[18]

[14] See H.G. Creel, *Confucius, the Man and the Myth* (John Day Company: 1949) for a solid study of Confucius.

[15] Carson Chang, *op. cit.*, ch. 3, considers the quest of sagehood (he calls it the science of sagehood) as one of the institutions or external manifestations of Neo-Confucianism. He also stresses the influence of Buddhism (the bodhisattva ideal in particular) on this aspect of Neo-Confucianism.

[16] Shao Shuo-chi (1059–1129), a perceptive observer of Northern Sung academic trends, particularly objected to this aspect of *tao-hsüeh* learning. See his letter to Yuan Chi-kao in *Sung-shan chi* 15, which gives his evaluation of the shortcomings of the individual *tao-hsüeh* scholars as well as their common weaknesses.

[17] In addition to Shao Yung, many of the disciples of Ch'eng I were known to have led hermit-like lives, e.g., Yin T'un (1061–1131), see his biography in SS 428; Lo Ts'ung-yen and Li T'ung (see Carson Chang, *op. cit.*, ch. 11, "The Period of Transition between Ch'eng I and Chu Hsi").

[18] The quotation is from James Legge's translation, *The Chinese Classics*, vol. I, p. 415. The same passage may be read in E.R. Hughes's translation; see *The Great*

It is only he who is possessed of the most complete sincerity that can exist under heaven, who can give its full development to his nature. Able to give its full development to his own nature, he can do the same to the nature of other men. Able to give its full development to the nature of other men, he can give their full development to the natures of animals and things. Able to give their full development to the natures of creatures and things, he can assist the transforming and nourishing powers of Heaven and Earth. Able to assist the transforming and nourishing powers of Heaven and Earth, he may with Heaven and Earth form a ternion.

In this passage, the key word is obviously *hsing* (nature). The sage was sage by virtue of the fact that he was able to fulfil his *hsing* completely. But what was *hsing*? It was what one was endowed with by Heaven (*t'ien ming chih wei hsing*),[19] so says the very first sentence of the *Chung-yung*. The quest for sagehood hinged upon two crucial concepts, *hsing* and *ming* (what Heaven decreed). The whole line of endeavor was therefore often referred to as the learning of *hsing-ming*.

The terminology of the *hsing-ming* learning went back to the classical texts. In their preoccupation with the *hsing* and *ming* concepts, however, the *tao-hsüeh* scholars were unquestionably influenced by Buddhist and Taoist thought. The ultimate goal of Buddhist aspiration, enlightenment (*wu*), was based on the possibility of attaining a higher level of perception so that the enlightened one sees through the flux of phenomenal life and grasps the true meaning of existence. Buddhist philosophising was therefore focused upon the concepts of reality, of different types of consciousness, of the nature of the phenomenal world and of the mind. These concepts were given different emphases by different Buddhist sects. However, all the varieties of Buddhism stressed an articulated cosmology or world view that could be applied to account for all conceivable things in Heaven and Earth. Steeped for centuries in a Buddhist atmosphere, the Chinese intellect invariably took on a Buddhist stamp. Buddhist axioms governed his perception of reality, his thinking processes and his canons of truth. The Northern Sung *tao-hsüeh* scholars, while repudiating the Buddhist goals and values, nevertheless could not repudiate the habits of thought which the Chinese intellect had been developing under the impact of Buddhism for hundreds of years. Thus when they disowned the Buddhist doctrine of reality (ontology), they could not help but try to set up a new one in its stead. This explains their preoccupation with the concepts of *hsing* and *ming*. Similarly Buddhist antecedents led them to clarify the ground of their Confucian truths, which brought them into the

---

Learning and the Mean-in-action (E.P. Dutton and Company, New York: 1943), p. 128.

[19] Legge, *op. cit.*, p. 383; Hughes, *op. cit.*, p. 105.

realm of psychology and epistemology. These several lines of inquiry, when integrated into a coherent world view, made it possible for them to account for everything in Heaven or on Earth, giving their doctrines a comprehensiveness which was the test of the ultimate truth, valid for all time and space.

In struggling to give birth to the subtle ideas in their cosmologies, *tao-hsüeh* scholars drew from the phraseology of the classical texts, where appropriate. But for the most part, they had to devise their own method of expression; there were really no adequate precedents to their type of inquiry within the Confucian tradition.[20] They were well aware of this fact, and used to say that they had made known truths which the sages of former times had not revealed.[21] Convinced of the overriding importance of their endeavors, many of them chose to put their ideas into self-contained treatises instead of trying to convey them by stretching the meaning of the existing Confucian texts. Thus came into existence the major *tao-hsüeh* works of the Northern Sung period such as *T'ung-shu* (Comprehensive Understanding) of Chou Tun-i (1027–1073), *Cheng-meng* (Correction of Youthful Follies) of Chang Tsai (1020–1077), and *Huang-chi ching-shih shu* (Cosmic Periods of the Great Ultimate) of Shao Yung. Before long, these works were to be recognized as major components of the *tao-hsüeh* ideology. Like the seminal minds of former times, their authors achieved immortality as founders of distinct schools of thought (*ch'eng i-chia-yen*).[22]

[20] Wing-tsit Chan has made a systematic study of the terminology of *tao-hsüeh*. See his article, "Neo-Confucianism, New Ideas in Old Terminology", in *Philosophy, East and West*, vol. 17, nos. 1–4.

[21] Ch'eng I, commenting on the Western Inscription of Chang Tsai, said, "It (i.e., the Western Inscription) extends the principles of reason to bring out the right meanings, thus revealing truths which the former sages had not revealed. It has made as much contribution to the [cause of the sages] as Mencius did with his idea of the goodness of human nature and his nurture of the all-pervading breath." See *Erh-Ch'eng ch'üan-shu*, section of I-ch'üan, Ch'eng I's letter to Yang Shih on the Western Inscription. Chu Hsi, commenting on the *T'ung-shu* of Chou Tun-i, voiced the same sentiment, although his phraseology was slightly different: "Somebody remarked, '*T'ung-shu* is a worthy successor to the *Analects* and the book of *Mencius*.' Whereupon Chu Hsi said, 'In comparison to the *Analects* and *Mencius*, it (i.e., *T'ung-shu*) is more analytical and profound, with a more tightly-knit structure. The sayings of the *Analects* and *Mencius* are not as instructive.'" See *Chou-tzu ch'üan-shu, T'ung-shu*, 2:43a.

[22] This interpretation is based on the self-revelations of Chang Tsai. "In elucidating the concepts on human nature [and other subjects], we should expound our ideas in self-contained treatises, and not seek to convey them by distorting the surviving words of the ancients. For instance, the ideas of the goodness of human nature and the four self-evident beginnings of goodness (*ssu-tuan*) originated with Mencius. They were not ideas which Confucius had briefly commented and Mencius elaborated. [Mencius gave expression to these ideas] because his mind was in communion with that of [Confucius]." See *Chang-tzu ch'üan-shu* 12:4a.

Wm. Theodore DeBary, in his introduction to the writings of Chou Tun-i, Chang

The innovating spirit of the *tao-hsüeh* scholars was manifested mainly in their efforts to probe into the recesses of psychological phenomena and in the construction of their cosmological systems. There were, however, no compelling reasons why this spirit should be kept within these confines. It could also conceivably operate in the realm of socio-political thought. After all, the Confucian sage was not a recluse but one who took upon his shoulders the problems of the world. Most of the *tao-hsüeh* scholars had strong views on how to cope with the social and political problems of their day.[23]

The most notable exponent of the innovating spirit in the realm of socio-political thought was Wang An-shih. The reforms which he preached and implemented were in substance not really earth-shaking; they had been advocated and partially implemented by other men in former times.[24] Rather, it was the resoluteness with which he pushed for his reforms that made him stand out above the crowd of reform-minded statesmen of the Northern Sung period. He was so sure of the righteousness of his cause that he would stop at nothing in crushing the opposition. According to Ssu-ma Kuang, Wang An-shih operated on the basis of the "Three not worths", namely, the founding fathers of the dynasty not worth imitating, celestial omens not worth fearing, and public opinion not worth heeding.[25]

Wang An-shih's phenomenal self-conceit was not merely due to an excess of gall. It was not explicable apart from the ideological climate in which he lived. He was never regarded as a *tao-hsüeh* scholar, and yet he was nurtured by the same intellectual milieu and shared in the same concerns. Like *tao-hsüeh* scholars, his self-image was dominated by the ideal of the sage.[26] Just as the sages of former times resolutely

---

Tsai and other Neo-Confucianists of the Sung period, discerns a composite pattern in Neo-Confucian writings, viz. textual exegesis combined with philosophical expositions. He does not, however, pursue the question of motivation — why some thinkers preferred to write philosophical expositions and others did not. See DeBary, *Sources of Chinese Tradition*, ch. 20, p. 511.

[23] See Wm. Theodore DeBary, "A Reappraisal of Neo-Confucianism", in Arthur F. Wright, ed., *Studies in Chinese Thought*.

[24] Precedents for Wang An-shih's reforms have been carefully studied by Williamson, *op. cit.* Whereas most of the reform measures advocated by Wang An-shih were not altogether new, his thinking on social and economic matters that inspired or justified these reforms did contain innovative features. See James T.C. Liu, *Reform in Sung China*, ch. 3, "Wang and the Political Thought of the Northern Sung".

[25] See Ssu-ma Kuang, *Wen-kuo Wen-cheng Ssu-ma Kung chi* 72, preliminary remarks on proposed examination questions.

[26] My view of the personality of Wang An-shih is very much influenced by Lin Yutang. Lin is not a recognized authority on Wang and his portrayal of Wang (whom he describes as the bull-headed prime minister) indicates prejudice. However, I think he has correctly located the dynamics of Wang's unconventional behavior, namely, in the latter's pretension to sagehood. See Lin Yutang, *The Gay Genius*.

brushed aside stiff resistance to their reform programs (for example, the sages I Yin and the Duke of Chou) so Wang An-shih, consciously following the footsteps of the sages, stood unflinchingly under the cross fire of adverse criticism.

This self-image was almost identical to that of Ch'eng I. The latter claimed to have rediscovered the *tao* from the surviving fragments of the classics which nobody in the preceding thousand years had been capable of doing. In a letter to his friend Tseng Kung (1019–1083), Wang An-shih expressed the same idea though in a milder tone:[27]

For a long time scholars have been denied the teaching of the classics in their entirety. If anybody reads the classics alone, it is unlikely that he can really comprehend them. That is the reason why I have read, in addition to the classics, the writings of the philosophers, the manuals of medical doctors, herbalists, story-tellers, and miscellaneous notes, not overlooking anything in my quest for knowledge. Nor have I missed any opportunity to raise questions with the lowly peasants and female servants. Having done that I am now able to understand the major import of the classics. Keeping in mind that scholars today live in different times from those of the ancient kings, there is no way to exhaust the [meaning of the] sages if they do not [follow my methods].

As Wang An-shih rose in his official career, his sense of accomplishment intensified. This is reflected in the title he chose for his commentaries on the classics, *San-ching hsin-i* (New Commentaries on the Three Classics). To us moderns, the title probably does not indicate anything unusual. Nevertheless we should try to view it in historic perspective. In traditional China most commentators on the classics hastened to demonstrate their credentials as the legatees of particular schools of interpretation, probably the only way to command a hearing. By choosing the title *hsin-i* for his commentaries, Wang An-shih was doing the inconceivable, openly advertizing his trail-blazing attitude. The concept "new" (*hsin*) was so unusual that it became a label for anything associated with him, his learning (*hsin-hsüeh*), his reform policies (*hsin-cheng*), and his party (*hsin-tang*).[28]

Self-confidence breeds a sense of mission, as demonstrated in the preface to his lexicographical work, the *Tzu-shuo* (Exegetical Explanation of Words):[29]

[27] Wang An-shih, *Lin-ch'uan chi* 73, "To Tseng Tzu-ku" (Letter in Reply to Tseng Kung).

[28] Wang An-shih's scholarship is presented in SYHA 98 under the label of *hsin-hsüeh*. An example of contemporary reaction to Wang's advertising of the newness of his scholarship is given by Shao Shuo-chi (1059–1129), *Sung-shan chi* 14:15a–b, "Ch'ih-hsin" (Ashamed of Newness).

[29] *Lin-ch'uan chi* 84, "Hsi-ning Tzu-shuo hsü".

...... For long, the literature of the former [sage] kings survived only in a mutilated form. [Hsu] Shen's work was not comprehensive, full of error. Even I, in my ignorance am able to perceive his shortcomings. Yet, who knows that it may not be Heaven's will to bring about a revival of culture in our times, making me the spearhead [in this revival]? For this reason, there is no alternative to this (i.e. *Tzu-shuo*) as the basis of instruction. Those who have mastered it are already in a position to comprehend nine-tenths of the underlying principle of virtue.

Wang An-shih undoubtedly believed what he worte in the above quotation. During the years of his retirement in Nanking, he was reported to have devoted his major effort to expanding and revising the *Tzu-shuo*. It was obviously the work that he expected posterity to remember him by, just as Confucius expected to be remembered for his editing of the *Ch'un-ch'iu*.[30] Considered as a work of philology, *Tzu-shuo* did not have much to recommend it. Wang An-shih seemed to have ignored the traditional Six Methods (*liu-shu*) in the evolution of the Chinese script, concentrating exclusively on the method of Ideograms (*hui-i*). Thus he often came up with interesting etymologies which cannot stand the test of history.

To evaluate the *Tzu-shuo* from the point of view of the lexicographer, however, is altogether inappropriate. From a cursory scrutiny of the surviving fragments,[31] as the work in its entirety is no longer extant, it is easy to observe that Wang An-shih was primarily interested not in the meaning of words *per se*, but in the realities that the words signify. His approach was therefore not descriptive or empirical but analytical and normative. In seeking to comprehend these realities, he demonstrated great versatility and an ability to draw from various sources of his cultural legacy. He applied, for instance, the classical *cheng-ming* approach (rectification of names) to concrete social and political institutions,[32] Buddhist and Taoist concepts to abstract ideas[33] and his

---

[30] Wang's obsession with this philological task is amply attested in Sung literature. For example, Ch'en Shih-tao, *Hou-shan hsien-sheng chi* 20, "Tan-ts'ung" (Miscellaneous Remarks); Lu Tien, *T'ao-shan chi*, p. 121; Su Chou, *Shuang-ch'i chi*, p. 221.

[31] Ironically the longest surviving list of Wang An-shih's etymologies is preserved in the collected works of his most unrelenting critic, Yang Shih, favorite disciple of Ch'eng I. Yang's *Tzu-shuo pien* (A Refutation of the *Tzu-shuo*) purports to reproduce the *Tzu-shuo*'s explanation of twenty-nine characters followed by Yang's refutation. This list, together with a few shorter ones, has been gathered together by K'e Chang-i. See his *Wang An-shih p'ing-chuan* (A Critical Biography of Wang An-shih), ch. 17, "Wen-tzu hsüeh" (Philology). Additional examples of Wang's etymologies may be found in the text of his *Chou-kuan hsin-i*.

[32] The philosophic basis of the "rectification of names" is based on the consideration that the name of things (and therefore the words that denote them) have normative as well as descriptive functions. The essence of the thing denoted by the word thus inheres in the word itself. For instance, the word "father" denotes not only a man with regard to a son he sires but also the proper manner he ought to behave towards

own powers of observations to natural phenomena.[34] In his rational mind, the myriad phenomena of the world were reduced to order and the gap between the natural and human world bridged. His *Tzu-shuo* was therefore a compendium of knowledge, his statement of the ultimate reality.

II

BY THE TIME of the Southern Sung, the innovative impulse of the Northern Sung appeared to have run its full course. Together with the withering of the innovating impulse, there was also a narrowing of the intellectual horizon. Activities which used to canalize much creative energy were pushed away from the center of the stage and allowed to languish. The dominant note of the intellectual history of the Southern Sung, therefore, was conservation. This was a selective process, not an indiscriminate commitment to everything that flourished in the past. Efforts were directed only at those legacies deemed worthy of salvaging. Such a drastic change in the mood of the Sung people was not fortuitous. It was in fact precipitated by a catharsis: a series of traumatic events overtook the Sung dynasty and China emerged much changed.

The chain of events started with the death of Emperor Shen-tsung

---

his son. The applicability of this principle to Wang An-shih's philology may be easily demonstrated. A Chinese word (*tzu*) is usually made up of several components. By analysing its components and knowing what these individually stand for, one should be able to know not only what the word means but also what it ought to mean. To illustrate, the word *pin* 嬪 with the female graph on the left and the guest graph on the right designates a certain rank among the palace women. The guest graph suggests courtesy extended to an honored guest and therefore palace lady *pin* ought to enjoy a fairly high status. On the other hand, another rank among the palace women, signified by the word *fu* 婦 with the female graph on the left and the broom graph on the right, obviously could not be held in high esteem as her appointed lot was to sweep the floor with the broom. See *Chou-kuan hsin-i* 1:7.

[33] A good example is Wang's explanation for the word *k'ung* 空 (emptiness): *wu t'u i-wei yüeh tse k'ung wu hsiang* (without a cave dug out of the earth there will not be an image of emptiness). The concept of an image (Sanskrit Lakṣana) is definitely of Buddhist origin. See *A Dictionary of Buddhist Terms* by William Edward Soothill and Levis Houdous, p. 309.

[34] The third longest list of surviving examples of Wang An-shih's etymology, as culled by K'e Chang-i, comes from Li Shih-chen, the famed Ming naturalist, author of the *Pen-ts'ao kang-mu*. The fact that Li Shih-chen quoted from the *Tzu-shuo* in the compilation of his masterpiece indicates that Wang An-shih had some success in his handling of botanical phenomena. An anecdote told by the Southern Sung poet, Lu Yu, indicates that Wang An-shih also made an effort to comprehend physical phenomena. According to Lu Yu, the *Tzu-shuo* explanation for the word *hsiao* 霄 (empyrean) is: "When water vapor rises to this level in the atmosphere, it vanishes of its own accord." See *Lao-hsüeh-an pi-chi* 2, p. 13.

in 1085.[35] During his entire reign, the Reform Party, in spite of Wang An-shih's retirement in 1076, was able to stay in power. The new emperor, Che-tsung, was still a minor, and for the next eight years (during the period of Yüan-yu, 1086–1093), the Dowager Empress, Hsüan-jen, was actually in charge of the government. Being implacably opposed to the Reformers, she had them dismissed, and brought back to court the conservative ministers who had suffered under the preceding reign. The Dowager Empress died in 1093 and her death marked another shift in the kaleidoscope of court politics. The way was again open to the Reform Faction to launch a comeback.

Men such as Chang Tun (1035–1105) and Ts'ai Ching (1047–1126) who dominated the court in the post-Yüan-yu era espoused the cause of reform mostly for reasons of political expediency. They had to wean Emperor Che-tsung away from the conservatives. On his part the young emperor, who up to the death of the Dowager Empress had been chaffing under her straitlaced ministers, was willing to co-operate. The Emperor's advisers had no difficulty convincing him that the Dowager Empress and her conservative ministers had betrayed the ideals of his sagely father, Emperor Shen-tsung. As a symbol of their determination to take the sagely Shen-tsung as their model, the reign title was changed to Shao-sheng (in imitation of the sage). Most of the reform measures which had been discontinued during the Yüan-yu era were revived. The premature death of Emperor Che-tsung called for no adjustment in the orientation of the party in power. His successor, Emperor Hui-tsung (reigned 1101–1125), a younger son of Shen-tsung, was equally receptive to the argument of the Reformers.

To consolidate their power, the Reformers carried out a thoroughgoing purge of their opponents. A black-list was drawn up, inscribed on rock pillars and made known to the public. This was the list known as the Yüan-yu tang-jen. Those whose names appeared on this list were to be summarily dismissed from government positions and their writings proscribed. In purging their enemies, the Reformers were not guided by ideological consistency: they went after those who had the most potential to cause trouble. The hardest hit among their victims were probably Ssu-ma Kuang and the Su brothers (Su Shih and Su Che). Although Ssu-ma Kuang was dead by this time, he remained a symbol of the opposition. His profound historical scholarship was also incompatible with the New Learning (the legacy of Wang An-shih) fostered by the Reformers. The Su brothers, particularly Su Shih, had always been a thorn in the flesh of the Reformers. Through his wit and

[35] For an account of these events, see Williamson, Wang An-shih, A Chinese Statesman and Educationalist of the Sung Dynasty (Arthur Prosthain: 1937), vol. 2, chs. 1–3.

indomitable spirit, he exposed the follies of the regime in his much loved and widely circulated poems.

Hence there was an element of literary inquisition in the determined campaign of the Reformers against their opponents. This literary inquisition was carried to considerable lengths against a few selected targets. Attempts were made to destroy the printing blocks of Ssu-ma Kuang's annalistic history *Tzu-ch'ih t'ung-chien* (Comprehensive Mirror in Aid of Government) in the imperial printing office. Severe warnings were issued to bookstores or printing firms not to print or possess works of the proscribed authors.[36] There was evidence that these governmental directives were generally complied with. The once ubiquitous works of Su Shih, for instance, became virtually unobtainable.[37]

The literary inquisition undoubtedly took a heavy toll of the cultural life of the Sung period. A good example was classical prose-writing (*ku-wen*). The Northern Sung was the high watermark of the *ku-wen* movement. Of the so-called Eight Masters of *ku-wen* of the T'ang and the Sung, six lived during the Northern Sung period, all contemporaries. This vibrant literary form, however, suffered a severe setback in the course of the literary inquisition. Because of the relatively simple requirement of the format, compositions in *ku-wen* put a premium on content. It was therefore most suited to the untrammeled exposition of ideas. Most of the celebrated *ku-wen* masters of the T'ang and Sung period were men of large minds, who poured their visions and emotions into their writings. This untrammeled expressiveness was inhibited by the literary inquisition. The Reformers in power managed to clamp a narrow orthodoxy on the intellectual life of the time. Anything they disliked could be brought under the category of "writings contrary to the sages" or that of "Yüan-yu scholarship" which they interdicted in edict after edict. Thus, discouraged by the authorities and deprived of good literary models, few scholars cared to cultivate the art of *ku-wen* writing. Hence, the *ku-wen* prose style, the finest literary

[36] An abridged version of many of these edicts warning the bookstore owners of severe punishment for possessing the prohibited books have been preserved in *Sung hui-yao chi-kao* (*hsing-fa* section), pp. 6519b, 6526b, 6539a.

[37] We have the testimony of Liu Ts'ai-shao whose life straddled the transition between the Northern and the Southern Sung. In the original preface to his collected works *Shan-ch'i chü-shih chi*, Liu was reported to have said, "In those days, bookstores, fearing to run afoul of the law, had their printing blocks of the writings of Su Tung-po and Huang Shan-ku destroyed. It was only the family of an imperial relative who dared make woodblocks for these prohibited writings. Ten essays of Su Tung-po sold for a thousand cash. Thus the more stringent the prohibition, the higher they were priced."

achievement of the Northern Sung, wilted in this hostile intellectual climate.[38]

Meanwhile, the self-seeking innovationism of the Reform Faction committed the dynasty to a course of action which just fell short of wrecking it completely. To pander to the aesthetic taste of Emperor Hui-tsung, who was probably the foremost connoisseur of art in the empire, the Reformers sent their agents scurrying to the provinces to ferret out exotic plants, stones and *objets d'art*. From everywhere, convoys of these rare items — the so-called *hua-shih kang* — converged on the capital. Agents of the Reformers availed themselves of the opportunity to rob the people and line their own pockets. To gratify their whims and search for glory, the Reformers pushed for an expansionist policy at the expense of the aboriginal tribes of Kwangsi and Tibet. Finally, as an act of supreme folly, they entered into an alliance with the rising power of the Jürchen and participated in the destruction of the Liao empire.[39]

The upshot of it all was the Jürchen invasion which in turn triggered widespread popular insurgency. The authority of the dynasty collapsed over large areas of the empire. The invading Jürchen army invested the Sung capital and made off with the Sung emperors and the imperial family. The dynasty, however, survived this catastrophe and henceforth ruled only the Southern half of China.

Living under the shadow of the Northern Sung debacle, Southern Sung scholar-officials were under a psychological necessity to explain away the national and dynastic humiliation. Surely something had gone wrong and someone was to blame. The protagonists of the Reform Faction naturally became prime targets. However, the search for culprits could not stop with their condemnation. In retrospect, the character of the age preceding the debacle was so irrational that it did not seem possible to attribute it simply to the machinations of a few self-seeking men. The follies committed by the Reform Faction were indicative of a deep-seated malaise which must be traced to its ideological

[38] For the decline of literary standards, the remark of the late Northern Sung writer T'ang Keng (1071–1121) is significant. In a letter to Ts'ai Ching (*Mei-shan T'ang hsien-sheng wen-chi* 23:4–6), he wrote, "In recent years, the art of prose writing has not been cultivated. In the examination halls, each student follows his own style, without conforming to any standard in his diction and manner of expression..." It may also be remarked that Wang Tsao (1079–1154), writing in the early years of the Southern Sung, specifically attributed the decline of literary standards of his time to the adverse influence of Wang An-shih's learning. See *Fou-ch'i chi* 21, "In Reply to the Letter of Wu Chih-lu".

[39] The sources bearing on the ill-fated alliance between the Sung and the Chin have been collected and analysed by Chao T'ieh-han. See his article, "Sung-Chin hai-shang chih meng shih-mo chi", *Ta-lu tsa-chih* 25:5–7.

roots. There can be no question that the legacy of Wang An-shih had a lot to do with it.[40]

Wang An-shih in his self-conceit was accused of treating the established practices of the dynasty embodying the wisdom of the founding fathers as if they were things of no account. His disciples followed his example and changed the dynastic institutions rashly until disaster finally struck. The wisdom of the founding fathers was clearly vindicated by the chain of events. In counter-argument to the Reform Faction who used to justify their innovations by claiming the sanction of the Three Dynasties of Hsia, Shang, and Chou, Southern Sung conservatives characterized their approach as *tsun Yao* (honoring the ways of Emperor Yao).[41] They were committed to the established ways of the dynasty just as the sage-ruler Shun was known to have honored the ways of his predecessor, Yao.

The *tsun Yao* mentality not only discouraged radical reforms inspired by utopian ideals but also frowned upon fresh approaches to administrative and social problems. The psychological scars left by Wang An-shih's reformism was still a factor to be reckoned with fifty years after the Northern Sung debacle. Chu Hsi (1130–1200), for example, the great Southern Sung scholar, was warned by a close friend when he implemented his public granary measure (*she-ts'ang*) in Chang-chou that he was running the risk of being misunderstood for attempting to revive Wang's discredited "green-sprout money" (*ch'ing-miao ch'ien*).[42] The *tsun Yao* mentality also had a considerable impact on Southern Sung historiography. For the people of Southern

[40] The most well-known attempt to expose the ideological roots of the regime of the Reformers during the reigns of Che-tsung and Hui-tsung was by Ch'en Kuan (courtesy name Ying-chung), author of the work *Ssu-ming tsung-Yao lu* (A Record of Reverently Following the Way of Yao). Ch'en's work was intended to be a critique and refutation of the *Jih-lu* (Daily Records) purportedly written by Wang An-shih himself during his retirement to justify his reform measures. Ch'en Kuan sought to prove that Wang An-shih practised chicanery and sophistry. Consequently the sanctions claimed by him and his self-styled disciples were untenable. For a lengthy statement of the rationale of the *Ssu-ming tsung-Yao lu*, which is no longer extant, see the preface of the work preserved in *Ho-nan Shao-shih wen-chien hou-lu* 23:147–155. In addition, revulsion against Wang An-shih gave rise to a voluminous body of slanderous literature. For a systematic treatment of this subject, see K'e Chang-i, *op. cit.*, ch. 23, "Shih-chuan chih shih-shih" (On the Inaccuracy of Historical Records).

[41] The first use of the *tsun Yao* expression to designate the conservative point of view was probably by the scholar Ch'en Kuan (1062–1126) who applied it to his book *Tsun-Yao chi*. See SYHA 35. Lo Ts'ung-yen kept up the tradition by writing the *Tsun-Yao lu*, dealing primarily with the events and personalities of the Northern Sung period. The mentality was also discernible in the common designation of Emperor Kao-tsung after his abdication, Kuang-Yao (making bright the virtues of Yao).

[42] There is a solid study of Chu Hsi's administrative success by Conrad Shirokauer, in *Etudes Song: Melanges offerts a la memoire d'Etienne Balazs*. Chu Hsi referred back to Chang Shih's warning in his letter to Chang. (See SYHA 49:11b.)

Sung, living under the shadow of dynastic humiliation, the scholar-officials of the Northern Sung period who presided over the heyday of the dynasty (that is, before the advent of Wang An-shih) were worthy objects of emulation. Considerable efforts were spent by some of the leading scholars in compiling what came to be known as *Ming-ch'en yen-hsing lu* (Records of the Words and Deeds of Outstanding Ministers).[43] These compilations purported to be serious historical works in contradistinction to the mass of *sui-pi* literature (random notes, memoirs, hearsay reports). In addition, the greatest monument of Southern Sung historical scholarship, *Hsü Tzu-ch'ih t'ung-chien ch'ang-pien* (A Continuation of *Tzu-ch'ih t'ung-chien* in Draft Form), was a clear manifestation of this mentality.

Revulsion against the legacy of Wang An-shih also brought about a new approach towards interpretating the classics. The classics by themselves were quite innocuous; they did not have the power to compel belief or disbelief. However, as they were still vested with a degree of sanctity, denied to other genres of literature, they still had the potential to do much damage if they fell into the wrong hands. Wang An-shih and his disciples amply bore this out. The imperative necessity to prevent the classic from being perverted is illustrated in the observation of T'ang Keng (1071–1121), a late Northern Sung writer. He wrote:[44]

A guest once addressed the following question to Tao, the Hermit, "I would like to annotate both *Chou-i* (Classic of Changes) and *Pen-ts'ao* (Manual of the Herbalist). [In your opinion], which should I start with?" "Start with the *Chou-i*," said the Hermit. Whereupon, the guest asked, "Why?" The Hermit replied, "Because if you annotate *Chou-i* erroneously, your errors will not cause men to die. But if you annotate *Pen-ts'ao* erroneously, many people would not be able to die of natural causes." The Hermit was generally commended for these prudent words, but I disagree with him. The Six Classics are nothing but the *pen-ts'ao* (guide or canon) for achieving orderly government... They do not deal with trivial matters and it is not easy to discourse on them. The purpose of *Pen-ts'ao* is to ascertain the properties of things. The purpose of the Six Classics is to ascertain the *tao*. The *tao* is the cause of the existence of things [and the principle] that men live by. If one makes an error with regard to things, [the harmful effects] will not extend to other things. If one makes an error with regard to *tao*, the consequences can be devastating. In ages gone by, there were Confucian ministers who, citing precedents in the Classics, committed the state to a

---

[43] The most famous of the compilations bearing this title is by Chu Hsi. Chao Ju-yü was also the author of a similar compilation.

[44] T'ang Keng, *Mei-shan T'ang hsien-shen wen-chi* 9:5a. There is a similar passage in Li Kou's collected works. See *Chih-chiang Li hsien-sheng wen-chi*, "Chang-yu hsia". According to him, Tao the Hermit was Tao Hung-ching (452–536).

ruinous path, with violence and bloodshed engulfing a thousand *li* of territory. How could errors in annotating *Pen-ts'ao* be greater than this?

Chu Hsi was in full agreement with T'ang Keng. In saying that it was imperative to guard against errors in annotating the classics, it is plain that neither T'ang nor Chu had abandoned the concept of truth as an objectively determinable entity. Theoretically it is possible for any scholar, without reference to what other scholars have said, to comprehend the truth by his own efforts. But the chance of his comprehending it in every instance is remote. Considering the awesome consequences that erroneous interpretations of the classics might give rise to, one could not afford to take chances. Interpretating the classics, therefore, had to be a co-operative enterprise. Ssu-ma Kuang, though he did not live through the darkest period of the literary inquisition and was spared the soul-searching that followed the Northern Sung debacle, nevertheless saw the path that classical scholarship was destined to take, when he said:[45]

Annotating the classics is like target-shooting. The chances of a single archer hitting the target are not as good as when many archers shoot at it together.

The co-operative nature of Southern Sung classical scholarship can be seen in the title of some of the published works. Chu Hsi, for example, entitled his commentary on the *Shih-ching* (Classic of Odes) and the *Analects*, the *chi-chu* (composite commentary). Another format frequently employed by annotators of classics is that known as *tse-chung* (reconciliation or mediation) in which the editor juxtaposed conflicting interpretations of the same text and sought to harmonize them.[46] Annotating the classics was thus a work of erudition rather than one of genius. It was not unknown for a man who aspired to prepare a definitive commentary on a classic to spend a life-time researching all the existing literature on that particular classic. Wang Yü-chih, author of *Chou-li ting-i* (Ascertained Meaning of *Chou-li*), prefaced his commentary with a list of the authorities known or consulted by him. The list includes fifty-one names, of which forty-five lived during the Sung period.[47]

In contrast to the *ku-wen* prose movement and the historical scholarship associated with Ou-yang Hsiu and Ssu-ma Kuang, which took a severe beating during the Northern Sung literary inquisition, *tao-hsüeh*

---

[45] Shao Shuo-chi, who was a faithful disciple of Ssu-ma Kuang, recalled this remark of his mentor. See *Sung-shan chi* 13:1, "Ti" (target).

[46] A good example is the *Chou-li tse-chung* by Wei Liao-weng, incorporated in his collected works.

[47] See Chu I-tsun, *Ching-i kao* 124:4b–7b.

emerged from the latter relatively unscathed. The immunity of *tao-hsüeh* was explained by the fact that it was not as big a target as those which caught the full fury of the inquisition. During the Yüan-yu period when the conservatives were in power, *tao-hsüeh* was still an *avant-garde* movement, little known outside the coterie of eccentric scholars. At a time when Su Shih and Ssu-ma Kuang had become household words, it is unlikely that the man on the street had heard of the name of Ch'eng I. That explains why it was permissible for Ch'eng I to carry on his normal life of writing and teaching in his native Loyang whereas the Su brothers and their more politically active associates were condemned to live as exiles in the far South.[48]

Still, the literary inquisition and the Northern Sung debacle had an incalculable effect on the subsequent development of *tao-hsüeh*. The impact was two-fold, viz. (*a*) in determining the subsequent direction of *tao-hsüeh* development and (*b*) in facilitating its rise as the mainstream of Southern Sung intellectual life.

It is not by chance that the type of *tao-hsüeh* propagated in Southern Sung times was derived almost exclusively from Ch'eng I, the least typical of the Northern Sung *tao-hsüeh* masters. The preponderance of Ch'eng I's influence is due, among other things, to the fact that his personality and scholarship were in line with the conservative bent of the times. Unlike Chou Tun-i, Shao Yung and Chang Tsai who channelled their efforts primarily into the writing and lecturing on their cosmological systems, Ch'eng I seemed to have operated within the framework of the Confucian classics. Although Ch'eng I deliberated with his disciples on typically *tao-hsüeh* themes and made significant contributions such as his elaboration of the *li-ch'i* (principle-material force) ontology and his formula for learning, his own writings dealt almost exclusively with exegesis and interpretation of the classics. It was he who lifted the *Ta-hsüeh* (Great Learning) out of *Li-chi* (Book of Rites), the anthology of ritualistic writings, and refurbished it to become the basic exposition of his philosophy — the gateway to virtue, as he called it.[49] His astuteness in turning existing Confucian classics to account

---

[48] Ch'eng I was, of course, not given an entirely free rein. In the inhibiting atmosphere of the literary inquisition, he wisely bided his time, cutting back on his writing and teaching activities. See the statement of Han Yuan-chi on this matter, *Nan-chien chia-i kao* 16, pp. 321–322, "Shu *Shih-shuo* hou" (After Inscribing on the Teaching of the Master).

[49] The importance of the *Great Learning* in the system of Ch'eng I is stressed by Mou Tsung-san. In his *Hsin-ti yü hsin-ti*, Pt. I, ch. 1, section 4, "Sung Ming ju chih fen-hsi" (On the Filiation of Sung and Ming Confucianists), he divides the prominent Neo-Confucianists of the period into two major camps. The first camp, based on the philosophy of the *Great Learning*, included only Ch'eng I and Chu Hsi. The second camp, based on the philosophy of the *Doctrine of the Mean*, included all

may also be seen in his promotion of the *Analects* and the *Book of Mencius*. Hitherto, these well-known works were regarded as minor classics fit only to be reading primers for children. With his promotion, the *Great Learning*, the *Analects*, the *Book of Mencius*, together with the *Doctrine of the Mean*, came to be known collectively as the "Four Books", indicating their exalted status rivaling that of the "Five Classics". In addition, Ch'eng I also directed his efforts towards interpretation and exegesis of the established classics. His commentary on the *I-ching* (The Book of Changes) was accepted as definitive by most scholars of the Southern Sung period.[50]

If Ch'eng I had not succeeded in anchoring *tao-hsüeh* firmly in a canonical basis, it is doubtful that the latter would ever have ceased to be an eccentric learning on the periphery of the mainstream of Confucian scholarship. *Tao-hsüeh* was an expression of the moral and intellectual ferment of the Northern Sung period. His fellow *tao-hsüeh* masters gave full rein to the innovating impulse of the times by creating new literature. Ch'eng I, however, directed the upsurge of moral intellectual ferment to revitalize the time-honored Confucian classics. By trusting to the sayings of Confucius, Tseng-tzu, Tzu-ssu and Mencius, instead of putting forward novel ideas on his own authority, Ch'eng I effectively demonstrated that *tao-hsüeh* was not a passing fad but a legitimate development in the best tradition of the ancient sages.

His pedagogical approach also contributed to his impact. He was highly successful in re-establishing the classical norm of master-disciple relationship. This success was due not so much to his severity as to his conception of the role of the teacher.[51] Although he claimed to have rediscovered the *tao* which had been lost to the world for the last thousand years, this *tao* did not consist of any specific doctrine which could be transmitted orally. It was essentially a condition of moral and spiritual attainment. What the master imparted, therefore, was not theoretical or practical wisdom but a piece of himself, as the living embodiment of *tao*. The aim was to steer the disciples onto the

other outstanding *tao-hsüeh* scholars. The significance of the *Great Learning* in Chu Hsi's system has been dealt with by E.R. Hughes.

[50] For example, the list of commentaries on the classics that Chu Hsi wanted the state to recognize as authoritative for examination purpose. See CWCKCC 69, "Hsüeh-hsiao kung-chü ssu-i" (Private Views on the School and Examination Systems).

[51] The severity of Ch'eng I as a teacher is illustrated by the well-known story of Yang Shih and Yu Tso, two of his favorite disciples. One winter day, it was the turn of these two disciples to wait upon the master when the latter suddenly dozed off. Upon waking, several hours later, Ch'eng I found that Yang and Yu were still standing nearby while the snow outside was already more than a feet deep. See *Erh-Ch'eng ch'üan-shu*, wai-shu section, 12:7b–8a.

right path of moral and spiritual development. To this end, the master explained the classics, lectured on specific themes and answered the questions of the disciples. These utterances of the master, however, must not be cherished for their own sake; they were only a means to an end. This instrumental view of knowledge is well illustrated in the following episode, reported in the collection of Ch'eng I's recorded sayings (*yü-lu*). Like the disciples of other charismatic teachers, Ch'eng I's disciples used to jot down his discourses. When some of them presented their version of his recorded sayings to him for emendation and endorsement, he said, "I am still with you; there is no need to read the recorded sayings."[52]

As there was scarcely any man who could not profit from the transforming powers of the master, Ch'eng I was willing to give instruction to all who cared to learn. As such, he contrasted sharply with other Northern Sung *tao-hsüeh* scholars who, as guardians of specific learnings, admitted disciples with great selectivity.[53] Ch'eng I, therefore, could transmit his influences through a larger following. Among his disciples, there were not only men of unbending minds who guarded his teaching tenaciously but also those of outstanding intellect capable of making contributions of their own.

Next to the intrinsic merits of Ch'eng I's teaching and efforts of his disciples, the legacy of Wang An-shih also played a crucial role in the rise of *tao-hsüeh*. There is no question that Ch'eng I's teaching was different from that of Wang An-shih on many vital issues and gained popularity in the general revulsion against Wang's legacy in the aftermath of the Northern Sung debacle. It seems possible, however, that in addition to the factor of reaction, Wang An-shih's legacy also helped the rise of *tao-hsüeh* in a positive manner.

To justify their policies and solidify their hold on power, the Reformers who dominated court politics from the period of Shao-sheng (1094–1097) almost to the very end of the Northern Sung period hailed Wang An-shih as the fount of wisdom. He was canonized "King of Shu", installed in the Confucian temple, taking a station immediately after Confucius and Yen Yüan but before Mencius in the sacrificial hierarchy.[54] Under these circumstances his teaching gradually attained the status of an orthodoxy. In this institutionalization of his

---

[52] The disciple in question was Yin T'un. See SYHA 16:6a.

[53] This statement is based on the assertion of Shao Shuo-chih, See *Sung-shan chi* 15, "Letter to Yuan Chi-kao". The actual propagation of the learning of the *tao-hsüeh* masters of the Northern Sung is the subject of a study by Ho Yü-shen who made a quantitative analysis on the data in the SYHA. See his article, "Liang Sung hsüeh-feng ti ti-li fen-pu", *Hsin-ya hsüeh-pao* 1:1.

[54] See Williamson, *op. cit.*, vol. 2, p. 23.

teaching, we may assume that elements conducive to the interests of the group in power received greater emphasis whereas incongruous elements were pushed into the background. The primacy of political interests necessitated a selective propagation of Wang An-shih's legacy. In this selective propagation, the most valuable elements were always excluded. The greatness of Wang An-shih lies essentially in his intrepid, critical spirit which dared to question all conventional wisdom, permitting nothing to stand in the way of reason. His self-styled disciples could not follow this course. The new policies that he advocated had become the shibboleths of the new orthodoxy and the party in power could not permit these to be scrutinized without jeopardizing its own base of power.[55] As a consequence, discussions of political or institutional questions were discouraged. This avoidance of political topics also explains its aversion to historical scholarship.[56] History is essentially "past politics". In passing judgement on historic events, one could not help reflecting on the "present". On the other hand, the philological legacy of Wang An-shih was innocuous enough to suit the convenience of the authorities. Stemming from Wang An-shih himself, it had prestige. Dealing with the profundities of the mind and natural phenomena, it was intellectually satisfying. Being apolitical, it was safe. Consequently, his philology was the part of his legacy most favored by the government of the Northern Sung Reformers.[57]

It must be borne in mind that there was more to the appeal of Wang An-shih's philology than its utilitarian value as the key to success in the civil service examination. There is irrefutable evidence that many people were moved by its intrinsic merits. Some men, for instance, used the *Tzu-shuo* in a manner that Wang An-shih had intended, namely, as a primer for moral and spiritual regeneration. In this

[55] It may be remarked that with a view to denying the would-be critics of the regime access to information on sensitive matters, the *Jih-lu* of Wang An-shih, like other writings on the administration of Emperor Shen-tsung, was prohibited from circulation. See *Sung hui-yao chi-kao* (*hsing-fa* section), pp. 6538b, 6539a.

[56] As an indication of the aversion towards historical scholarship, prefectural school libraries bearing the name of *ching-shih* (classics and history) were ordered to have the name changed. See Li Tao, *Hsü Tzu-ch'ih t'ung-chien ch'ang-pien*, addendum 28:11a.

It seems likely that the downgrading of historical scholarship is closely linked to the substitution of *ching-i* (knowledge of the classics) for *shih-fu* (poetry and rhymed prose) as the basis of the examination system. See the Southern Sung work, *Ch'ü-wei chiu-wen* 3, p. 20, for a statement. Robert Hartwell, in a well documented article, "Historical Analogism, Public Policy and Social Science in 11th and 12th Century China", *American Historical Review* 76:3, also notes the decline of historical scholarship and historical consciousness during the ascendancy of the Reform Faction.

[57] See Lu Yu, *Lao-hsüeh-an pi-chi* 4, p. 33.

connection, the poet Lu Yu (1125–1210) told of an instructive anecdote:[58]

Hu Chun-ming, a former scholar of my native place, was particularly fond of *Tzu-shuo*. One day, upon taking a bath, he was overcome with joy, saying, "Just then when I was in the bath-room, I found enlightenment (*wu*). The *Tzu-shuo* explanation for the character *chih* (integrity) is 'Integrity is what one does in private which can yet stand the scrutiny of ten eyes'. It is only after thirty years of persistent effort that I come to this understanding."

In another anecdote, Lu Yu showed how *Tzu-shuo* provided imagery and inspiration to the poets of old.[59]

The literary inquisition and the aversion of the party in power towards historical scholarship produced a cultural vacuum which could only be filled by Wang An-shih's philological legacy. Whole generations of scholars were brought up on Wang An-shih's *San-ching hsin-i, Tzu-shuo* and other writings. It cannot therefore be denied that the ways of thinking characteristic of Wang's philology left an indelible mark on Sung intellectual history.

With the disgrace of the Reform cause after the Northern Sung debacle, Wang An-shih's ideas became untenable and were readily rejected. But the ways of thought or mental attitudes that his legacy nurtured could not be rejected overnight. In the fashion of Professor Franz Schurmann,[60] we may refer to Wang An-shih's ideas as his pure ideology and the mental attitudes nurtured by his legacy as his practical ideology. His practical ideology survived the downfall of his pure ideology and provided a genial atmosphere for the propagation of *tao-hsüeh* doctrines.

The points of similarity between Wang An-shih's philological mentality and the *tao-hsüeh* mentality are instructive. Both shared a common orientation, namely, their concern for self-cultivation and cosmological theorizing, as well as a common aversion, namely, their downgrading of historical, empiricist scholarship. In regarding *Tzu-shuo* as a primer for moral regeneration, Wang An-shih undoubtedly subscribed to the

---

[58] *Ibid.*, 2, p. 19.
[59] *Loc. cit.*
[60] Schurmann formulates his concept of pure and practical ideologies in his monumental work on the Chinese Communist Party and government. On the basis of his interviews with Chinese refugees in Hong Kong who have fled from Communist China, he comes to the conclusion that it is possible for practical ideology to be divorced from pure ideology. The refugees, long exposed to the Communist system, have learnt to analyse situations in terms of the Marxist dialectic and other approved Marxist methods. After reaching Hong Kong they are likely to retain these perceptual and analytical tools for a long time although they may have immediately given up conscious Communist goals and values. See Franz Schurmann, *Ideology and Organization in Communist China* (University of California Press: 1966), ch. 1.

instrumental view of knowledge. His etymological endeavors represented a systematic approach to the *ke-wu* (investigation of things) problem of the Ch'eng-Chu school of *tao-hsüeh*. The downgrading of historical, empiricist scholarship by the philological and *tao-hsüeh* mentalities was rooted in a common approach to China's cultural heritage. Both subscribed to the view that Chinese culture had been deteriorating steadily from the pristine days of the Three Dynasties and both committed themselves to a process of complete innovation. From their point of view, nothing in the historic traditions of China subsequent to the Three Dynasties was worth salvaging. History was but a sorry record of human frailty. We may therefore assume that when a man switched his allegiance from Wang An-shih's New Learning to *tao-hsüeh*, there was no need for a re-orientation of the mind, no radical change in the habit of study or philosophizing. The mind nurtured by *San-ching hsin-i* and *Tzu-shuo* had no difficulty in accepting the *T'ung-shu, Cheng-meng* and the recorded sayings of *tao-hsüeh* masters.

With the ground thus prepared, the propagation of *tao-hsüeh* during the early years of the Southern Sung period met with little resistance. Political patronage during the critical moment also helped to build up its momentum. Although Ch'eng I died in obscurity during the supremacy of the Reform Party, his disciples in and out of government service were on hand during the agonizing last days of the Northern Sung period.[61] Reacting to the imminence of the dynastic debacle, they led a concerted attack on Wang An-shih's legacy and recommended a new course of action for the dynasty. The men who played leading roles in the founding of the Southern Sung regime in Hangchow were also on the whole well-disposed to Ch'eng I. The most notable were Chang Chün (1097–1164) and Chao Ting (1085–1147). The latter, in his capacity as Prime Minister, was particularly known to have favored the students of Ch'eng I so that men looking for official appointments

---

[61] Among his disciples who held important posts in court just prior to the Northern Sung debacle were Yang Shih (1053–1135) and Hsü Ching-heng (1072–1128). Yang Shih held the post of Librarian of the Imperial Library and Expositor of Classics of the Mi-ying Palace which gave him easy access to the emperor (SYHA 25:1b). Hsü Ching-heng was successively Drafting Official of the Secretariat and Executive of the Secretariat (SYHA 32:3a). Another disciple, Yin T'un (1061–1131) had been twice invited to the capital but did not serve for any length of time (SYHA 27:1b).

Yang Shih took the lead in denouncing Wang An-shih's legacy in memorials to the throne and in writings for the general public, such as his "San-ching i-pien" (A Critique of the *San-ching hsin-i*), and the "Tzu-shuo pien" (A Critique of the *Tzu-shuo*). Part of the latter has been incorporated into Yang's collected works. Yang's own disciples joined him in this assault. See Li Kuang, *Chuang-chien chi* 8:21b–23b, "Lun Wang shih chi Yüan-yu chih hsüeh" (On the Learning of Wang An-shih and Those of the Yüan-yu Scholars); and Liao Kang, *Kao-feng wen-chi* 1:20–21, "Lun Wang shih hsüeh cha-tzu" (On the Learning of Wang An-shih).

would falsely claim to be the latter's students to augment their chance of success.[62]

[62] The ascendancy of Ch'eng I's learning during the early years of the Southern Sung period was clearly linked to the patronage extended to it by the powerful prime ministers Chao Ting and Chang Chün (See SYHA 44). With the rise of Ch'in Kuei, official patronage shifted surreptitiously back to the learning of Wang An-shih. See Li Hsin-ch'uan, *Chien-yen i-lai hsi-nien yao-lu* (Chronicles of Events Since the Time of Chien-yen, subsequently to be cited as *Chronicles*), p. 5577. However, by then the learning of Ch'eng I had achieved sufficient momentum that the withdrawal of official favor did not seem capable of checking its progress. From time to time voices were raised, referring to it by the perjorative term *chuan-men chih-hsüeh* (narrow or sectarian learning). See *Chronicles*, pp. 2886, 5133, 5305, 5762.

CHAPTER TWO

A Budding Scholar of Practical Learning

EIGHT YEARS before Yeh Shih was born, the hostilities between the rival powers of the Sung and the Chin came to an end with the signing of the peace treaty of 1141.[1] The treaty established a pattern of coexistence which was to endure in its essential form for almost a hundred years.

A peace settlement at this juncture was welcomed by the Jürchen rulers of the Chin empire as a solution for their mounting problems. During the initial years of their military operations in China, their armies had been able to move almost at will, encountering only token Sung resistance. After capturing K'ai-feng and most of the Sung imperial clan, however, as they moved down to the South, Sung resistance stiffened. Loyalist forces rallied around Prince K'ang, lone scion of the imperial line, known in history as Emperor Kao-tsung (reigned 1127–1162), and managed to make a stand behind the Yangtze River. Before long, Sung forces grew sufficiently strong that they were capable of launching counter-offensives into enemy held territories. In addition, the Jürchen presence in North China was also harrassed by widespread bandittry. A peace treaty that legitimated their conquests and allowed them to consolidate their rule was therefore in their best interests to strive after.

The Southern Sung court wanted to put an end to the hostilities for different reasons. The tide of war was indeed turning in its favor. However, the primacy of military considerations which developed during the years of crisis was basically distasteful to the dynasty. Traditionally the Sung dynasty opted for security rather than expansion, and had an ingrained prejudice against military men. During the heyday of the Northern Sung dynasty, army commanders and provincial governors were subjected to stringent control from the center, under a policy of centralization known as *chiang-kan jo-chih* (strong trunk, weak branches).[2] In contrast, the armies now fighting for the Sung cause

---

[1] See SSCSPM 72; also, Herbert Franke, "Treaties Between Sung and Chin", in *Etudes Song* Ser. 1, pp. 55–84.

[2] For the stringent control of the provincial administrators, see Miyasaki Ichisada, "Sōdai shu-ken seido no yurai to sono tokushoku", *Shirin* 36:2 (July 1953). For

after the Northern Sung debacle were almost entirely the personal creations of their commanders who held them together with their charismatic personality, improvised ways for provisioning them, with only token central supervision.[3] This drastic departure from the dynastic tradition naturally gave rise to misgivings to tradition-minded ministers of state. Their misgivings are easy to explain. They claimed that the greatest menace to the security of the dynasty did not come from the Jürchen armies in as much as the latters' drive had been contained but from the commanders of these autonomous Sung armies on the field. If these commanders went from victory to victory, riding the crest of popularity, there was no way to deter them from the ultimate prize — the emperor's throne.[4]

Much of the credit for persuading the emperor to nip the potentially dangerous situation in the bud belonged to Ch'in Kuei (1090–1155), a man of exceptional ability.[5] The field armies which had been rolling back the tide of Jürchen invasion were recalled, their commanders cahiered and a humiliating peace signed with the enemy. With Ch'in Kuei's ascendancy, the Peace Party achieved undisputed power for almost twenty years. Former advocates of war and internal reform were hounded from office.[6] The primary preoccupation of the faction in power was self-preservation which depended upon the preservation of the status quo. Gradually an atmosphere of smug decadence settled on the court, nestling behind the beautiful hills of Hangchow, the new capital.[7]

However, with Ch'in Kuei's death in 1155, the mainstay of the Peace Party was lost. Men of integrity gradually returned to government service. This change in the complexion of Southern Sung politics quickened in 1160 when the threat of an invasion from the North suddenly became imminent. An ambitious man, King Hai-ling (reigned

---

the control of the army, see Lo Ch'iu-ching, "Pei-Sung ping-chih yen-chiu", *Hsin-ya hsüeh-pao* 3:1 (1957).

[3] The most dynamic of the commanders of the autonomous armies was Yüeh Fei. For a scholarly study, see the doctoral dissertation by Edward Kaplan, *Yüeh Fei and the Founding of the Southern Sung*, University of Iowa: 1970.

[4] For the anxiety that ministers of state felt, see Chiang Fu-ts'ung, "Sung-tai i-ko kuo-ts'e ti chien-t'ao", *Ta-lu tsa-chih* 9:7 (1954).

[5] See his biography in SS 473. Also SSCSPM 72, "Ch'in Kuei chu-ho".

[6] The most well-known of those forced into retirement was Chang Chün (died 1164) who had served as Pacification Commissioner Plenipotentiary of Shensi and Szechwan, had been Prime Minister twice, sometimes concurrently as Military Commissioner (*shu-mi shih*) and played a crucial role in devising the overall defensive posture of the dynasty against the Jürchen and their allies. See his biography in SS 361 as well as his *hsing-chuang* (draft biography for the deceased) in CWCKCC 95–1 and 95–11.

[7] See J. Gernet, *Daily Life in China on the Eve of the Mongol Invasion* (Macmillan, New York: 1962), Introduction and ch. 1.

1149–1160), usurped the throne of the Chin empire and decided to conquer the Southern Sung.[8] Rudely awakened to face this peril, the aged Emperor Kao-tsung reversed his time-honored policy of appeasement, and entrusted the reins of power to the advocates of war. By a stroke of good fortune, the Chin army's initial attempt to cross the Yangtze at Ts'ai-shih was foiled, and this minor reverse triggered a *coup d'état* in the Chin camp, resulting in the assassination of the Chin ruler. The new Chin ruler, eager to consolidate his position, sought peace.

Meanwhile, Emperor Kao-tsung abdicated his throne to his adopted son Hsiao-tsung (reigned 1162–1189). The latter, uninhibited by the experience of personal and dynastic humiliation, determined to take advantage of the temporary disarray in the Chin empire and took the offensive. However, his troops were defeated north of the Huai river, and he was forced to accept peace terms. For the remainder of his reign, he refrained from bellicose gestures.[9] Nevertheless, the succession of events had helped to bring into existence a climate of opinion favorable to the *hui-fu* ideology. A new generation of scholar-officials sprung up, who, although too young to stand in the front line of combat during the first years of the Northern Sung debacle, matured and were elated at the prospect of ultimate victory evoked by the heroic exploits of Yüeh Fei (1103–1141) and Han Shih-chung (1089–1151), only to be frustrated later by the slump during the regime of Ch'in Kuei. Their long, pent-up emotions could now find an outlet. Their ranks were swollen by defectors from the North, who, although born in Chin territory, were never reconciled to their alien conquerors, and had availed themselves of opportunities to fight their way to the South and place their services at the disposal of the Southern Sung emperor.[10]

This was the "Augustan Age" of the Southern Sung dynasty. Emperor Hsiao-tsung was a conscientious monarch, and, as emperors went, amenable to Confucian morality. His court was graced by a galaxy of brilliant men who eventually made their way into the halls of fame in their respective fields of achievement: Fan Ch'eng-ta (1126–1193), Yang Wan-li (1127–1206), Lu Yu (1125–1210), and Hsin Ch'i-chi (1140–1207) in poetry; Chu Hsi and Lu Chiu-yüan (1139–1192) in philosophy; Lü Tsu-ch'ien (1137–1181) and Chang Shih (1133–1180) in classical studies. Although we cannot exclude the factor of accident

---

[8] For a comprehensive treatment of this war, see Tao Jing-shen, *Chin Hai-ling-ti ti fa-Sung yü Ts'ai-shih chan-i ti k'ao-shih.*

[9] See SS 33, "Annals of Emperor Hsiao-tsung" and SSCSPM 77, "Lung-hsing ho-i" (The Peace Settlement of Lung-hsing).

[10] Lu Yu and Hsin Ch'i-chi exemplified the former and the latter types admirably.

or chance in attempting to account for the disproportionately large number of talented men in this period, we must also give due acknowledgement to the character of the times. It was a time of guarded optimism and healthy-mindedness: the genial sunshine without which the frail plants of genius could not blossom.

The creative minds of the age drew much of their inspiration from the myth of *hui-fu*, which was an official ideology scrupulously observed by the court. The relevance of this ideology to the lyrical poetry of Lu Yu and Hsin Ch'i-chi needs no explanation. What needs to be kept in mind is the fact that all the other men listed above, without exceptions, were also ardent champions of the *hui-fu* ideology. All took it seriously, and each went on record in expressing his support of the dynastic goal. They differed only with regard to the means for the attainment of the end. Such was the ideological context in which Yeh Shih grew up.

Yeh Shih, whose courtesy name (*tzu*) was Cheng-tse, was born into a family of poor village school-teachers. His great-grandfather, whose given name was Kung-chi, had once attended the Imperial University (*t'ai-hsüeh*) but failed to win any recognition. With a view to improving the life prospects of his children, Kung-chi moved his residence from the ancestral home in Lung-ch'üan in Southwestern Chekiang to Jui-an, in the prefecture of Yung-chia (also known as Wen-chou) on the southern coast of Chekiang, an area of rising prosperity.[11]

We have no information about Yeh Shih's grandfather. His father, Kuang-tsu, seemed to have had more than his share of adversities. At the time of his marriage, for instance, a disastrous flood swept away his house with whatever material possessions the family had accumulated during the past two generations. In addition, all the other plans of his youth seemed to have miscarried.[12] His straitened circumstance was reflected in the frequency with which he moved his residence. During the lifetime of his mother, Yeh Shih recalled, in a span of about forty years, the family moved twenty-one times. Often, they lived in dilapidated houses with missing pillars or beams.

The succession of misfortunes seems to have broken the spirit of Kuang-tsu. There was, however, one bright spot in his life — his marriage which produced five grown sons. His wife, née Tu, was a level-headed and strong-willed woman, and it was she who provided the necessary sense of direction in the family struggle for survival.

The young Yeh Shih was undoubtedly moulded more by maternal than paternal influences. The Tu family, from which his mother came,

---

[11] YSC 15, "Tomb Inscription of the Honorable Mr. Yeh of the Rank of Chih-cheng Chao-ch'ing-lang".
[12] YSC 25, "Tomb Inscription of Yeh's Mother, Neé Tu".

had for generations made their living by serving as *yamen* clerks. In Sung times, the profession of *yamen* clerks was financially rewarding but socially undesirable. They were classified as "mean" people, and as such, they and their children were barred from the civil service examination, the regular avenue for social advancement. Yeh Shih's maternal grandfather broke with this family tradition and sought to live by the more acceptable profession of a farmer. Other members of the Tu clan probably had not abandoned the ancestral occupation and could have used their influence to procure a position in the clerical service for Yeh Shih's father.[13] They had compassion on the plight of the Yeh family and wanted to help. Yeh Shih's mother, however, steadfastly declined their good-will, preferring the poverty of school-teaching to suffering the social stigma of the *yamen* clerks. She wanted her family to remain respectable and looked forward to the day when all her toils and tribulations would be redeemed in the examination halls by her sons. Her faith in study and the examination system as the proper avenue for advancement was eventually vindicated; and she lived just long enough to witness the great happening.

Wen-chou in Southern Sung times was one of the more culture-conscious prefectures in the empire.[14] The ranks of the local literati were swollen by immigrants fleeing from the invading Jürchens in the North.[15] This large literati element had a leavening effect on the overall population. Culture and scholarship were highly esteemed, and there was no lack of wealthy men willing to give employment to an indigent scholar or to help support a talented child. Many wealthy men established colleges (*shu-yüan*), built the premises in secluded scenic areas, endowed them with funds and libraries, and hired competent teachers for them. These colleges and teaching groups, rather than the public educational facilities (*chou-hsüeh* or prefectural schools, for instance), were the main arena of academic activities.[16] They provided the points of contact between the aspiring young men and the more mature scholars of established reputation, and so helped to impart a definite outlook to scholars from the same region.

[13] *Loc. cit.*

[14] The rise of culture consciousness in Wen-chou is traditionally dated to the latter half of the eleventh century when nine scholars from this area travelled North to study under the great teacher Ch'eng I. See SYHA 32.

[15] The family of Yeh Shih's father-in-law was among the emigrès from the North. See YSC 15, "Tomb Inscription of Mr. Kao, Prefect of Yung-chou". The powerful Prime Minister Ch'in Kuei, though strictly speaking not a Northerner (native city, present-day Nanking), also located his residence in Wen-chou. See SS 377, biography of Ch'en Chüeh.

[16] For examples of the private colleges in Wen-chou, see YSC 17, "Tomb Inscription of Liu Tzu-i" and YSC 16, "Tomb Inscription of Lin Cheng-chung".

Judging by available evidences, despite the grinding poverty of his parents, Yeh Shih's childhood was not unhappy. He was not a precocious child, and had the normal boy's love of play.[17] The solicitude of his parents, however, enabled him to make good use of the splendid opportunity for learning that the prefecture of Wen-chou offered. After acquiring the rudiments of reading and writing at home, he ranged far and wide within his prefecture in search of more advanced reading materials and competent teachers. He was blessed with a sweet disposition, and everywhere met with a cordial reception. It was perhaps owing to this fact that, in spite of his humble origin and straitened circumstances, he grew up without the least bitterness against men of wealth. The image of the rich man that was formed through his youthful experiences was of one who made his money the hard way, practised extreme economy himself but manifested liberality towards others.[18]

We have no precise information of the type of educational influences that shaped Yeh Shih's intellectual development during his adolescence. However, in view of the generally advanced conditions of Wen-chou, it may safely be assumed that he was early exposed to the major currents of Sung thought. For example, Liu Yu, a wealthy and public-minded resident of Wen-chou whom Yeh Shih claimed as one of his early mentors, was known to have cherished the legacies of Ch'eng-Chang and Su-Huang.[19] Ch'eng I and Chang Tsai, as leaders of the *tao-hsüeh* movement of the Northern Sung period, stood for a more demanding morality and relentless self-discipline; whereas Su Shih and his disciple Huang T'ing-chien (1045–1105) were literary giants of their time. It is conceivable that Liu Yu had imparted his moral passions and love of literature to the impressionable young Yeh Shih.

In the house of a rich man of Jui-an, Yeh Shih chanced to meet a young scholar who was employed as the tutor to the children of the householder.[20] This chance encounter was to have an incalculable effect on Yeh's life. The young scholar was Ch'en Fu-liang (1137–1203), who was thirteen years older than Yeh and had already acquired a reputation as a master of classical prose. This was in the 1160's when Yeh was still in his teens. Ch'en was to be Yeh's mentor and friend for the next forty years.[21] It was probably at about the same time, or even earlier, that Yeh made the acquaintance of another brilliant young man, Ch'en Liang (1143–1194) of Yung-k'ang, in the central Chekiang prefecture

[17] YSC 18, "Tomb Inscription of Li Chung-chü".
[18] YSC 14, "Tomb Inscription of Mr. Lü".
[19] YSC 17, "Tomb Inscription of Liu Tzu-i".
[20] YSC 16, "Tomb Inscription of Lin Cheng-chung".
[21] YSC 28, "Sacrificial Ode to Ch'en Chün-chü, Drafting Official of the Secretariat".

of Chin-hua. He was closer to Yeh's age and was therefore more likely to receive him on terms of equality. He remained one of Yeh's closest associates till his death, and must have made an indelible impression on Yeh. In the popular mind, Yeh Shih's name was often coupled with Ch'en Liang's, suggesting more or less a single image.[22] Through Ch'en Fu-liang and Ch'en Liang, Yeh Shih was introduced to the cultural elite of Wen-chou.

The tone of intellectual life in Wen-chou was set by two men, Cheng Po-hsiung (1128–1181) and Hsüeh Chi-hsüan (1134–1171), who were very unlike in their life-styles, exemplifying the serene scholar and the dynamic man of action respectively.[23] Significantly, the intellectual antecedents of both men could be traced to the school of Ch'eng I. Cheng Po-hsiung approached the legacy of Ch'eng I through the inspiring example of Chou Hsing-chi (born 1067), a personal disciple of Ch'eng I who spent the greater part of his life teaching in his native city of Wen-chou.[24] Cheng's life was uneventful. He distinguished himself as a scholar of the classics, specializing in the subtle shades of their meanings (i-li). His writings have practically all been lost. But he was remembered as the first person to arrange for the printing of yü-lu (selected sayings) of the Ch'eng brothers in Fukien, and as the scholar who submitted a disturbing memorandum on the subject of hui-fu during the ascendancy of Ch'in-Kuei which brought his official career to an abrupt end. For the rest of his life, until he was recalled to government service in his twilight years, he did nothing except to make his counsel available to all aspiring young men of his prefecture.[25]

Hsüeh Chi-hsüan, six years younger, was caught up in the vortex and tumult of the times.[26] He was orphaned at five and grew up with his paternal uncle, wandering from place to place in the course of his official career. Hsüeh claimed that his studies owed a great deal to Yüan Tao-chieh, an unconventional scholar excelling in the practical arts of military strategy and hydraulic engineering who had studied under Ch'eng I in his youth. The central fact of his life, however, was

[22] A good example is that furnished by Han Hu who enumerated the great men of the Southern Sung in various fields of achievement. The name of Yeh Shih is coupled with that of Ch'en Liang under the category of po-i (rhetoric). See his Ch'ien-ch'üan jih-chi 4:10.

[23] Yeh Shih acknowledged the importance of these two men in the intellectual life of Wen-chou in an essay commemorating the founding of the prefectural school. See YSC 10, "Wen-chou hsin-hsiu hsüeh chi".

[24] For a short biographic account of Chou Hsing-chi, see SYHA 32.

[25] Loc. cit. Pertinent data on Cheng Po-hsiung have been gathered by Sun I-yen in his Ou-hai i-wen 5 (Anecdotes of the Ou Coast, subsequently to be cited as Anecdotes).

[26] Biographic information on Hsüan Chi-hsüan is available in his hsing-chuang by Ch'en Fu-liang in his Chih-chai hsien-sheng wen-chi 51. See also Sun I-yen, Anecdotes 6.

that he was serving as personal secretary to the governor of a frontier prefecture when the Jürchen megalomaniac, King Hai-ling, launched his invasion of the Southern Sung. He acquitted himself well in crucial situations and made the acquaintance of military men who had been comrades in arms of the great generals Yüeh Fei and Han Shih-chung. It was thus in the school of living reality that Hsüeh came to develop a genuine appreciation for the practical sciences, such as military strategy, geography, land revenue, etc. He excelled so much in these fields that his admirers regularly compared him to Chang Liang (d. 189 B.C.) and Chu-ko Liang (181–234), lieutenant and principal adviser to the founders of the former Han and the Shu-Han dynasties respectively. In the midst of his busy life, Hsüeh could not afford the luxury of studying for the civil service examination. Nevertheless, on the strength of his war merits, he was admitted into the regular official hierarchy, and left an impressive record as a prefectural governor. He died unexpectedly before he was forty years old. The example of his life must have been a source of inspiration to younger men of his prefecture. Moreover, he went out of his way to help them. Through correspondence and personal contact, he made an effort to direct them along the right path. His most cherished disciple was Ch'en Fu-liang.

Cheng and Hsüeh thus stood for two distinct approaches to the purpose of education. Cheng was no doubt closer to the central concern of Ch'eng I, viz., the quest for moral truth and unrelenting self-discipline. Hsüeh, on the other hand, emphasized learning for practical use (*ching-shih chih-hsüeh*). These two strains of scholarship actually were not mutually exclusive but complementary, corresponding to the classical Confucian polarities of inner sageliness and outer kingliness. To a considerable extent, both Cheng and Hsüeh seemed to have achieved a proper balance between these two strains. For example, although Cheng was primarily interested in the unraveling of moral truth, he did not neglect the utilitarian aspect of learning. We find him making an effort to tap the expertise of Hsüeh on the potentials of the rivers and lakes of the Huai area for irrigation and defense.[27] By the same token, Hsüeh Chi-hsüan, who excelled in practical learning, also sought to apply to himself the most rigorous moral standards. His commitment to moral self-cultivation may be seen in his efforts to annotate the *Analects*, the *Book of Mencius*, etc.[28]

These two stalwarts of Wen-chou and their disciples had a powerful

[27] Among the letters written by Hsüeh Chi-hsüan is one dealing with Cheng's inquiry on rivers and lakes of the Huai area. See *Lang-yü chi* 24.

[28] See Hsüeh Chi-hsüan's preface to his commentaries on the *Analects* and the *Book of Mencius, Lang-yü chi* 31.

ally in Lü Tsu-ch'ien from Chin-hua. The prefecture of Chin-hua, though located in central Chekiang, was administratively within the eastern circuit of Chekiang. For this reason, these great scholars from Wen-chou, Chin-hua, and their disciples were sometimes referred to collectively as the "Che-tung" (Eastern Chekiang) group. Lü Tsu-ch'ien was a nationally renowned scholar of the classics, and for practically his entire official career, was associated with the Imperial University and the Bureau of Historiography.[29] He was also a man of great versatility, suave and likeable, on excellent terms with nearly all the outstanding men of his age. Chu Hsi, for example, esteemed him so highly that he entrusted him with the education of his own son.[30] Lü was thus in an ideal position to mediate between the men of Wen-chou and the less kindred spirits of the outside world. Consequently, no account of the intellectual pattern of Wen-chou is complete without reckoning with Lü.

Unable to pursue a career of active service to the dynasty, Lü probably sought self-fulfilment in teaching and writing. He was a highly successful teacher. Hundreds of young men walked in his company. His academy, the Li-tse shu-yüan, ranked as one of the foremost in the empire, and the regulations of this academy were widely imitated as a model.

Perhaps the best known of his writings is *Tung-lai po-i* (The Extensive Deliberations of Tung-lai).[31] This is a collection of essays on various episodes of the Ch'un-ch'iu period (722–484 B.C.) as reported in the *Tso chuan*. This period was a time of social and political tumult when the traditional ethic was subject to severe strains. In these essays, using the concrete situations as materials for thought, he explored the realm of moral responsibility. He fathomed the motivations behind the deeds of the protagonists, suggested viable alternative courses of action, and exercised the historian's function of praise and blame. It is the kind of study — a moralistic approach — dear to the heart of Ssu-ma Kuang and Chu Hsi, derived from the tradition of *Ch'un-ch'iu* scholarship which dated from the Confucian revival of the Northern Sung.

However, there is also another side to his learning, as expressed in the less well-known work, *Li-tai chih-tu hsiang-shuo* (A Comprehensive Discussion of the Institutions of the Successive Dynasties).[32] This work,

---

[29] See his biography in SS 434 and his *nien-p'u* (annalistic biography) in *Chin-hua ts'ung-shu.*

[30] See CWCKCC 33, p. 520, "Letter to Lü Po-kung".

[31] *Tung-lai po-i* was intended as a model of examination questions on the classic of *Ch'un-ch'iu.* See Lü's preface.

[32] Some authorities have questioned the attribution of this work to Lü Tsu-ch'ien, as it is neither mentioned in his *nien-p'u* nor in his official biography. However, the mere fact that this work was attributed to him indicated that he had succeeded in

as transmitted to the present day, comprises fifteen chapters dealing with civil service examination, schools, taxation and corvee labor, grain transport, salt administration, statutes relating to the state monopoly of wines, money (metal and paper currency), relief administration, the land tenure system, agricultural colonization, the military system, horse administration, merit rating for officials, imperial clansmen, and ceremonial sacrifices. It should be noted that these topics related to vital government functions of all pre-industrial regimes. Their relevance to the Sung dynasty was particularly marked. Each chapter is divided into two sections, respectively entitled *chih-tu* (systems or institutions) and *hsiang-shuo* (comprehensive discussions). The first section gives a concise chronological account of the evolution of pertinent institutions. The second section applies the lessons of history to a discussion of contemporary systems of the Southern Sung dynasty, pin-pointing their merits and defects. In most cases, the author's judgment was expressed in unequivocal terms. There is no mistaking his point of view. The focus of interest shifted from individual moral responsibility to the institutional framework in which man lived and moved. This concern with the external sphere, the ordering of state and society (corresponding to the *ching-shih* learning of the Wen-chou scholars), was undoubtedly in the *Chou-li* tradition, minus perhaps, an unbridled utopian enthusiasm. Lü kept in mind the paramount factor of feasibility and sought to urge reform within the framework of the dynastic configuration of the Southern Sung.

It was probably difficult for Yeh Shih to attach himself to any permanent teachers for any protracted length of time. He had to work for a living and help support the large family of his father. He probably took up teaching in his late teens or early twenties. His school-house could be a temporary hut or the hallway in a Buddhist temple. The peasant folks whom he attracted to his school could not pay him much. To secure a more steady income, he sometimes sought employment as tutor to the children of more well-to-do families. This took him away from home for long periods of time. We find him, for instance, spending over a year in this capacity in the city of Wu-i, in the prefecture of Chin-hua.[33]

projecting onto the public mind the image of a scholar conversant with both historic and contemporary institutions.

[33] For references to his early teaching activities, see YSC 27, "Letter to the Venerable Mr. Lü" and YSC 14, "Tomb Inscription for Ting Shao-chan". The latter provides the earliest dated reference to Yeh Shih's teaching career (1176) when he was twenty-six. Among the localities away from Wen-chou where he probably worked as a private tutor were Yung-k'ang (See Ch'en Liang, CLCC 25, "Sacrificial Ode to the Mother of Yeh Shih") and Wu-shang (YSC 14, "Tomb Inscription for Mr. Yao").

However, he did find time to pay visits of varying length to those he considered as his mentors, particularly Cheng Po-hsiung and Lü Tsu-ch'ien. We do not have much information on Yeh's relationship with Cheng, but some of the latter's austere moralism must have rubbed off on the youthful Yeh Shih.[34] We have more information bearing on Yeh's relationship with Lü.[35] During the many occasions that they were together, stimulating discussions took place which often centered on the themes or even the specific wording of passages of Lü Tsu-ch'ien's *Sung wen chien* (Anthology of Northern Sung Authors). It was probably due to the influence of Lü, with his emphasis on empirical and concrete learning, that Yeh Shih began to tackle Li Tao's monumental chronological history of the Northern Sung period entitled *Hsü Tzu-ch'ih t'ung-chien ch'ang-pien*.[36] Thus from the start, Yeh Shih's learning was erected on a solid empirical foundation. Apart from Cheng and Lü, he also sought guidance from other quarters, mainly through correspondence, for example, with Hsüeh Chi-hsüan.[37]

Among the diverse strains of learning of the Che-tung masters, it was undoubtedly that of practical statecraft (or, *ching-shih* learning) that had the greatest appeal to young Yeh Shih. It is permitted to youth to have visions, and faith that gives substance to their visions. To Yeh Shih, as to others in the same stage of life, action was more to be valued than contemplation, and positive exertions in the interest of state and society more than dispassionate deliberation for the benefit of moral self-cultivation. Besides, the times (the early years of the reign of Emperor Hsiao-tsung) were propitious and seemed to lend credibility to their visions. Great deeds were what they were hankering after, if not in real life, at least in their fervid imaginations.

Their preoccupation with concrete results in the ordering of state and society naturally found an outlet in their writings. As young men actively preparing for the civil service examination, they had to cultivate the art of essay-writing. However, unlike the typical examination essays (*ch'eng-wen*) which were characterized by generalities and meaningless platitudes, their essays were suffused with a note of contemporary

[34] Yeh Shih acknowledged his discipleship to Cheng in the sacrificial ode he composed for him (YSC 28, "Sacrificial Ode for Cheng Ching-wang"). However, the acknowledgement was couched in such terms that, modesty apart, seems to suggest an intermittent contact, not a sustained master-disciple relationship.

[35] The extent of Yeh Shih's association with Lü Tsu-ch'ien may be gauged from (*a*) his poem, commemorating his visit to Lü in YSC 6, "Yüeh-ku" (Moon-lit Valley) and (*b*) YSC 27, "Letter to the Venerable Mr. Lü". For the tenor of Yeh's intellectual discussion with Lü, see HHCYHM 49:36 and HHCYHM 50:6.

[36] Yeh claimed that he studied the *Hsü Tzu-ch'ih t'ung-chien chang-pien* in his youth. See YSC 12, "Preface to *Sun-yen chi*".

[37] *Lang-yü chi* 25.

relevance. The pertinence of their observations made their work read more like official communications (*cha-tzu*) than examination essays.[38]

The most notable example was Ch'en Fu-liang. Combining immense erudition with a logical and systematic mind, he ranged over the entire gamut of political problems faced by the imperial government of Sung China. His essays were carefully thought-out expositions, supported by an impressive array of appropriate historical analogies. Their most conspicuous character was an undisguised amorality. He wasted no ink on the discussion of ideals. He advocated the optimum efficiency of the bureaucratic government with the emperor in control. From this vantage point, he explored the mechanisms and processes of the imperial government and came up with specific suggestions. Ch'en Fu-liang had studied history well. The dexterity with which he applied historical and cultural analogies is reminiscent of the great writers of classical times, such as Hsün-tzu. And, like the cogently argued essays of Hsün-tzu, his writings had a grandeur and persuasive power that often swept the reader off his feet.[39] They could not be dismissed as academic exercises of a mere literatus; they were a manual for the instruction of the prince. In the popular edition which achieved wide circulation, these writings were in fact entitled *Tai-yü chi* (Expecting to be Appreciated by a Prince).[40]

Likewise, Ch'en Liang aspired to be the teacher of kings.[41] At the age of eighteen, he wrote the *Cho-ku lun* (Treatises on the Ancients), which dealt with the heroic deeds of the great men of former times. He singled out the critical moments of their careers, commented on the merits and perils of the alternative courses of action open to them,

---

[38] The statement about examination essays reading like communications of officials (*cha-tzu*) refers specifically to Wang Tzu-chung whose *hao* was Tao-fu. See YSC 24, "Combined Tomb Inscription for Ch'en Tung-fu and Wang Tao-fu".

[39] The thinking of Ch'en Fu-liang became more conservative as he grew older. To signify his repudiation of the writings of his fire-breathing youth, he consigned them to a ceremonial bonfire. His collected works, *Chih-chai hsien-sheng wen-chi*, is therefore of little use for re-constructing the early phase of his political thought. However, much of his early writings, particularly those pertaining to political commentary, have survived on account of their intrinsic merits. A substantial work, in twelve *chüan*, under the title of *Yung-chia hsien-sheng pa-mien feng* (Eight Cutting Edges of the Master of Yung-chia) is generally attributed to him. Having examined its contents in considerable detail, I have no reason to question the appropriateness of this attribution.

[40] From a statement in *Wen-hsien t'ung-kao* 32, p. 302 which refers to the banning of the books of Yeh Shih and Ch'en Fu-liang, we know that the latter's book was so entitled.

[41] Ch'en Liang attained fame early in life but was repeatedly frustrated in his attempt to pass the civil service examination. SSCSPM 79, the whole chapter, is devoted to his several attempts to sell his ideas on *hui-fu* to Emperor Hsiao-tsung. Ch'en's patriotism has inspired a number of biographic studies of which the most substantial is his *nien-p'u* by Yen Hsü-hsin.

and indicated what he would have done if he were in their place. Seven years later, his penchant for armchair advice gave rise to his *Chung-hsing wu-lun* (Five Treatises on Restoration). These treatises were intended for Emperor Hsiao-tsung, professing to show him how to achieve the dynastic goal of *hui-fu*; to wit, the defeat of the Jürchen enemy and recovery of lost territories.

Yeh Shih was obviously in tune with this overriding concern for relevance. As he confessed in his twenty-fourth year, "Concerning the matters of the army, the penal code as well as the appropriate relationship between law and morality, though I be unworthy, these are the fields of study that I truly devote myself to. . . ."[42] To Yeh Shih in his early twenties, the advice received from his elders was to talk less about generalship and statesmanship but pay more attention to moral self-cultivation. This in effect was the message that the most *ching-shih* oriented of his mentors, Hsüeh Chi-hsüan, had for him.[43]

In his twenty-third year, 1173, he had an opportunity to visit the capital of the dynasty, Hangchow. It is possible that he attended the Imperial University at this time.[44] If he was not formally enrolled as a student, he probably made an attempt to associate himself with this academic community. We have little information about his motives for going up to Hangchow; probably, like all country boys, he yearned for the glamour and excitement of the capital, not to speak of the opportunities for intellectual development. This University was regarded as a respectable avenue for entrance into officialdom.[45] Theoretically, it took a minimum of five years to graduate; but in actual practice, few ever did so. Theoretically too, the University was to provide instruction in the classics and to supervise the study of students through monthly evaluations. But, in actual fact, a large proportion of the students were absent most of the time, and the majority of the remainder were less interested in academic matters than in currying favor with the high and the mighty, or in enjoying a brisk social life. After one year, Yeh became disenchanted. He had nothing but contempt for the mercenary-minded, gay youths of the University. Even the life of the obscure village school-teacher appeared more palatable.[46]

---

[42] YSC 27, "Shang Hsi-fu shu" (Letter to the Military Commissioner).
[43] Hsüeh's letter to Yeh Shih in *Lang-yü chi* 25.
[44] YSC 27, "Shang Hsi-fu shu". This letter was written at the end of his sojourn in Hangchow when he was twenty-five.
[45] See a comprehensive study of this institution by Wang Chieh-ch'iu, *Sung-tai t'ai-hsüeh yü t'ai-hsüeh-sheng*.
[46] His vehement denunciation of this Imperial University in his *Wai-kao*, though written more than ten years later, was probably a reflection of his disenchantment at this time, as he had no further direct contact with this institution.

His experience in the capital does not seem to have helped him mature much. If it made any impact on him at all, what he saw in the University and in the court probably strengthened his self-conceit. He believed that he was the only one (perhaps excepting other members of the Che-tung group) who cared, and who could find a way out of the malaise for the state and society of Southern Sung China. It was in this frame of mind that he addressed a letter to the Commissioner of Military Affairs, offering a general program of reform. It was fairly common practice for men in humble circumstances to try to write to the ranking ministers, hoping to win recognition. We may indeed consider Yeh Shih one of such fame-seekers. Nevertheless, it is more likely that he was consciously following the powerful example of Ch'en Liang, who, five years before, had the temerity to address his *Chung-hsing wu-lun* for the restoration of the dynasty to the emperor.

Yeh's letter had little to commend it as a piece of political commentary; except for felicity of expression, it probably did not differ much from the dozens, if not hundreds, of unsolicited proposals which reached the high ministers every year. He harped upon conventional themes without spelling out his own understanding of them, and gave the impression that he was merely mouthing platitudes. Nevertheless, the letter actually foreshadowed the specific proposals which he was to work out in greater detail in his later, more mature, writings. He emphasized the theme of dynastic disgrace, the causes leading to it, the necessity of avenging it, and the requisite steps that must be taken in striving towards the ultimate objective of defeating the enemy and recovering the ancestral lands. He called for rationalizing the fiscal structure, cutting back expenditure to within the limit of regular revenue, reducing taxation to relieve the burden of the people, investing the provincial governors with greater responsibility, broadening the base of recruitment for government service and delegating authority to the military commanders in the field to increase the effectiveness of the defense system.

Meanwhile, he was building up his reputation as a budding essayist and serious scholar in his home prefecture. As a young man of promise, in spite of his poverty and undistinguished antecedents, he was able to marry the daughter of an immigrant family from the North which was related to the distinguished Northern Sung Dowager Empress Hsüan-jen.[47]

The ultimate badge of respectability and the normal channel for self-fulfilment of the literati class was the passing of the civil service examination. In Sung times, the examination system was not as elaborate

[47] See YSC 18, "Tomb Inscription for Kao Ling-jen".

as that of the Ming and the Ch'ing. There were no academic degrees corresponding to *sheng-yüan* and *chü-jen*. Nevertheless, there were still preliminary examinations at the prefectural level before one qualified for the metropolitan examination. They were a formidable hurdle in prosperous, cultured prefectures where the number of scholars was disproportionately large.[48]

Yeh Shih was under increasing pressure to succeed. He was probably the only one among the many sons of his parents who stood any chance of winning recognition for the family. He had to pass the examination for the sake of his mother who had toiled so hard for her sons and who was now old and suffering from palsy. It is therefore highly probable that he prepared himself for the scheduled triennial examinations of 1173 and 1175, but apparently did not clear the first hurdle, the prefectural examination.

Perhaps fearing that he might be held up indefinitely by the bottle-neck of a preliminary examination, where competition was intense and luck, more than anything else, seemed to be the deciding factor, he began to put his hopes in the *chih-chü* (Decree) examination.[49] This special examination, accessible both to commoners and to low-ranking officials, was theoretically held in greater esteem than the normal civil service examination, and gave the successful candidate a considerable advantage in the struggle to get ahead in his official career. Moreover, the scope of the examination was limited to *ts'e-lun*, that is, treatises and discussions on themes of classical-textual, historical and contemporary interests. Though the prescribed subject matter was practically limitless and the standard of passing extremely rigorous, it was never-theless an endeavor much more congenial to Yeh Shih's *ching-shih* propensity than the criteria of elegant phraseology, prosody, meter and rhyme that the ordinary civil examination required. Since the *chih-chü* examination was held at infrequent intervals at the wish of the emperor, Yeh proceeded to write a cycle of about fifty practice essays on themes and topics most likely to occur in this kind of examination. Writing such essays not only served to clarify his ideas on the most pressing problems of state and society, but was also the only way to secure pre-liminary recognition from someone in a responsible position necessary to qualify him for this examination. These essays have been preserved under the name *Chin-chüan* (Presented Scrolls).

Yeh Shih did not make his way to fame and success via the route of

---

[48] For a comprehensive account of the examination system of the Northern Sung, see Chin Chung-shu, "Pei-Sung k'o-chü chih-tu yen-chiu", in *Hsin-ya hsüeh-pao* 6:1.

[49] See Nieh Ch'ung-ch'i, "Sung-tai chih-chü k'ao-lüeh", in *Shih-hsüeh nien-pao* 2:5 (1938).

the *chih-chü* examination. But his labor had not been in vain, for his essays earned him the endorsement of Chou Pi-ta (1126–1204), one of the better known prime ministers of the reign of Emperor Hsiao-tsung. Chou deplored the fact that a man of such ability should be frustrated by the inequitable system of the prefectural examinations. Therefore, as an expedient, he acknowledged him as his kinsman and so enabled Yeh Shih to participate in the *ts'ao-shih* (examination held by the Fiscal Intendant of the circuit), thus bypassing the prefectural bottleneck.[50] Competition in this examination was less severe and Yeh Shih won first place among those who passed. This was probably early in 1178. Subsequently, he went on to pass the metropolitan examination of the same year.[51] Less than six months after his triumph, his mother died.[52]

Yeh Shih's first official assignment was as the *t'ui-kuan* (Staff Supervisor) of P'ing-chiang in present-day Soochow area. He probably served for a very short period, if he served at all in this capacity, for he resigned from the office as soon as his mother died. By 1181, he had received a new appointment as *p'an-kuan* (Prefectural Judge) of Wuchang (in the present-day Wuhan area).[53] It is not known how long he stayed in this new post, probably for the whole three-year term. He was now in his early thirties, and had just finished mourning for his mother. Then both Cheng Po-hsiung and Lü Tsu-ch'ien, who, of all Yeh's mentors, meant most to him, died in rapid succession within a single year. This series of tragedies and the fact of assuming real administrative responsibility (although in a limited way) for the first time in his life probably had a sobering effect on him. He realized he still had a long way to go in scholarship. Besides, there was the imperative need to master the immense body of government regulations and bureaucratic precedents if he wanted to succeed in his long-term political ambition. Wuchang

---

[50] Sun I-yen, *Anecdotes* 8:1. According to Li Hsin-ch'uan (*Chronicles*, pp. 4539–4540), the ordinary prefectural examinations were a hundred times as competitive as the *ts'ao-shih*, undoubtedly an exaggeration. During the early years of the Southern Sung, the quota for the *ts'ao-shih* was set at one for every seven candidates.

[51] The year he passed the examination was the fifth year of Hsün-hsi (1178–1179).

[52] YSC, "Pen-chuan".

[53] There are evidences that Yeh was present at the funeral of Cheng Po-hsiung and probably also at that of Lü Tsu-ch'ien — both died in 1181. It is therefore justifiable to assume that he had not taken up his appointment at Wuchang before these events. The evidence in the case of his presence at Cheng's funeral who died in his office at Chien-ning is furnished by Ch'en Liang in his letter to Chu Hsi (CLCC 27): "Cheng-tse (Yeh Shih's courtesy name) is making rapid progress in learning. He has come a long way and is no longer the same scholar whom you used to know at Chien-ning."

For Yeh Shih's probable attendance at Lü's funeral, see HHCYHM 50:10, "After the burial of Master Lü at Mount Ming-chao, [Ch'en] Liang and Pang Ching-yü desired me to succeed to the position of the master. In view of the fact that I received instructions late in the master's life and among the disciples there are many outstanding persons, I declined the offer."

was a remote, isolated town with few distractions. His official duties were light, leaving him plenty of time to attend to his own studies. For the moment, he was content to stay where he was. It was perhaps not altogether for form's sake that he declined the recommendation of the Junior Preceptor of the Heir-Apparent, Shih Hao (1106–1194) which could have resulted in an appointment in the capital for him.[54]

When the tenure of his appointment at Wuchang duly expired, he was able, with the backing of influential friends, to obtain the appointment as *kan-pan kung-shih* (Executive Assistant) to the Judicial Intendant of Che-hsi (Western Chekiang).[55] This was the first real challenge to his administrative and judicial ability. The office of Judicial Intendant had jurisdiction not only over purely judicial matters, but also over a wide range of business, such as the supervision of the money and grain to be forwarded to the central government, suppression of banditry, operation of the *pao-chia* system, administration of arsenals, and supervision of river and canal maintenance. Moreover, Che-hsi was one of the most densely populated circuits of the empire, containing the imperial capital of Hangchow. The seat of the office was at Soochow, then probably second only to Hangchow in prosperity. As Executive Assistant to the Intendant, Yeh Shih's primary responsibility was general administration rather than jurisdiction over criminal matters;[56] consequently he was bombarded with a constant stream of business of such volume and complexity which would have overwhelmed a lesser man. Even with his previous experience at Wuchang, Yeh found it necessary to carry with him a copy of the official regulations and to make reference to it unceasingly.[57] This was very embarrassing, but somehow he muddled through. He stayed fully three years in Soochow. These years of struggle with the intricacies of bureaucratic practice must have left an indelible imprint on his mind. His understanding of governmental institutions and processes attained a depth which he lacked previously.

Yeh Shih was a genial man and was back in his element in the familiar

[54] Sun I-yen, *Anecdotes* 8:39a, "Shih Wen-hui Recommended Shui-hsin". Yeh Shih's reason for declining the recommendation is set forth in a letter to the Prime Minister Chao Hsiung (YSC 27).

[55] Ch'en Liang in a letter to Prime Minister Wang Huai (CLCC 19) commended Yeh Shih strongly. Chou Pi-ta, Yeh's first patron, probably also helped. Chou's letter to Yeh Shih, dated the ninth year of Hsün-hsi (1182) shows that he continued to hold Yeh Shih in high regard. See *Chou I-kuo Kung chi*, "Shuo-kao (Correspondences) II".

[56] For the delineation of responsibilities between the two principal assistants to the Judicial Intendant, see the statement by Liu Hou-ts'un, *Hou-ts'un hsien-sheng ta-ch'üan chi* 79, "P'i Yung-ning chih-ch'eng ch'ung pen-ssu kan-kuan shen sheng chuang".

[57] YSC 23, "Tomb Inscription for the Former Prefect of Yüan-chou, Mr. Lo". Also YSC 28, "Sacrificial Ode to the Vice-Minister, Mr. Lin".

climate and accent of Kiangnan and the bustling life of Soochow. The
slight touch of decadence in the quality of city life was not sufficient
to depress him, but on the contrary seemed to have a mild, stimulating
effect on his spirits, making him more conscious of his high resolve.

His friends had been abetting him as far as possible. After the death of
Lü Tsu-ch'ien and Cheng Po-hsiung, Ch'en Fu-liang was undoubtedly
the senior Che-tung scholar. He sent Yeh Shih off when the latter was
leaving his home in Jui-an to take up his new post in Soochow, composing a valedictory poem for the occasion. It opens with the following
lines:[58]

> It has been a busy year,
>> sending friends off on their travels.
> The wine has run out,
>> and the poetry is no longer elegant.
> You are the last to part from me.
> How a welter of feelings throng into my mind!
> There was a sage in Mount Ch'i,[59]
> With the powers of government and religion,
>> making the crude people of Pin good.
> You and I are men of mature years,
> And we come from the same place on the shore of the sea.
> Surely we will not fall into the same predicament
>> as Liu Pei, who, while quaffing wine with Ts'ao Ts'ao,
> Changed countenance,
>> upon a single remark from his drinking partner.

The reference is, of course, to the celebrated boast of Ts'ao Ts'ao:
"The only heroes of the world are you and I."[60] While it is advisable
to make allowance for what is known as poetic license and not take the
language literally, Ch'en's high esteem for Yeh is unmistakable. Years
later, as we will see in Chapter Seven, he was to pay Yeh one of the
highest compliments that one scholar could accord another.

During these years in Soochow, Yeh Shih was certainly well occupied.
In addition to his onerous official duties, he also made himself available
to all students who were eager to learn. This was the first peak in his
teaching career. We will deal with this subject at greater length in
Chapters Four and Eight. It was probably as a result of the interaction
with his students that he came to see many of the problems of contem-

---

[58] *Chih-chai hsien-sheng wen-chi* 2, "Sending Yeh Cheng-tse Off to Join the Staff
of the Judicial Intendant of Che-hsi".

[59] Mount Ch'i was the place of origin of the ancestors of King Wen and the Duke
of Chou, revered sages in Chinese history. It is therefore reasonable that Ch'en
Fu-liang had the sage-ruler in mind when he used the expression "the singing phoenix
of Mount Ch'i".

[60] See *San-kuo chih* (Dynastic History of the Three Kingdoms) 32, "Biography of
the First Ruler of the Shu Kingdom".

porary state and society in a new light. He would seek relief from his anxieties by meditating on what he was going to do if he indeed had a chance to run the imperial government, sharpening his views on various facets of government operations, military and fiscal reform, and so forth.

Meanwhile, his stock was definitely rising. His first patron, Chou Pi-ta, was beginning his ascendancy at court. The prime minister, Wang Huai (1127–1190) was also favorably disposed towards him. Yeh Shih's reputation as a scholar and essayist spread gradually,[61] enhanced no doubt by his high placement among the examination graduates of his class. After the death of Yao Ying (1150–1183), who had been placed first in the metropolitan examination in which Yeh was placed second, Yeh Shih was at the head of his class.[62] Candidates passing the examination in high ranks were usually selected for posts in the Imperial University or other academic agencies, a shortcut for rapid promotion. Yeh's turn came before long. Recommended by Kung Mou-liang, Assistant Privy Councilor in 1185, he received the appointment of *t'ai-hsüeh cheng* (Rectifier of the Imperial University).[63]

This was a significant landmark in his life, almost as significant as his passing the examination six years before. Appointments in the university carried a prestige far above their nominal rank — they were stepping stones to higher things. As Rectifier of the Imperial University, he would be part of the academic community and would have opportunities to attend to his own studies. Moreover, in the course of time, he would be called upon by the emperor to deliberate on matters of state and society. This access to the ear of the emperor, in the capacity of personal advisor, was what he cherished most of all. It was to be the occasion for the fulfilment of his lifelong dream — putting his *ching-shih* ideas into practice through an appreciative emperor. Anticipating that moment when he would find himself face to face with his "Prince", he reviewed all the operations of the government which had a bearing on the fortunes of the dynasty and reduced his thoughts to writing. This effort resulted in about forty essays, preserved under the title *Wai-kao* (External Draft).[64]

---

[61] We have the text of an appointment letter for Yeh Shih for a position in the Board of Personnel, written by Lou Yüeh (*Kung-ku'ei chi* 38, p. 357). Lou Yüeh singled out Yeh's literary talents as particularly worthy of mention.

[62] Yao Ying (1150–1183) was the son-in-law of the Prime Minister Wang Huai and a close colleague of Yeh Shih at the time of his death. See YSC 13, "Tomb Inscription for Mr. Yao, Staff Supervisor of P'ing-chiang Prefecture".

[63] YSC, "Pen-chuan".

[64] Years later, Yeh Shih himself gave a precise account of the circumstances under which he wrote the *Wai-kao*. See YSC PC 15:843.

It was in the thirty-fifth or thirty-sixth year of his life that he wrote his *Wai-kao*. His official career had barely begun, and was to continue until his early sixties. However, he never again had the same inclination or opportunity to address himself directly to the problems of the dynasty on such a vast scale and in such a comprehensive manner. *Wai-kao*, therefore, together with *Chin-chüan*, could be regarded as a fair epitome of his *ching-shih* ideas.

We will have to postpone discussing the greater part of the ideas of *Chin-chüan* and *Wai-kao* until the relevant chapters later on. Meanwhile, to appreciate fully the state of mind which Yeh Shih reached at this juncture and to see his subsequent career in the proper perspective, it is necessary to consider the program or grand strategy that he worked out in his *Wai-kao* for the realization of the *hui-fu* objective. *Hui-fu* was the compelling goal to which everything else was subservient.

CHAPTER THREE

A Plan for Complete Restoration
of the Sung Dynasty

IN EXPLAINING why the dynastic objective of *hui-fu* had not been accomplished, Yeh Shih alluded to two inhibiting factors, viz. (*a*) a procrastinating attitude known as *tai-shih* (waiting for opportunity) and (*b*) a rash approach to military operation known as *ch'in-cheng* (expedition led by the emperor himself).[1]

In view of the magnitude of the task, procrastination is an understandable attitude. Pretexts for non-action can always be found. As usual, Wang An-shih's legacy was a useful whipping-boy. His notorious dictum of the "three not worths" was irrefutable proof that he and his partisans were impious men who feared neither Heaven nor man. Altering at random the institutions of the dynasty and causing harm to the multitudes, they defied the laws of Heaven. Heaven therefore allowed the Jürchen cause to prosper as a chastisement to the Chinese. As long as the wrath of Heaven persisted, there was nothing that man could do except to wait patiently and make amends. Eventually, it was hoped that Heaven would relent (*hui-huo*) and permit a revival of Sung fortunes.[2]

Another useful pretext for procrastination was supposedly provided by historic precedents. It was argued that no previous barbarian regime in China had been able to perpetuate itself peacefully for more than several generations.[3] As the Chin empire was already several decades old, its impending end could not be very far off. It was therefore prudent to wait a few more years until the enemy started to disintegrate.

The second of the inhibiting factors that Yeh Shih adduced is also easy to substantiate. It was generally known that Emperor Hsiao-tsung esteemed the military arts of horsemanship and archery and practised

---

[1] YSC PC 10, "Hsi-hsü lun I, II" (The Silencing of Impractical Views).

[2] For a clear exposition of this mentality, see Ts'ao Hsün, *Sung-yin chi* 25:3b–10b, "Discourse on War and Peace, Fearing Heaven and Protecting People".

[3] Ch'en Liang alluded to this view in his series of letters to Emperor Hsiao-tsung. See CLCC 2, "Chung-hsing lun".

them himself.[4] It is therefore possible that he cast himself in the role of Emperor T'ai-tsung of the T'ang dynasty (reigned 627–649) personally leading his troops to victory. His desire to play a direct role in military action against the Jürchen enemy is clearly indicated in his parting instruction to Yü Yün-wen, the hero of Ts'ai-shih, whom he sent to be viceroy of the Szechwan circuits.[5] Capitalizing on the emperor's weakness, men with an eye for self-advancement often posed as strategists or knights-errant claiming that they knew of a secret route for rapid troop movements or they had cultivated contacts within a certain strategic city facilitating its capture.[6] The emperor's absorbing interests in the purely tactical aspects of war undoubtedly detracted from the dynasty's ability to make long range preparations for war which alone held out promise of a sure and permanent victory. With no guarantee of victory, military operations against the enemy were not unlike gambling and it is no wonder that some of the most esteemed of the prime ministers of the emperor were adamantly opposed.[7]

Yeh Shih was not the only person who traced the failure of the dynasty to implement its *hui-fu* objective to psychological reasons. The poet statesman, Hsin Ch'i-chi, for instance, dealt with the prevalent myth that Southerners made poor soldiers and could not be a match for the sturdy peasants of North China, traditionally the best recruiting grounds of Chinese armies.[8] The inhibiting effect of the myth is indisputable: the Southern Sung regime which had to depend on the unsoldierly material of the Southerners could never hope to defeat the Chin empire which had access to the best troops of China. To demolish the myth, Hsin Ch'i-chi produced a countervailing one, namely, the inability of barbarians to rule in China permanently:[9]

---

[4] See Li Hsin-ch'uan, *Chien-yen i-lai chao-yeh tsa-chi*, Pt. II, p. 10.

[5] Among other instructions, the emperor exhorted Yü Yün-wen to pay special attention to the army so that when the order for mobilization came, the Szechwan army under Yü Yün-wen could effect a conjunction (*hui-shih*) with the army under the direct command of the emperor. See SS 383, biography of Yü Yün-wen.

[6] Yeh Shih commented on this matter in his *Chin-chüan*. See YSC PC 4, "Ping-ch'üan II" (Expediency in Military Matters).

[7] The most well-known of the prime ministers opposing the use of force for attaining the *hui-fu* objective were Shih Hao and Wang Huai (1127–1190). See notes 2 and 3 of ch. 4.

[8] Hsin's program for dynastic restoration was set forth in his *Mei-ch'in shih-lun* (Ten Discourses Presented in Humility), preserved in *Chia-hsüan shih-wen ch'ao-ts'un*. See section 4, "Tzu-ch'ih" (Putting One's Own State in Order).

[9] *Loc. cit.* Hsin's anti-fatalist sentiments was also strongly mirrored in Lu Yu's poetry, for instance the following couplet: 南人孰謂不知兵 ， 昔者亡秦楚三戶 in *Lu Fang-weng chi*, vol. 2, ch. 11, "Shih-yüeh erh-shih-liu jih yeh meng-hsing Nan-cheng tao-chung".

Your minister has heard those who make observations on the condition of the empire say, "The potentialities of the North and the South are fixed. The frailty of Wu and Yüeh (i.e. the South) cannot be pitted against the robust strength of the Middle Kingdom (i.e. the North)." In reply, your minister ventures to say, "There is a constant principle operating both in former and present times: the barbarians with their stinking filthiness cannot permanently feel at home in China."

To support his anti-fatalist posture, he marshalled a series of historic precedents to shatter the widely held misconception of the Southerner. It may be observed that this psycho-historical approach which he used so effectively was also extensively employed by other Southern Sung advocates of the *hui-fu* ideology.[10]

By debunking the inhibiting myths, advocates of the *hui-fu* ideology generally pressed for immediate action. Ch'en Liang, for instance, warned that the sentimental attachment of the people in North China to the Sung dynasty would soon vanish when the generation who personally lived under Sung rule passed away.[11] If the emperor procrastinated, it was possible that ambitious men would rise, overthrow Jürchen rule and set up their own regimes. If these possibilities materialized, the moral claim of the Sung dynasty to North China would be much weakened.

Both Ch'en Liang and Hsin Ch'i-chi dealt with issues beyond the military sphere and offered suggestions for reform. However, institutional reform was a minor theme in their writings. The main thrust of their effeort was to sway the will of the emperor to take prompt action in the military sphere. By contrast, Yeh Shih of the *Wai-kao* seems to take the will of the emperor for granted and proceeded to show him how to work towards the *hui-fu* objective. His emphasis was not on the end but the means.

Like modern geo-political strategists, Yeh Shih did not see the struggle with the Chin empire primarily in military terms.[12] The outcome of the struggle did not depend so much on the relative valor of the contestants as on the material resources available to them. In this regard, he pointed out the Southern Sung enjoyed an overwhelming advantage over the Chin empire. Due to differences in the development of their respective economies, the territories of the Chin empire, though amounting to half of China, produced no more than two or three tenths of the total revenue compared to seven or eight tenths produced by territories of

[10] See Ch'en Liang CLCC 2, "Chung-hsing lun"; Yang Wan-li, *Ch'eng-chai chi* 88, "Lun ping shang" (First Section, Discussion of Military Matters) and Wang Chih, *Hsüeh-shan chi* 1, "Shang huang-ti shu" (Memorial to the Emperor).
[11] See YSC PC 10, "Shih-mou" (Practical Planning) which presents a succinct account of his vision of the struggle between the Southern Sung and the Chin empire.
[12] *Loc. cit.*

the Southern Sung. However, in spite of this advantage, the Southern Sung was militarily weak. Why? Yeh Shih's explanation was that the potential superiority was dissipated through the perverse practices of the dynasty. It is only by purging the body polity of these evils that the potential superiority of the dynasty could be translated into actual superiority. In Yeh Shih's terminology, this was *shih-mou* (practical planning).[13]

In line with this practical planning, Yeh Shih visualized a reorganization of the state in four vital areas: finance, army, essential institutions of the dynasty (*fa-tu*) and the structural principles of the body politic (*chi-kang*). His prescription for reform in each of these areas might be of questionable value. However, in putting his emphasis on these structural-functional aspects of the current regime, he was at least on the right track in his attempt to rejuvenate the dynasty.

In his diagnosis, the malady that afflicted the body politic of the dynasty in each of these areas was a simple case of over-exertion. Overtaxation of the people resulted in an unwieldy, inefficient fiscal structure and in chronic impoverishment of the people. Over-recruitment of troops resulted in a rabble army which consumed state revenue but lacked fighting ability. Excessively regimented institutions resulted in increasing bureaucratic red-tape. Excessive regimentation of personnel (*chi-kang*, signifying stringent discipline or submission to a hierarchy of authority) resulted in a lack of responsibility on the part of officials. The logical remedy for this disease was to reverse the process that caused the malady. Yeh Shih therefore counseled a general retreat — a drastic retrenchment of central governmental activities. Given the premises, this was the only rational solution.

The problem of finance remained in the forefront of governmental concern throughout the three hundred years of the Sung dynasty. It was a principal focus of controversy in Wang An-shih's reforms. The urgency of the problem increased with the Northern Sung debacle. In the period of transition before the consolidation of the regime in Hangchow, the regular sources of revenue were slow in coming; there was consequently no way of raising army funds except through irregular levies. When the exigency eased, no attempts were made to repeal these levies. The tax burden of the people thus grew by gradual accretion. As an indication of their plight Yeh Shih pointed to the increase of government revenue. He claimed that the money revenue of the Sung dynasty in its heyday, before the reign of Emperor Shen-tsung (1068–1085) was double that of the Han and the T'ang, that Wang

---

[13] YSC PC 11, "Ts'ai-tsung" (Overall Comment on Revenue).

An-shih, with his rapacity, boosted it to several times the previous amount, that his self-styled disciple, Ts'ai Ching (died 1126) doubled it again and since the dynasty was established South of the Yangtze, it doubled again so that it reached an unprecedented height.

This enormous amount of tax money was collected by a multiplicity of agencies and the burden computed on a variety of bases. Yeh Shih did not indicate in what way the method of collection was responsible for the unsatisfactory performance of the whole fiscal system. But he alleged that in consequence of the obsession with money, all worthy projects had to be suspended because there were never sufficient funds for them. The greater the sum of money that was raised in taxes, the more additional money was needed — there was always the feeling of insufficiency. By contrast, he argued, in former times, when the tax receipts were low, there was always a surplus. During the most prosperous days of the Han dynasty, the reigns of Wen-ti (179–157 B.C.) and Ching-ti (156–141 B.C.), the wealth of the empire was in fact not funneled into the metropolitan region of Kuan-chung. Even when the Chinese world split up into the Three Kingdoms or into the Northern and Southern Dynasties, well regulated systems of appropriation and distribution were still in operation. He clinched his argument that money never was the crucial factor of success or failure of empires by pointing out that the Sui dynasty (589–618) was the richest and yet failed to perpetuate its rule whereas the T'ang (618–905) was the poorest and yet rose to power.

Yeh Shih then gave an historical account of the proliferation of levies which had the effect of concentrating all public revenue under the central government. The resource base of the prefectures and counties was progressively diminished. He had no intention of undoing all that had transpired since the heyday of the dynasty; he merely wanted to do away with what he regarded as unwarranted accretions. The most pernicious of these accretions was known as *ching-tsung-chih ch'ien*, a levy for army rations.[14] The revenue so raised was mainly earmarked for the support of the four field armies and managed on their behalf by the *tsung-ling-so* (comptrollers). To raise the required revenue, each prefecture and county was assigned a quota which it had to remit from proceeds collected within its area of jurisdiction under a variety of indirect taxes such as a sales tax on documents, on houses and on other income-yielding properties. Unlike the yield of the "Double Tax", the regular tax on land which was collected twice a year, the collection of the *ching-tsung-chih ch'ien* was all year round, with the consequence

[14] For a study of the importance of this tax, see Hisatomi Ju, "Nansō no zaisei to keiso seisen", in *Hakudai shigaku* 9 (1964).

that the prefectures and counties were under pressure to remit funds on a monthly basis. It is this feature that made the levy particularly irksome. Yeh Shih listed three serious consequences. Firstly, demoralization of the officialdom: all that was on the mind of the district magistrates and prefectural administrators was that the *ching-tsung-chih ch'ien* quota be remitted on time as the higher authorities gave them no respite in their relentless drive to get them to deliver their quota.[15] They were fighting a losing battle and could never extricate themselves from the mounting pressure.[16] Little energy was left to attend to other important affairs of local government. Secondly, increasing impoverishment of the people. Yeh Shih claimed that with the proliferation of direct and indirect taxes which hit the people at every turn of their business transaction, the formerly wealthy people became less wealthy and those in less comfortable circumstances were reduced to dire straits. Thirdly, the impoverishment of the state: with the ruinous level of taxation, the government was depleting the resources of the state.

He proposed that the total *ching-tsung-chih ch'ien* quota be reduced by half. This drastic reduction would afford welcome relief both to government officials and to the people. Next, he proposed that the tax known as *ho-mai* (harmonious purchase) be abolished altogether. *Ho-mai*, as the name indicated, originated in the government actually paying in advance for the commodities (usually silk cloth) requisitioned. Later on, the advance was withheld but the commodities were demanded all the same. Sometimes the people were required to commute their commodity obligations to cash payments, known as *che-pi* (commutation) so that the people actually ended up paying an additional

[15] The manner of the remittance of this revenue was probably related to the manner of collection. As income from the revenue yielding sources, such as excise tax, stamp duty etc., was generated all the year round, so remittance was spread out evenly over the year. For the *tsung-ling-so*, see Ide Tatsuro, "Sōryō kō", in *Saitama Daigaku kiyo* 5 (1956).

[16] Hu T'ai-ch'u, a late Southern Sung official, in his manual for the offices of *hsien* magistracy, *Tsou-lien hsü-lun* 9, pp. 14–15, "Li ts'ai pien" (Management of Finances) enumerates the revenue sources available to the *hsien* magistrate. He does not seem to share Yeh's desperate view of *hsien* finance because, among other reasons, he wanted to impress his readers with his skill as an administrator. Yeh Shih, however, was probably not exaggerating the plight of this office. Throughout the Southern Sung period, there were indications that qualified officials were reluctant to take up this assignment with the result that many *hsien* magistracy positions remained unfilled and there was a rapid turnover rate. Among remedies proposed for the situation, were suggestions to vest the *hsien* magistrate with greater authority and exhortations to the superior offices, viz. the prefectural and circuit administrators, to moderate their financial demands. See *Huang-Sung chung-hsing liang-chao sheng-cheng*, p. 1320. For the responsibilities of the magistrate's office, see Brian E. McKnight, *Village and Bureaucracy in Southern Sung China* (University of Chicago Press: 1971).

tax in money. Yeh Shih argued that if this unjustifiable tax were removed, the people would be eternally grateful.[17]

He also wanted to put a stop to the abuse-ridden practice of *che-pi*. Often this commutation was pegged to inflationary prices and when the prices fell, the hapless tax-payers had to sell two or three times the stipulated length of silk cloth to make up for the price differential. There is no reason why the people should be penalized for the vagaries of the market.

Finally he touched on the matter of state monopoly of tea and wine. He believed that something should be done in this area also, but the time had not come for him to discuss the details. With the halving of the *ching-tsung-chih ch'ien* and the abolition of *ho-mai* and *che-pi*, if one were to abolish the tea and wine monopolies also, there would not be any money left to run the government. He promised to come back to this topic in one or two years after the rest of the blueprint of his reorganization plan had been implemented.[18]

He commenced his discourse on the army by making the point that it was wrong to idolize the military systems of the past and disregard the realities of the present. Within the framework of the current dynasty, he tried to drive home the lesson that so far as the army was concerned, it was quality rather than quantity that should be cherished. The astounding victories of Emperor T'ai-tsu (reigned 960–975) were achieved with an army totaling less than two hundred thousand. It was only when the military power of the dynasty showed signs of weakness under increased Khitan and Tangghut pressure that the army was swollen to about a million men. Numbers were therefore an indication not of strength but of weakness.[19]

Since the establishment of the court south of the Yangtze, the best troops had been those stationed in four strategic locations along the Northern frontier, known as *ssu-t'un chu ta-ping*. They were formed of the nuclei of the autonomous personal armies of the celebrated generals of the era before Ch'in Kuei. In addition, there were the palace guards protecting the capital and many categories of provincial and local troops. Together they approximated to one million men. Yeh Shih alleged that this enormous army was impressive only on paper. Not only was it unable to function as an effective deterrent against foreign encroachment, as the abortive invasion of the Chin emperor

[17] YSC PC 11, "Ts'ai-tsung". Practically all Southern Sung writers concurred with Yeh Shih that the level of taxation was excessive. Among the more vocal spokesmen were Chao Ju-yü (died 1195) and Ch'en Fu-liang.
[18] YSC PC 11, "Ho-mai", "Che-pe", "Ch'a-yen".
[19] YSC PC 11, "Ping-tsung lun I, II" (Discussions of the Army).

Hai-ling indicated; it was also hopelessly inefficient in coping with internal troubles. Yeh Shih alluded to the unedifying incident some ten years ago when a band of several hundred tea smugglers decided to defy the dynasty, rose in revolt and roamed at will over the country-side.[20] The uprising was not put down for two or three years, until, after repeated failures by the local authorities, the poet-statesman Hsin Ch'i-chi was specifically appointed by the court to co-ordinate local efforts. The ineffectiveness of the frontier armies was due to their size. Their nominal strength was over three hundred thousand. This large standing army could not be maintained on an adequate basis of remuneration. To supplement their meager stipends, troopers took to trades and officers to roll-padding. The consequence was that the effective fighting strength of the armies was no more than four or five tenths of the nominal strength.[21] Another debilitating factor was the system of control over the armies. The armies were placed under the direct command of the emperor who guarded his prerogatives jealously even against his own ministers. All appointments and promotions of personnel were decided by him in consultation with his close attendants who constituted what was known as the inner court.[22] Yeh Shih charged that because of this system, the army officers could not hope for preferment through recognition of their merits — the emperor had no independent access to the pertinent facts except through his attendants. The officers therefore hastened to ingratiate themselves with the denizens of the inner court, and as a result, incompetence and corruption were rampant in the higher echelons of the army command system.

If the frontier armies were in a sorry state, the provincial and local troops were more so. Originally the various categories of troops such as *hsiang-chün* (rural troops), *chin-chün* (imperial troops), *kung-shou* (archers) and *t'u-ping* (native troops) were each supposed to perform a different function and financed in a particular way. The archers and native soldiers, for instance, were usually assigned to police and patrol duties and were financed as militia of local communities and consequently not a charge on county and prefectural treasuries. The *hisang-chün*

---

[20] Yeh Shih alluded to this incident in the *Chin-chüan*, not in the *Wai-kao*. See YSC PC 4, "Wai-lun III" (Discussion of External Affairs). For Hsin's part in this campaign, see his biography in SS 401.

[21] The rampant corruption in the frontier troops was a matter of common knowledge. Yang Wan-li, for instance, referred to the padding of the army rolls. See *Ch'eng-chai chi* 88, "Lun-ping shang" (First Section, Discussion of Military Matters).

[22] The direct control of army personnel by the emperor was an imperial prerogative which even the enlightened Emperor Hsiao-tsung guarded jealously. See Lou Yüeh, *Kung-ku'ei chi* 93, "Tomb Inscription for Chung-wen (i.e. Chou Pi-ta)", p. 887.

was a public works corps and the *chin-chün* a corps of professional crack troops. Eventually these functional differences were blurred and all of them came to depend to varying degrees on prefectural and county government support. Meanwhile their organizational structures and lines of authority remained distinct so that they could not be effectively mobilized to act in concert to a common end.

Yeh Shih's remedy for the ills plaguing the military establishment of the dynasty was to reduce the size of both the frontier and the prefectural-local armies. Reduction and simplification of structure would result not only in tremendous savings but also in improved quality. Without reducing the frontier armies, no relief could be brought to the finances of the central government; without reducing the prefectural and local troops, no relief could be extended to the finances of the local government.

Yeh Shih's analysis of the major civil institutions (*fa-tu*) will be discussed in detail in Chapter Six.[23] To summarize the main points here, it may be said that he made an attempt to expose the absurdity of the dynasty's effort to arrange everything with a view to forestalling the evils that had plagued the Late T'ang and the Five Dynasties, namely, the insubordinate military governors. He tried to show that under the warping influence of this obsession, the vital institutions of the state had all been malfunctioning. This was the ultimate cause of the discomfiture of the dynasty. It was analogous to the case of the stupid man who, to use a well-known Chinese expression, for fear of hiccoughs, refrains from eating altogether. Yeh Shih then took up the major institutions of the dynasty one by one, viewing them in this light and came up with general suggestions for reform. He called for a reduction in the emphasis on rules and favored giving more power to the Board of Personnel in the matter of merit evaluation. He also made some daring recommendations such as the abolition of the whole sub-bureaucratic service of the office clerks (*hsü-li*) and reduction of superfluous circuit intendants (*chien-ssu*).

Yeh Shih's section on *chi-kang* is the shortest of the four principal divisions into which his analysis of the ailments of the body politic is divided.[24] He was of the opinion that *fa-tu* and *chi-kang* actually meant the same thing, differing only in their scope and connotation. In this respect, while *fa-tu* denoted the various political institutions, *chi-kang* signified the configuration of the political and military forces, or the structural principles of the body politic. In theory, *fa-tu* and *chi-kang* are conceptually seaparate; but in practice, it is often difficult to separate

[23] See ch. 6, sections 3 and 4.
[24] YSC PC 14, "Chi-kang I–IV" (The Structural Principles of the Dynasty).

them. Yeh Shih therefore repeated much of what he wrote in other sections.

However, in bringing the disparate pieces together and making them fall in place, Yeh Shih was trying to see his subject-matter in proper perspective. In so far as he tried to see the Sung dynasty as a totality, we may call his approach a "macro" one. The macro approach is not new in Chinese historiography. In a crude way, Confucian scholars had long been accustomed to visualize historic periods, for example, the Hsia, Shang and Chou of the Three Dynasties grouping, as concrete wholes. Each of these dynasties was thought to be characterized by one particular virtue, namely, loyalty, sincerity and refinement respectively. These virtues were not predicated of the actions of any one man but of all who then lived, probably as a function of the total institutional arrangement of the times. Similarly, it had long been recognized that the invincibility of the Ch'in army in the Warring States period was not entirely due to the innate martial prowess of the Ch'in people, but was a function of the institutional arrangement of the Ch'in state.

This macro approach was also frequently applied to the subsequent dynasties. By general consensus, the Han dynasty had the ideal polity, well balanced between central control and provincial autonomy. The following dynasty, the Chin (265–317), sought to erect bulwarks for the imperial house by establishing enfeoffed kingdoms of collateral lines. This decision resulted in internecine warfare and weakened the dynasty. The T'ang dynasty began with a well-balanced polity but had gone to the extreme of decentralization after the An Lu-shan Rebellion (755–763). Military governors with plenary powers within their areas of jurisdiction were originally appointed to bolster and co-ordinate frontier defense. After the rebellion, a great number of these military governorships were set up in the interior, with the result that the whole empire passed under the rule of arrogant satraps. The T'ang dynasty perished because of the excessive strength of the provinces.

Historical commentators of the Sung dynasty realized that their own dynasty had swung to the other extreme and erred in reducing the provinces to utter impotence.[25] To illustrate their point of view they often used a favorite analogy — a country house. The encircling outer ramparts, intended as a main line of defense, should be tough and forbidding whereas the inner apartments, intended as the living quarters, should be soft and comfortable. In their opinion, the troubles of the T'ang dynasty after the An Lu-shan Rebellion were due to the

[25] A good example of this line of historical theorizing is that of Su Che, in his *Luan-ch'eng ying-chao chi*, chs. 1–3.

fact that the inner apartment were treated as if they were the outer
ramparts, hard throughout. The troubles of the current dynasty were
due to the fact that the outer ramparts were treated as if they were
the inner apartment, and made soft. With the voluntary demolition of
the protecting bulwark, the dynasty had a hard time keeping the wolf,
i.e. the enemies, from the door.

Yeh Shih's analysis of this subject was not much superior to other
commentators of the Sung period. But he seemed to have a greater
conviction of the relevance of his insight to the contemporary scene.
If the woes of the dynasty were due to the disarming of the provinces,
why not rearm them? The course was not without peril. It could conceivably lead to a return of the situation when powerful satraps held
their own court in regal fashion, with the emperor completely powerless
to restrain them. Yeh Shih tried to put these fears to rest by saying that
the danger of insubordinate military governors was grossly exaggerated.
In this connection, he stated that during the Five Dynasties period,
the rapid change of regimes was not brought about by ambitious
governors, as was generally supposed, but by ambitious petty officers.[26]

The stage was now set for Yeh Shih to reveal his astounding program
of reform. The many debilities under which the dynasty labored had
all been probed, their causes diagnosed. All indeed was not well with
the dynasty. There were problems and weaknesses almost everywhere.
Moreover, the problems were so numerous and interconnected that it
would be futile to try to deal with them one by one. Individual solutions
to individual problems were like palliatives. They had no efficacy
against the disease of the entire polity. What was required was a gigantic
effort to reshape the structure of the polity, "cutting the Gordian
Knot", so to speak. With the built-in debilities of the polity removed,
a polity of strength instead of weakness would emerge and all the
troubles hitherto plaguing the dynasty would vanish.

For the emperor to apply himself to this gigantic task of reshaping
the polity of the dynasty, the difficulties were both psychological and
practical. There were the mental inhibitions to overcome, the fear that
once the accumulated wisdom of the ancestors was disregarded, the
evil genie which they had with so much difficulty confined to the bottle
might be uncorked to stalk the unhappy land again. The practical
aspects of the problem were no less formidable. How and where was
the emperor to begin in this overhaul of the machinery of government?
The problem was complicated by the fact that, unlike the overhauling
of an automobile or a ship which is usually done in a garage or in dry

[26] YSC PC 14, "Chi-kang II".

docks, the overhauling of the machinery of government had to take place while the engine was still running — a shutdown was impossible. The vital functions of the state could not be suspended while the vital organs were taken apart and mended. For this reason, it might be more apt to compare the proposed regeneration of the dynasty to surgical operations on a sick man. To provide for an extra margin of safety, extraneous help, in the form of an artificial heart or lung was often necessary. Yeh Shih believed that this extraneous help to cushion the shock of conversion to the new regime (i.e. the rejuvenated dynasty) was available and should be applied.

When all parts of his blueprint were implemented and functioning normally, he alleged, there ought to be a perfect equilibrium — no shortage of funds or intolerable strains. Meanwhile, in the thick of the conversion process, while the yield of those revenues scheduled for reduction had diminished as expected, the revenue-consuming activities might not have retrenched at a similar rate — a time lag was to be expected. It is here that the extraneous help was to be applied. He calculated the scheduled reduction of revenue over a two-year period to be around sixty million strings of cash. After two years, the retrenchment of consumption should have caught up with that of production and the extraneous help could be withdrawn. The emperor should have no difficulty paying for the sixty million strings of cash out of his personal purse.[27] By so doing, he could demonstrate a selflessness greater than any ruler since remote antiquity and signify his unshakable purpose of persisting with the regeneration of the dynasty. All the evil practices plaguing the dynasty for two hundred years would be swept away. The people who benefitted from drastic tax-reduction would remain forever his devoted subjects. The bureaucracy, purged of debilitating practices such as the mechanical operation of promotion by seniority, would become the emperor's supporters, eager to advance the interests of the dynasty. The prefectural and county governments, relieved of the need to support troops, would acquire greater freedom of action, and become resourceful in dealing with local problems. The army, greatly reduced in size and improved in efficiency, would become an army of crack troops, disciplined and yearning for the excitement of combat. The polity of weakness would surely be transformed into a polity of strength.

One final item in Yeh Shih's reorganization plan remains to be discussed. He probably felt that the frontier defense could not become really strong and the army really efficient unless the frontier army

[27] The private treasury of the Sung emperors was known as the *nei-tsang*. For a study of this aspect of Sung finance, see Umehara Kaoru, "Sōdai no naisō to sasō", *Tōhō gakuhō* 42 (1971), pp. 127–176.

commanders were given complete control over everything that had a bearing on the success of the army. He therefore counseled a form of "feudalization" of the frontier. On the basis of the existing four frontier armies, four autonomous commands were to be established, located in Liang-Huai (modern Kiangsu-Anhui), Kiangnan (modern Kiangsi), Ch'ing-Hsiang (modern Hupei), and Szechwan, each with complete charge over military and civil affairs within the area. Within the areas of their jurisdiction, the central government would not intervene in any way. The only thing required of them was that their armies be strong and victorious. There was no need for them to have big armies. Bigness was in itself an obstacle to efficiency. It sufficed for these armies to number thirty to forty thousand men each so that their combined strength would be around one hundred and thirty thousand, more than enough to cope with the standing army of the Chin empire. With this level of armament, it was not necessary for the commands to extend their authority to the hundred odd prefectures of Szechwan, Ch'ing-Hsiang, Kiangnan and Liang-Huai. The revenues of a few prefectures would suffice to support a command army of this magnitude. Consequently only a minority of these prefectures would be placed directly under the jurisdiction of the commands; the others would be attached to them in name only. With this arrangement, the rest of the empire would be completely exempted from the obligation of supporting the frontier armies.[28]

Yeh Shih presented his plan for the feudalization of the frontier as if it was an entirely new concept. As a matter of fact, something similar to it had been implemented by the dynasty not too long ago. During the turbulent years following the initial Jürchen invasion, the Southern Sung court established a system of autonomous commands under the name of chen-fu shih (Commissioner of Stabilization) in strategic areas. The poor performance of these commissioners against the enemy and fear of their potential for self-aggrandizement led the dynasty to phase them out after a few years. Probably anticipating strong resistance on this score, Yeh Shih wrote:[29]

At present, it is a very serious matter to assign troops and territories to [the generals]. However, without alarming the empire and without agitating the multitudes, it could be done in a single day if Your Majesty so wills it. Having accomplished it, the effect will persist, and will be accepted willingly by [the multitudes] as the normal order of things. Within a few months, all the afflictions of the people would be removed and in two years, the soldiers would be brave and the officers spirited, fearless of death.

[28] YSC PC 15, "Chung-lun" (Concluding Remarks).
[29] Ibid., p. 819.

If all the obstacles were overcome, Yeh Shih promised, the cherished dynastic goal of complete restoration would be in sight. In two to five years, the full benefit of the reorganization would be felt and the whole state ready for action. It would be a struggle in which the Southern Sung empire would be able to bring its full preponderance of material resources to bear. Szechwan of the Sung would confront Shensi across the Chin border and would overcome the latter; Ch'ing-Hsiang of the Sung would confront Han and Wei (Western portion of Honan) across the Chin border and overcome the latter; Liang-Huai of the Sung would confront the Liang and Pien (Eastern portion of Honan) and would overcome the latter. The powerful Sung navy (*yen-hai chih-chi ssu*) would confront Chin naval units stationed in Shantung and overcome the latter. This left the rich provinces of Liang-Che, Fukien, Liang-Kwang and others uncommitted in the reckoning of strength and would vastly boost the Sung margin of preponderance over the enemy. Thus, in this anticipated war of total mobilization, the victory of the South over that of the North was a foregone conclusion.

In coverage and cogency of argument, there is no question that Yeh Shih's *Wai-kao*, in which he set forth his reorganization plan, is an outstanding specimen of writing. It is easy to disagree with him on detailed points of fact. However, factual errors do not seriously detract from the force of his argument. He was basing his case on premises, the validity of which most of his contemporaries were inclined to concede, bringing in empirical data only by way of illustration. For instance, when matching the geo-political units of the Sung and Chin empires in his vision of total warfare, he used not the contemporary names of the circuits or prefectures but the ancient designations and in descrying the phenomenal growth of unwarranted taxation, he gave not the actual figures in strings of cash or other countable units of account but the proportions of increase. Yeh Shih was therefore not likely to be vulnerable to criticism of his facts. Once his premises were conceded, it was difficult to find fault with his logic.

One might indeed question the wisdom of his specific recommendations such as the immediate halving of the *ching-tsung-chih ch'ien* quota or the soundness of his estimates such as his claim that the revenue of a few prefectures would suffice to support an army of thirty odd thousand. One might also criticize him for his failure to anticipate and make provision for the possible incompatibility between the proposed innovations and the basic stock on which they were to be grafted, e.g. the difficulties likely to be caused by the autonomous commands on the frontier. Was the head of the command to serve a definite term or to serve for life? If the former, how was his position to fit into the civil-military hierarchy of the central government, and what would have to be done to prevent him from engaging in intrigues in the inner court as previously? If serving for life, what inducement would he need to give his last ounce of energy to the job? Admittedly, these were serious objections and could nullify the avowed benefit of the whole reorganization plan unless resolved. Nevertheless, they were still of a technical nature and cast no doubts on the soundness of the plan in principle.

Yeh Shih's reorganization plan could only be accepted or rejected as a whole. It appears that the chances of its acceptance were slim in view of the fact that its unstated assumptions were anachronistic and contrary to historic realities.

We began this chapter with a discussion of the apparent difference of approach towards the *hui-fu* objective between Ch'en Liang and Hsin Ch'i-chi on the one hand and Yeh Shih on the other. The remark was made that whereas Ch'en and Hsin concentrated on persuading the emperor to make up his mind to strike at the enemy right away, Yeh Shih was mainly interested in showing him how to do it. Nevertheless after this long detour, the differences between Yeh Shih and the others which formerly loomed large now seem to have evaporated into thin air. The image of the emperor that Yeh Shih revealed is that of the omnipotent monarch whose commands all mortal men hastened to perform. When all the rhetoric has been discounted, Yeh Shih's reforms seem to boil down to this: it was the will of the emperor, not the impersonal collective will of the complacent, career-minded bureaucrats, that decided whether the rule by seniority could be abrogated, whether superfluous official posts and sinecures could be abolished, whether the proliferation of taxes and tax-gathering bureaux could be halted. It was the sense of propriety, or gratitude for imperial grace, not calculation of advantage that bound the frontier commanders and interior administrators in allegiance to the emperor, even in the face of seductive enticements from a rival regime. The conjunction of these assumptions produced the illusion of the Gordian Knot which Yeh Shih wanted the emperor to cut.

In the final analysis, so far as Yeh Shih was concerned, whether the dynasty could be regenerated and the *hui-fu* objective achieved still remained a question of whether the emperor would or would not, not whether he could or could not.[30] Yeh Shih thus fell into the same fallacy as Mencius in the latter's attempt to persuade King Wei of

---

[30] The *locus classicus* of this distinction between non-ability and non-willingness is the remark by Mencius (*The Work of Mencius*, translation of James Legge, p. 142): "Therefore Your majesty's not exercising royal sway is because you do not do it, not because you are unable to do it."

Liang to implement "Kingly Government". Mencius' exposition of its feasibility is by itself a logical, well-reasoned argument, but it is unrealistic because it did not take into account the nature of the polity within which the king operated. Given the semi-feudal structure of Chinese society during the Warring States period, no reform had any realistic chance of success unless it had the blessing of the noble houses which often disposed as much wealth as the king.[31] By the same token, it is unlikely that the emperor of Sung China could have accomplished anything against the will of the scholar-official class.

As the civil service examination by the Sung period had become the principal channel of recruitment for the civil service, the relationship between the ruler and the scholar-officials may be characterized as one of "Symbiosis".[32] The emperor could not do without the scholar-officials who provided structure for both state and society, and supplied qualified manpower to keep the machinery of the state running as well as moral leadership to keep the people under control. By the same token, the scholar-officials could not do without the emperor, for it was he who justified their position by certifying their competence to play their role in state and society through the civil service examination.

With the consolidation of this partnership between the emperor and the scholar-officials and with diminishing faith in an anthropomorphic or theistic Heaven undermining the traditional rationale of the emperor as the mediator between Heaven and Man, the Chinese monarchy emerged into a new light in which the emperor was not so much above the polity as part of it, in the sense that the scholar-officials were also part of it. Contemporary Sung usage underscored this point. In popular parlance, the emperor was known as "Kuan-chia" or "Chao Kuan-chia" projecting not the image of an awe-inspiring, transcendental ruler, but that of a man, an official and as such, more kindred and accessible to the people.[33] This de-mythologization of the emperor made it possible for him to be the object of warm affection, but it also diminished his

---

[31] The state in the Warring States times was evolving in the direction of the absolute monarchy. However, with the exception of the state of Ch'in, the tendency towards centralized control did not gain complete ascendancy. There is no question that at the time of Mencius, the families of the great ministers shared power with the titular ruler in most states. For an excellent study of Chinese society at that time, see Hsü Cho-yun, *Ancient China in Transition* (Stanford University Press: 1966).

[32] For a succinct account of the relationship between the emperor and the literati, see Joseph Levenson, *Confucian China and Its Modern Fate* (University of California Press: 1964), vol. 2.

[33] The Dowager Empress Hsüan-jen, for instance, referred to her grandson, Emperor Che-tsung, as *kuan-chia*. See SSCSPM 44. Popular literature also frequently attests to this usage. For example, *Shui-hu chuan* (Water Margin) 19, the hero Yüan Hsiao-wu sang a song ending with the line "chung-hsin pao-ta Chao Kuan-chia" (striving loyally to repay the kindness of the emperor).

traditionalized charisma. He was no longer a god demanding unreasoning submission. As a man, he had to deal with the people in human terms. The consequence was that he had to win and hold their support by his largesse or else they might defect from his cause.

The loyalty of the subject to the throne was thus a conditional one. Under the stress of external aggression and internal turmoil, the conditionality of this loyalty became manifest. With the exception of a handful of unusually idealistic men, few high officials were willing to risk their life for the cause of the dynasty. Self-sacrifice was not part of their bargain. The old feudalistic ethic of paying the ultimate price for one's lord was now supplanted by the ethic of contract of which self-preservation was the supreme law. This lack of backbone was the primary reason for the rapid collapse of the Sung defense north of the Yangtze River at the time of the Northern Sung debacle. Weighing their personal advantage, many officials abandoned their charge and fled at the approach of the enemy; others capitulated and took service under their new lord. Quite a number of Sung officials, civil and military, who lost out in the power struggle at home, defected of their own accord to the Chin empire or to the puppet Chinese regime that the Jürchens set up.

By the time the dynasty was re-established in the South, especially after the Ch'in Kuei interlude, prudence dictated that one did not do anything to jeopardize the comfortable circumstances of the present in pursuit of a doctrinaire good. The uncertainties of war discouraged a bellicose posture. Yeh Shih was not unaware of the indifference of most scholar-officials to the dynastic goal of *hui-fu*. In fact he was the author of a revealing analogy in which he likened their moral obligations to avenge the disgrace of the dynasty to isolated patches of fungus infection on the body.[34] The fungus would not cause serious trouble if one did not scratch it. The routine of life therefore went on: scholars continued to pass the examination, became officials, enjoyed handsome emoluments and displayed a righteous indignation whenever the disgrace of the dynasty was alluded to. But concrete action in prosecution of the *hui-fu* objective was unimaginable. It was tantamount to scratching the itch, bringing infection to the whole body.

In the context of the prevailing, pacifist mood, the decision early in Emperor Hsiao-tsung's reign to take the offensive might be regarded as a temporary aberration. It followed in the wake of a series of traumatic events: the abortive attempt of the Chin King Hai-ling to conquer the Sung, Emperor Kao-tsung's abdication to his adopted son Hsiao-

[34] YSC PC 10, "Shih-i" (Initial Discourse), p. 760.

tsung and the turmoil in the Chin empire after the assassination of Hai-ling. The familiar framework of reference of the Sung ruling elite was jostled out of focus for the time being and the advocates of a knockout blow against the Jürchen power momentarily gained the upper hand. Nevertheless the decision to take the offensive was not backed by an all-out effort, by total mobilization of troops. The offensive was more in the nature of a probing movement, and when the Sung forces met the first sign of stiff resistance, the faint-hearted enterprise was called off. Peace was soon concluded and normalcy, i.e. the situation *ante bellum*, was re-established.[35] The consequence of this abortive attempt to reconquer the North was further to confirm the wisdom of abiding by the *status quo* and to damn the few hotheads who took the *hui-fu* myth seriously.

However, the emperor himself did not seem to have given up hope. While sharing the same reluctance of gamble with the last remaining possessions of the dynasty, he was more conscious of the moral duty incumbent upon him. After all, it was his ancestors that were taken prisoner and it was the possessions of his house that were despoiled by the Jürchen invaders. Doubtless his sense of propriety was outraged, permitting him no real peace until the wrongs were redressed. He could not count on the support of his court, which held to a different order of priorities. The only way he could hope to achieve his objective was to rely on himself, on his personal resources and make the whole enterprise a private, not a public concern. It is only with this end in mind that we can account for the phenomenon of the rapidly swelling sources of revenue that were diverted into the emperor's private purse, the *nei-tsang-k'u* (Inner Storehouse). Emperor Hsiao-tsung was extremely frugal; he was building up a monetary reserve so that one day, when the appropriate moment came, he could put together an army and lead it himself, without calling upon the reluctant scholar-officials and the country to share in the risk and the expenses. It would be his own war, not that of the state over which he presided.

[35] SSCSPM 37, "Lung-hsing ho-i" (The Peace Settlement of Lung-hsing).

CHAPTER FOUR
The Untiring Activist

YEH SHIH was probably born too late for the role which he had marked out for himself — namely, as the right-hand man for Emperor Hsiao-tsung, guiding him in the great enterprise of Restoration. By 1185, when Yeh Shih was brought to the capital as Rectifier of the Imperial University, the emperor had been on the throne twenty-three years. His youthful enthusiasm had long since evaporated. As he grew older, his generosity and capacity for trust in his ministers also diminished. Men of strong views who clashed with him and with one another over matters of policy, such as the prime ministers Yü Yün-wen[1] and Shih Hao,[2] were gradually removed from office. They were replaced by men of a more conformist, sycophantic type such as Wang Huai,[3] whose greatest ambition was to hold the line against further institutional and personal rot. Radical reform was out of the question.

Yeh Shih was undoubtedly disappointed by the situation he found at court. The emperor did not grace him with a visit. He had to wait for his turn in accordance with the regular procedure for a court audience — the Sung dynasty had perpetuated the practice whereby all capital officials, regardless of rank, took turns in addressing the throne on matters of grave importance every five days.[4] Yeh Shih's opportunity did not come until his third year in the capital.

Following the established rule, Yeh Shih prepared a well-written text for his address, known as *cha-tzu* which was then submitted for the perusal of the emperor.[5]

[1] Yü Yün-wen was the hero at the battle of Ts'ai-shih where the Sung forces foiled the attempt of the Chin emperor Hai-ling to cross the Yangtze River. This exploit was his springboard for a great political career. See his biography in SS 383.

[2] The most complete biographic account of Shih Hao is his *shen-tao pei* (tombstone inscription) by Lou Yüeh (*Kung-ku'ei chi* 93, pp. 874–883). Shih was the tutor of Emperor Hsiao-tsung before his accession and was known for the vehemence with which he contradicted the emperor and other high ranking ministers.

[3] Lou Yüeh portrayed his character very well in the *hsing-chuang* he wrote for Wang. See *Kung-ku'ei chi* 87, pp. 800–810.

[4] See Li Hsin-ch'uan, *Chien-yen i-lai chao-yeh tsa-chi*, Pt. I, 9:6.

[5] YSC PC 15, "Report to the Throne".

His *cha-tzu* was a powerfully written document, covering essentially the same points as his *Wai-kao*. He again commenced by emphasizing the imperative need to avenge the wrongs of the dynasty and enumerated what he called *ssu-nan* (four problems) and *wu pu-k'o* (five perversities) which had hitherto held up all efforts towards this goal. The "four problems" were: (*a*) the disinclination of the ruling house to take action, rationalizing the failure to avenge the dynastic wrong as a mark of compassion and a reluctance to involve the people in further suffering; (*b*) dissension of opinions among the officialdom; (*c*) lack of talent, namely, capable and dedicated officials; and (*d*) the perverse rationale behind the government institutions which were all designed to forestall bygone evils (such as those prevalent in the Five Dynasties), but were oblivious of the calamity of the present day. This rationale in turn was responsible for the "five perversities": (*a*) the abundance of troops as a source of weakness; (*b*) the abundance of money as a source of destitution; (*c*) not trusting officials but trusting clerks; (*d*) relying not on men but on law; and (*e*) evaluating officials not on the basis of merit but on that of seniority.

He wound up his address with a rousing call for action, alleging that these "problems" and "perversities" would be removed in due course, if the emperor was in real earnest. It is to be noted that Yeh Shih had dropped his concrete suggestions for a radical revamping of the body politic, the immediate halving of the *ching-tsung-chih ch'ien* quota and the feudalization of the frontier defense system. Perhaps by this time Yeh Shih had reservations on their feasibility. Nevertheless, there was no apparent diminution of his optimism and he confidently predicted that if his diagnosis was accepted and proper remedial actions taken (without telling his imperial reader what they were), the long cherished dream of the dynasty of recovering the lost territories would be realized within five years.

The pledge of a five-year limit was perhaps sheer bravado. Emperor Hsiao-tsung literally raised his eyebrows and remarked, "I am now afflicted with an eye ailment and my ambition has vanished. Who would be equal to this task? It is appropriate that we speak with such frankness to you."[6]

Shorn of his specific recommendations and his systematic treatment of political institutions, Yeh Shih's proposal for the Restoration of the dynasty could not have had much impact on the emperor. Needless to say, no appreciable action ensued. Nevertheless, with his enthusiasm and eloquence, Yeh had probably projected a favorable image. Thus,

[6] YSC, "Pen-chuan", p. 7.

following this court audience, he was promoted to the more prestigious position of Professor of Imperial Sacrifices (*t'ai-ch'ang po-shih*) and concurrently Reviewing Officer (*chien-t'ao*) of the Bureau of Veritable Records (*shih-lu yüan*).[7]

As Rectifier of the Imperial University, and later on as Professor of Imperial Sacrifices, Yeh Shih was in charge of educational functions. However, it was not in these official capacities that he made the greatest impact on the younger generation. The Imperial University was an integral part of the official hierarchy and relation between faculty and students was rather stiff. It was in his capacity as a private teacher that he made his influence felt. Initially he went into teaching out of necessity. Later on, as he advanced in learning and as his material circumstances improved, teaching to him became a means of self-realization and a vocation. He was probably a gifted teacher, and eager students living several hundred *li* away would come to study under him.[8] As was the custom of the time, many of them chose to "live in" with their master and travel with him in the course of his official career. Most of his students would eventually take the civil service examination and enter into official life; consequently Yeh Shih had to shape his curriculum with this objective in mind. However, it is plain that his appeal did not consist primarily in his superior skill in getting people through the examinations. His students were attracted by his youthful idealism. They followed him because they felt he was sincere in his quest of *tao* — the way of the sage kings which had the ultimate objective of perfecting the individual and putting the world in order. Probably they were also impressed by his breadth of interest.[9]

The stories of Chou Nan and Wang Chih were good illustrations of Yeh Shih's effectiveness as a teacher. Chou Nan (1159–1213), a native of Wu-hsien of the Soochow area, had a brilliant, inquisitive mind. In his eagerness to fathom the mysteries of Heaven and Earth, he had little patience with the pedantry of most school-teachers. It was said that in a single year, he changed his teacher five times. This man became a faithful disciple of Yeh Shih and followed him for many years after the termination of his post in Che-hsi.[10] Wang Chih was

[7] *Loc. cit.*

[8] YSC 13, "Tomb Inscription for Mr. Li".

[9] His breadth of interests is attested by the following facts: (*a*) He claimed to have instructed the Meng brothers in the art of making a living, YSC 25, "Tomb Inscription of Meng Ta-fu". (*b*) His association with men of heroic temperaments, knights-errant, strategists, YSC 12, "On Sending Lu Jih-hsin Off". (*c*) One of his most devoted students eventually passed the military examination and had a successful career as a military commander and weaponry expert, YSC 22, "Tomb Inscription for Li Ling-wei".

[10] YSC 20, "Tomb Inscription for Chou Nan-chung".

the nephew of the retired prime minister Wang Huai. Having studied under Yeh Shih for some time, he made it a point to return to his mentor once a year and stayed several days to renew his studies. Nothing could keep him from his annual rendezvous: not the threat of political persecution when the learning of the foremost scholars of the land, including Yeh Shih, was castigated by their enemies in power as "bogus learning"; not even the imminent delivery of his pregnant wife.[11]

Yeh Shih's philosophy of education will be discussed in greater detail in Chapter Eight. Suffice it to say here that he was in close touch with the current trends in the scholarly world. His mentor, Lü Tsu-ch'ien, in an attempt to direct the upsurge of *tao-hsüeh* interests into appropriate channels, had taken the initiative to arrange for the meeting at Goose Lake (1175) between Chu Hsi and Lu Chiu-yüan, leader of the rationalist and the idealist wings of the *tao-hsüeh* movement respectively. To counteract the extreme idealism of Lu Chiu-yüan, Yeh Shih seemed to have laid particular emphasis on utilitarian studies and developed a program of instruction tailored to individual needs and capabilities. His goal was to enable each student to reach his maximum potential instead of insisting that each student strove to become a sage.

Nevertheless, for practical purposes, Yeh Shih's views on education were not radically different from those of his more illustrious contemporaries, such as Chu and Lu. Like them, his emphasis was not on imparting technical skills but on the training of knowledgeable men of superior moral sensibility and stamina. It was this basic affinity of outlook that prompted Yeh Shih to spring to the defense of Chu Hsi when the latter came under one of the most vicious attacks of his life. When Chu Hsi apparently declined a significant appointment in the Board of War, a severe indictment was brought against him by Lin Li, vice-president of the Board of War, a protégé of the powerful prime minister Wang Huai, who had been permitted to retire recently. Lin's charges against Chu Hsi were based on the following grounds: (*a*) that by refusing to take up his appointment in the Board of War, he was playing the game of brinkmanship, angling for fame and higher position; (*b*) that essentially he was without learning himself, having plagiarized the ideas of Chang Tsai and the Ch'eng brothers, and yet he deported himself as if he were a sage. The text of this indictment was widely circulated, and what had begun as the impeachment of an individual developed into an indiscriminate attack on an entire intellectual movement. This was a significant landmark in the so-called *tao-hsüeh*

[11] YSC 16, "Tomb Inscription for Madame Chuang".

controversy.[12] It is to be borne in mind that at this juncture and for some time to come, the term *tao-hsüeh* covered a much broader range of meaning than was the case later on. Not Chu Hsi alone, but all men of lofty ideals were put on trial.

Yeh Shih submitted a clearly written document to the emperor in defense of Chu Hsi, in which he rebutted the charges point by point.[13] He had done his homework well. His firm command of the intricate bureaucratic procedures enabled him to expose specious arguments. To illustrate: Lin Li charged that Chu Hsi was malingering (under the pretext of a foot ailment) in his refusal to accept the seal of the office of Section Chief (*lang-chung*) in the Board of War, to which he had been appointed. Yeh Shih replied that Chu was not malingering. His foot ailment was not imaginary but real, and on account of that he had been granted a leave of absence by the court. Since he had not yet taken up his office, he certainly could not accept the office seal.

In trying to vindicate the scholarship of Chu Hsi, Yeh Shih took the stance that a vital principle was at stake. If Chu Hsi was truly as Lin Li had alleged — a man without learning — he could not deceive people for long. If, on the other hand, he was indeed a man of great learning, his eagerness to instruct people could only be regarded as a boon to society. There never was a ban on private teaching in the course of the current dynasty, except during the dictatorial regime of Ts'ai Ching. In general, scheming, unprincipled men never lacked pretexts in presecuting upright persons. They could charge them with fame-seeking or with promoting factionalism. The current attack on *tao-hsüeh* must be viewed in this light. Men in positions of power were in league with one another, branding all those who showed the slightest concern for moral integrity as partisans of *tao-hsüeh*, and having them spied upon and ostracized. This led to a situation whereby some officials deliberatively sought dissipation in order to escape from the charge of *tao-hsüeh*. These perversities could result in irreparable damage to the dynasty.

The logic of Yeh Shih's argument is irrefutable. However, he was pitted against a power structure which was not amenable to reason. His memorial was probably not even permitted to reach the emperor. The upshot of it was that Chu Hsi again withdrew from the turbulence of the court and returned to teaching and writing. Yeh Shih was tough-minded enough to take his disappointment in his stride. He stayed on in the capital until the next year (1189).

[12] A comprehensive account of the *tao-hsüeh* controversy is found in SSCSPM 80, "Tao-hsüeh ch'ung-ch'u" (On the Elevation and Suppression of *tao-hsüeh*).

[13] YSC 2, "In Defense of Chu Yüan-hui, the *lang-kuan* of the Board of War".

By now, Emperor Hsiao-tsung was weary of the heavy responsibility of the august throne and early in the year he abdicated in favor of his son. The new emperor, Kuang-tsung, was already a grown man and naturally brought his own clique to power. Chou Pi-ta was ousted from the premiership.[14] Originally a protégé of Chou, Yeh Shih found it increasingly difficult to steer clear of factional strife. Although he was promoted to the post of Librarian of the Imperial Library (mi-shu lang),[15] a key position with access to the emperor, conditions were becoming increasingly intolerable for him.[16] He began to seek a provincial appointment and was eventually appointed Consultant (ts'an-i) in the remote city of Chiang-ling in present-day Hupeh.[17] The position of Consultant was a crucial one in the general staff of the frontline army organization and Yeh Shih reacted to the appointment with alacrity.[18] Chiang-ling, also known as Ching-chou, was one of the strategic points on the front line of Southern Sung defense against the Chin empire. It was a place with rich historical associations, and, in the youthful mind of Yeh Shih, the mystique of this land loomed large.[19] It was nothing less than the new lifeline of the Southern Sung empire.[20]

However, reality again proved to be intractable. The Jürchen elements of the Chin empire had mellowed and were loath to disturb the status quo. Nor were the Sung inclined to take the initiative in provoking hostilities. The two sides maintained an uneasy peace for over forty years. Similarly no significant steps had been taken to develop the vast resources of Hupeh. It remained both culturally and economically the backwater of the Southern Sung empire. Yeh Shih's desire to be

[14] Biographic sources for Chou Pi-ta are the following: (a) Kung-ku'ei chi 93, pp. 883–890, "Tomb Inscription for the Venerable and Honorable Chung-wen". (b) Kung-ku'ei chi 94, pp. 890–902, "Tomb Inscription of the Junior Preceptor, the Duke of I-kuo". (c) SS 391, his official biography. This is the only source that specifically states that he was ousted from his premiership in 1189.

[15] The function and personnel of the Imperial Library is the subject of a doctoral dissertation by John H. Winkelman, The Imperial Library in Southern Sung China (1127–1279), University of Chicago: 1968. See also his article in Library Quarterly 39:4.

[16] A valedictory tz'u poem by Ch'en Liang (CLCC 17) "Sending Yeh Cheng-tse Off to Chiang-ling" furnishes proof that Yeh Shih was elbowed out of his court post by factional politics.

[17] Loc. cit.

[18] Sun I-jang pointed out some of the inaccuracies in Yeh Shih's SS biography. For instance, his biography did not mention the appointment of ts'an-i of Chiang-ling (Chou-kao shu-lin 6). The usual sources on Sung government systems are reticent on the nature of the office of ts'an-i. For pertinent information on this office, see Wu Yung's Ho-lin chi 21:1a–b.

[19] YSC 6, "Sending Feng Ch'uan-chih Off".

[20] For a more detailed statement of the significance of Ch'ing-chou and Hupei in Yeh Shih's vision of dynastic recovery, see ch. 6.

in the thick of action was thwarted. Somehow the focus of Yeh's historic consciousness shifted from the stirring days when the armies of Liu Pang (reigned 206–195 B.C.) and Hsiang Yü (233–202 B.C.) fought on this land for supremacy in China to the declining years of the ancient state of Ch'u when a solitary figure, his loyalty and merits unappreciated by his sovereign, wandered on the banks of the Mi-lo river.[21] It dawned upon Yeh Shih that like Ch'ü Yüan (332–295 B.C.), he might never meet with an opportunity for his talents to be put into use.

To alleviate the oppressive monotony of the days, Yeh Shih turned to Buddhist doctrines as a distraction. This was the first revelation of his weakness for Buddhism, and it created quite a stir among his friends. His flirtation with Buddhism seems to indicate that the traditional orthodoxy of Confucian ethics and ideology had ceased to satisfy him.[22] He was launching out in search of truth in the wider world. This does not mean that he was disenchanted with Confucian orthodoxy altogether. Nevertheless he could not but feel that something vital was lacking, and it was this sense of inadequacy that predisposed him to Buddhism, and he admitted it frankly even to the most uncompromising custodian of Confucian values, namely Chu Hsi.[23]

Chu Hsi was thankful for the vigorous defense which Yeh Shih had rendered on his behalf against the indictment of Lin Li. Since that time the two men were close enough to communicate on an intellectual level. Chu Hsi was twenty years Yeh's senior, a man of imperious temperament and a recognized leader of the scholarly community. In their correspondences, of which only the letters emanating from Chu Hsi have been preserved, Chu Hsi naturally put on a superior, didactic tone. There was much in Yeh Shih's writings which he obviously disapproved, urging the latter to bridle his ambition and concentrate on the essential principles of the classics.[24] Chu Hsi's advice was well-founded, as Yeh Shih's understanding of the classics was certainly less than perfect. However, in his present state of mind, it is doubtful

---

[21] YSC 6, "Sending Feng Ch'uan-chih Off". In this poem, Yeh revealed his aspirations, frustrations and the succession of changing moods during his stay in Ch'ing-chou. Strictly speaking, it is perhaps incorrect to say that the consciousness of these historic recollections occurred in a clearly definable time sequence. They were probably all encompassed simultaneously within the threshold of his consciousness: depending on the objective circumstances and the subjective state of mind, now one episode would come to the forefront of attention, now another.

[22] Ch'en Fu-liang registered his reaction to the news in a poem, "Poem with the Ke Rhyme Dedicated to Yeh Cheng-tse on Hearing His Reading the Buddhist Tripiṭaka" (Chih-chai hsien-sheng wen-chi 3).

[23] Chu Hsi, in his fourth letter to Yeh Shih, reproduced portions Yeh's letter dealing with his attitude towards Buddhism (CWCCCC 56, pp. 1001–1002).

[24] Loc. cit.

whether this advice brought any comfort. In any case, the slump in Yeh Shih's spirit was only of a short duration. He was soon transferred to the Prefectural Administratorship of Chin-chou, a frontier town in the western sector of the Huai valley and not far from Wuchang. This was the first time in his career that he found himself with sole responsibility for a considerable unit of government. The area all around was potentially rich and Chin-chou was formerly a great city of the Huai valley. But it had fallen upon evil days, having been ravaged twice in the past seventy years, and was liable to further predatory inroad from the Jürchen army. Rehabilitation had been slow. There was still a great deal to be done.[25]

The most pressing task confronting Yeh Shih was the stabilization of the currency in this area. Chin-chou was in the iron belt of the empire where only iron coins were in circulation. The establishment of the iron belt by the government was a security measure designed to keep precious copper coins in the empire by minimizing their seepage to foreign lands. However, this separate currency was poorly managed. A chaotic situation prevailed due to rampant counterfeiting activities as well as the erratic operations of government mints which turned out coins of varying quality and even varying sizes. When the government took vigorous measures to crack down on counterfeiting, a full scale monetary crisis resulted. The harassed shopkeepers, unable to distinguish the genuine from the counterfeit coins, went so far as to shut down their shops in desperation.[26]

A government mint was located in Chin-chou and from the start of his appointment, Yeh Shih took upon himself the solution of the monetary crisis as his first order of business. His action could only have limited effectiveness, as he was dealing with an empire-wide problem on a local level. Nevertheless, the vigor that he exhibited in combatting the problem must have impressed those in power because he was soon promote to be *t'i-chü* (Intendant of Ever Normal Granary, Agriculture and Water Conservancy) of Huai-hsi.[27]

[25] Yeh Shih set forth his initial reaction to the Chin-chou appointment in "A Memorial Acknowledging Imperial Grace upon Assumption of Office in Chin-chou", YSC 2. In addition, there are a number of other items, both prose and poetry in YSC relating to the Chin-chou period.
[26] SS 133 (Shih-huo) mentions the establishment of the iron belt and the four government mints to service it. There are several references to the monetary crisis in YSC, viz.: (a) YSC 24, "Tomb Inscription for Mr. Chao, Former President of the Board of War". (b) YSC 22, "Tomb Inscription for Shu Yen-sheng". (c) YSC 18, "Tomb Inscription for Mr. Ch'ien, Prefect of Lu-chou". This is the most detailed account of the genesis of the monetary crisis.
[27] YSC 2, "Memorial Acknowledging Imperial Grace for being Appointed the *t'i-chü* Intendant of Huai-hsi".

As *t'i-chü* of Huai-hsi, his jurisdiction extended to a much larger area so that he was better placed for dealing with the monetary crisis. He set forth his proposed solution of the problem in a five-point memorandum.[28] He started this memorandum with a program of mass education. The doubts of the people about the appearance of the legal coin should be permanently put to rest by having samples of each issue of each government mint in display in prefectural and district offices, and in important points of transit, such as river crossings. The second point deals with the enforcement of the counterfeiting laws. Yeh Shih was of the opinion that the enforcement of laws should proceed efficiently without undue interference in the daily routine of the people. The third point deals with the convertibility of iron coins. Hitherto, possessors of copper coins could readily convert their money into local currency in the iron belt, but no similar facilities existed for the possessors of iron coins in the copper belt. Yeh Shih alleged that this inequity, the inconvertibility of iron, was a permanent depressant on the economy of the iron belt. The currency was practically worthless south of the Yangtze river, in the heartland of the Southern Sung empire. Consequently, rather than keep it, merchants would seek to dispose of it even on the most unfavorable terms. Yeh Shih's proposed solution was to remove this inequity by making the currency convertible. The fourth point deals with the varying sizes and weights of successive issues of legal coins. This was the cause of much mischief. They should be standardized and the personnel of the mint be held to the highest standard of workmanship. The fifth point concerns the administrative setup for managing the currency. Yeh Shih advocated no drastic changes but insisted that each unit be held responsible for its production.

We have no specific information on the final disposition of the issues Yeh Shih raised in this memorandum. He probably worked at this task for more than a year. The crisis was over, and conditions were returning to normal. Referring to this episode years later, Yeh Shih claimed credit for it. His only apparent regret was that commodities were becoming more expensive now. This is perhaps an indication that his proposal concerning the convertibility of currency was ultimately put into effect and commercial, investment capital flowed into the iron belt, boosting up prices.[29]

His impressive record in the provinces eventually led to his return

---

[28] YSC 2, "Five Point Memorandum on the Iron Coins Belt of Huai-hsi".
[29] YSC 24, "Tomb Inscription for Shu Yen-sheng". The rise of the price level in the Huai iron belt was in line with the overall inflationary trend in the Southern Sung period. See Ch'üan Han-sheng, "On the Inflation Towards the End of the Sung Period", *Bulletin of the Institute of History and Philology* 10:3.

to the capital. There he served as Chief of the Left Section (*shang-shu tso-hsüan lang-kuan*) of the Board of Personnel.[30] Shortly afterwards, he was appointed Vice-Director of Education (*kuo-tzu ssu-yeh*) in charge of instruction of the Kuo-tzu Academy, the second highest educational office in the empire.[31] He was thus on the spot when a great political crisis shook the court.

The crisis originated in a minor squabble in the imperial family but developed into an open challenge to Confucian ideology. For some time past, the reigning Emperor Kuang-tsung (reigned 1189–1194) had been estranged from his father, the abdicated Emperor Hsiao-tsung. Consequently the visits he paid his father as prescribed by custom became fewer and less regular. The estrangement came to be an open secret among the court and the populace of Hangchow. Sympathy was all with the abdicated emperor. He had been on the throne twenty-eight years and people still remembered his unfailing, meticulous devotion to his predecessor, the abdicated Emperor Kao-tsung, in stark contrast to the unfilial ways of the reigning emperor.[32]

Increasing pressure was exerted to get the emperor to relent, but to no avail. The crisis at court intensified when Hsiao-tsung became seriously ill and lay on his death-bed. Normally it is to be expected that at this juncture, petty feelings would be put aside and the estranged son would pay last homage to his departing father. But the court and the inhabitants of Hangchow were not so sure of the emperor and, as he tarried in his palace, tension mounted rapidly.[33] Filial piety was the cornerstone of Confucian ethics and such flagrant violations could not be condoned even in high places. On the contrary, because he was emperor, he was expected to exemplify the moral order. The court and the people were thus faced with a particularly poignant situation. Could they continue to owe allegiance to a ruler who had actually undermined China's cultural heritage which by law and by his position he was expected to defend? Pernicious rumors were circulated about disaffection in the ranks of the troops and among the people. The crisis finally came to a head when Hsiao-tsung died, and no provisions were made by the reigning Emperor Kuang-tsung to perform the mourning and

---

[30] YSC, "Pen-chuan".

[31] His official biography indicates that this appointment came after the abdication of Emperor Kuang-tsung. This is in conflict with other sources, for instance, Wu Tzu-liang's *Lin-hsia o-tan*. The discrepancy was noted by Sun I-jang in his *Chou-kao shu-lin*.

[32] The most detailed account of the estrangement and the maneuvers leading to the abdication of Emperor Kuang-tsung is SSCSPM 81, "Liang chao nei-ch'an" (The Abdication during Two Reigns).

[33] For example, see YSC 17, "Tomb Inscription for Ts'ai Pi-sheng".

burial rites incumbent upon a son and heir of the deceased emperor.
Throughout this crisis, the general response of the court officials
was one of circumspection. They tried to deter the emperor from his
perversities by reasoning with him, in reverently worded memorials
submitted either jointly or singly.[34] When that failed, some of them
resigned from their posts as an act of remonstrance. The prime minister,
Liu Cheng (1129–1206), unable to keep the chaotic situation under
control, panicked and departed from the scene without having his
resignation approved.[35] The court was verging on disintegration.

Then events moved with amazing rapidity. The recalcitrant ruler
abdicated in favor of his son, Prince Chia, who duly performed the
mourning rites on behalf of his father. The requirement of Confucian
morality was satisfied and the crisis was over.

Perhaps the true story of the abdication will never be told. It was
certainly masterminded by a few individuals, of whom the most well-
known were Chao Ju-yü (died 1195),[36] an imperial clansman, and Han
T'o-chou (died 1207),[37] an imperial relative. Chao was generally credited
with being the prime mover, who made use of Han's connections in the
palace to secure the blessing of the Dowager Empress Hsien-sheng[38]
(who was Han's aunt) for the enterprise. Apart from these principals,
many lesser men were certainly involved, among whom Hsü I (1144–
1208) and Ts'ai Pi-sheng (1140–1203) probably deserved special mention. Hsü was a close associate of Chao and had probably helped the
latter make up his mind for the momentous enterprise.[39] Ts'ai was
a palace postern attendant, hence a colleague of Han, and helped to
secure the latter's support for the project.[40]

In his official biography, Yeh Shih was credited with playing a
significant role in the whole abdication episode. Undoubtedly there was
a factual basis for this claim. We know that both Hsü and Ts'ai were
natives of P'ing-yang district of Wen-chou prefecture and were therefore
fellow-provincials of Yeh Shih. This factor was of added significance
for the men of Wen-chou who spoke a dialect virtually unintelligible
to men from other parts of Chekiang. In addition, both Hsü and Ts'ai

[34] A good example of the memorials submitted on this subject may by found in
Kung-ku'ei chi 23.
[35] Liu's biography in SS 391, reflecting a point of view favorable to him, puts a
different interpretation on the same action.
[36] See Chao Ju-yü's biography in SS 392.
[37] See Han T'o-chou's biography in SS 474.
[38] For a statement of her relation to the reigning emperor, see her biography in
SS 243.
[39] See YSC 21, "Tomb Inscription for Hsü I". Biographic information may also be
found in Sun I-yen, *Anecdotes* 15.
[40] YSC 17, "Tomb Inscription for Ts'ai Chih-ko".

were upright, idealistic men, slightly senior to Yeh who must have looked to them for guidance and companionship. As part of an informal group of kindred spirits, Yeh probably helped, in an intangible manner, to influence the views and outlooks of the other two men.

Also, we have no reason to question the claim advanced by his biography, that Yeh Shih was privy to the plans of the protagonists. It was mentioned that he officiated as the *shou-i ts'ao-lang* (Master of Ceremony) during the coronation ceremony and that, together with Chao Ju-yü, he helped to draft all the pertinent documents. His biography goes further and claims a more positive role for him. It casts him in the role of the prime mover, triggering a chain reaction which culminated in the accession of the new emperor. He is depicted as the gadfly, chiding prime minister Liu Cheng and exhorting him to action. The biography says that it was he who suggested to Liu that Prince Chia was a grown man and should be formally installed as the heir-apparent so that he might perform some of the imperial functions on behalf of his father, and so help to placate the critics. Liu was said to have taken up this suggestion and so provoked an unanticipated reaction from the emperor, who, after prolonged delay, issued two terse statements: (*a*) "This is quite all right", and (*b*) "I have been shouldering the affairs of state for a long time and am contemplating stepping down." The emperor's response was said to have unnerved Liu Cheng who then slipped away, leaving the court further demoralized. It is moreover known that later on the architects of the abdication seized on these terse statements to justify their action.

Apart from his official biography, general Southern Sung literature makes occasional reference to Yeh Shih's role in the abdication episode. The most comprehensive description is found in *Lin-hsia o-t'an* (Occasional Remarks under the Trees) by Wu Tzu-liang, a disciple of Yeh Shih's disciple. Here, Wu identified a contemporary of Yeh Shih, Yu Chung-hung by name, as the ultimate source of his information.[41] According to this source, Yeh Shih applied the rigorous "performance test" of Mencius to the mounting crisis at court and, like Mencius of old, refused to acknowledge the legitimacy of a ruler who had transgressed the moral law. The same source also claims that the impetus towards the final solution of the crisis came from the consultation between Yeh Shih and Hsü I.

Yeh Shih was silent on the role he played in this affair. There is, however, one passage among his voluminous writings in which he seems to be referring to himself. In the funerary inscription (*mu-chih ming*)

---

[41] Sun I-yen, *Anecdotes* 8:1b–2b.

which he wrote for Ts'ai Pi-sheng, he commenced his account of the abdication episode with a description of the predicament of prime minister Liu Cheng. Perplexed by the unexpected turn of events, Liu Cheng did not know what to do, but finally took action under the prompting of an unnamed person. Yeh Shih recounted the conversation between this unnamed prompter and the prime minister in this funerary inscription as follows: "There was someone chiding the prime minister, saying . . ." and "Then again, someone chiding the prime minister said . . ." This conversation is almost exactly the same as that reported in Yeh Shih's biography between Yeh himself and the prime minister.

Yeh's reticence about his role in this affair was probably due less to his ingrained modesty than to deliberate policy. In the ideological milieu of imperial China, one simply did not use blunt and straightforward expressions with regard to the imperial institution. The emperor was supposed to be the paragon of all mankind. Theoretically, there were only two categories of persons who could depose or suspend emperors, a great sage such as the Duke of Chou, or a great villain such as General Tung Cho (died A.D. 192) of Latter Han. Ordinary mortals could not afford to be sages nor did they relish being classified with the villains. Thus, even if the outcome had been fortunate, one should be wary of laying claim to the dubious honor of having helped depose a previous emperor of the same ruling house. This was especially the case if the outcome turned out to be less fortunate.

Prince Chia, later known in history as Emperor Ning-tsung (reigned 1194–1224) after his enthronement, was a well-intentioned, but weak man. Throughout his reign of twenty-nine years, he was dominated by a succession of strong ministers. The first was Chao Ju-yü, the man who took most credit for his accession. Chao became Prime Minister of the Right and proceeded to give a new complexion to the government. Prominent scholars, including the inimitable Chu Hsi, were brought to the court and given employment; rewards were dished out to all who had a part in the successful abdication maneuvers. His right-hand man was probably the idealistic and dynamic Hsü I, who became Acting Vice-President of the Board of War and concurrently Governor of the capital city.

But Chao's star was in the ascendant for only a short while. He failed to consolidate his regime. His enemies were those who felt that they had been snubbed or under-rewarded. Their rallying point was Han T'o-chou.[42] In the early stages of the factional struggle, Chu Hsi spoke out against Han. Thus both he and Chao Ju-yü became prime targets

[42] The chief figures in the anti-Chao coalition, besides Han T'o-chou himself, were Chao Yen-yü and Ching T'ang. See SSCSPM 82.

of the Han forces. In the showdown between Chu and Han, the former was the loser. He was relieved of his court position and those who protested against his dismissal were branded his partisans and suffered a similar fate. Chao's strength was gradually whittled away, whereas Han continued to pack his men into court positions. Finally the anti-Chao forces felt strong enough to launch a frontal assault on Chao himself. He was compelled to relinquish his post as Prime Minister of the Right on the ground that, as an imperial clansman, his continual occupancy of the post would be detrimental to the dynasty.

The anti-Chao forces thus scored a total victory. Chao's supporters and all those who spoke out on their behalf were hounded from court, and quite a few of them were exiled to far-off places. As it was impossible to bring trumped up charges against all the associates and sympathizers of Chao and Chu individually, it was decided to make use of a blanket indictment. The learning cultivated by these men was castigated as *wei-hsüeh* (bogus learning), capable of doing great mischief to state and society. A list was drawn up containing the names of fifty-nine individuals identified as practitioners of *wei-hsüeh*. They were to be dropped from whatever posts they were currently holding and barred from holding office again in future.[43]

This was the climax of the anti-intellectualist movement in the Southern Sung dynasty. The arguments against *wei-hsüeh* were generally of the same nature as those employed by the detractors of *tao-hsüeh* some time ago. There is no question that the primary motivation of the crackdown on *wei-hsüeh* was political partisanship. As a matter of fact, historians refer to this episode as "the Proscription of the Partisans of Ch'ing-yüan" (*Ch'ing-yüan tang chin*), Ch'ing-yüan being the reign-title of Emperor Ning-tsung. The connotation of this designation was obviously that those proscribed were guilty of partisanship. Thus, as often happens in history, the persecutors attributed to their victims the crime of which they themselves were guilty.

The victims of the Ch'ing-yüan Proscription were as motley a group as could be found among the ruling class of imperial China. There was little homogeneity either of political interests or of intellectual outlook among them. In fact, they covered the whole spectrum of the intellectual world of Southern Sung China, ranging from a representative of the extreme idealistic tendencies, Yang Chien[44] (1141–1226), through the centrist position of Chu Hsi, and then to the empiricist position of Ch'en Fu-liang, Yeh Shih and Huang Tu (1138–1213). In social and

---

[43] The list was drawn up in response to the memorializing of Wang Ch'ung in the third year of Ch'ing-yüan (1197). See SSCSPM 81.
[44] See ch. 8.

political status, they ranged from the retired prime ministers, Liu Cheng and Chou Pi-ta, to those without academic degrees, such as Lü Tsu-t'ai and Ts'ai Yüan-ting (1135–1198). The only common ground was the fact that they were all considered enemies of the regime of Han T'o-chou and his associates, either because they had spoken out against the regime or because they were closely associated with Chao Ju-yü and Chou Pi-ta, who, as retired prime ministers of a previous reign, might conceivably launch a comeback.[45]

Yeh Shih was also involved in the Ch'ing-yüan Proscription. But, compared with other men on the proscription list, his punishment was relatively mild. Both Chao Ju-yü and Hsü I were banished to the far south, Hunan and Kwangtung respectively, at that time still relatively undeveloped lands. Chao died en route and Hsü was destined to spend several long years in that uncongenial climate, supporting himself by practising medicine and divination.[46] Yeh Shih escaped banishment altogether and was moreover allowed to enjoy a sinecure for some time. If he was indeed a close associate of Chao and Hsü, how did he manage to get off so easily?

Hitherto, we have cast Yeh Shih mainly in the role of an activist, keen to thrust himself forward into the thick of action and uncompromising on moral issues. However, there was another side to his character which we must not ignore — his adaptability and tolerance of differences. He did not relish contention for its own sake. The way of the martyr had little appeal for him.

According to Yeh's official biography, he declined the reward which Chao Ju-yü was prepared to offer him for his part in the abdication episode. He alleged that he was merely doing his duty and therefore acquired no special merit. He was soon allowed to leave court to take up appointment as Comptroller (*tsung-ling chün-ma ch'ien-liang*) of Huai-tung. By assuming this provincial post, he surrendered his opportunity of exercising influence on the vital center of power (an opportunity which he would normally hold on to in order to put his ideas of statesmanship into practice). However, by the same act, he also disclaimed responsibility for the regime which was destined to be dashed to pieces.

Yeh Shih's voluntary dissociation with Chao's regime was probably prompted by a disagreement over policy or by a clash of personalities. The source quoted by Wu Tzu-liang in *Occasional Remarks under the*

---

[45] Lü Tsu-t'ai, for example, got himself included in the list by submitting an audacious memorial to the throne indicting Han T'o-chou for his abuse of power and requesting that Chou Pi-ta be restored to the office of Prime Minister. See SSCSPM 82.

[46] YSC 17, "Tomb Inscription of Ts'ai Chih-ko".

Trees claimed that Yeh Shih had forebodings of the wrath that was to come. This could be a reference to the intransigent and foolhardy manner in which Chao and his associates exercised power. Given the futility of attempting to change the course of events, the most prudent thing was to get out in time.

As Comptroller of Huai-tung, Yeh Shih strove to put its finances in order. He cut down on the irregular requisition of funds and secured an imperial rescript to this effect.[47]

He had intended to steer clear of the murky waters of court politics but he was too big a target to be missed by Han T'o-chou's partisans. An indictment was brought against him by the censor Hu Hung who had already initiated prosecutions against Chu Hsi. Yeh Shih was accused of *lèse majesté* on the basis of his essay "Chün-te" (Princely Virtues) included in his *Chin-chüan*.[48] In this essay, Yeh Shih upheld the highest ideals for the ruler and debunked the myths and hypocricies of contemporary practice. A case indeed could be made that his essay was subversive literature, undermining the credibility of the ruling house. Since Yeh Shih posed no serious threat to the regime, he was let off lightly, and was appointed to the sinecure post of Supervisor of Chung-yu Temple.[49] He declined the next substantive appointment as Administrator of Chü-chou in Southwest Chekiang.[50]

---

[47] *Sung hui-yao chi-kao*, p. 8198, "T'ai-fu ch'ing Huai-tung tsung-ling Yeh Shih" (Minister of Grand Treasury, Comptroller of Huai-tung).

[48] Sun I-yen, *Anecdotes* 8:33b.

[49] For a study of the sinecure system of the Sung dynasty, see Liang T'ien-hsi, "Sung-tai chih ssu-lu chih-tu", *Ta-lu tsa-chih* 29:2 (1964).

[50] YSC, "Pen-chuan".

CHAPTER FIVE

The Culmination of Yeh Shih's Career

FOR HIS motivation in not accepting the appointment as Administrator of Chü-chou, an inquiry into changes of his personal circumstances may be in order. Unlike some scholar-officials who came from well-established families, Yeh Shih and his family depended exclusively on his official emolument for their living. Moreover, as none of his brothers seemed to have made any headway in life, he was probably also burdened with their support as well as that of his parents. It was therefore unusual for him to decline a substantive appointment, especially one in the provinces which involved no direct commitment to the faction in power.

His passing the examination in 1178 did not bring an immediate improvement in his fortunes. Positions at the bottom of the official hierarchy paid only meager salaries. We have a glimpse of his family's way of living from the tomb inscription which Yeh Shih wrote for his wife.[1] We learn that the family lived in a rented house. His wife prepared a substantial meal every day, consisting of dishes of meat, fish, and vegetables for Yeh Shih and his students; she herself ate little more than green onions, mustard, and cabbage. Every month, she would turn over portions of her husband's income to her parents-in-law and then her brothers-in-law, neglecting no one in the family. Though she seldom bought new clothes for herself over the years, she always appeared neatly dressed, as she managed to keep her clothes well-laundered and well cared for.

This magnanimous and self-sacrificing woman had more than her share of afflictions. Her first two children, both female, died shortly after birth. The third child, also a daughter, was an epileptic who died when she was old enough to talk. She did not give birth to three sons till she was in her mid-thirties.

It is to be expected that as Yeh Shih rose in the official hierarchy, the financial situation of the family continued to improve.[2] However, it was not until 1198, twenty years after he passed the examination, that

---

[1] YSC 18, "Tomb Inscription for Madame Kao". In praising the virtues of his wife, Yeh Shih also showed us glimpses of his other kinsmen.
[2] YSC 16, "Tomb Inscription of Madame Chuang".

he was able to buy an estate in his home prefecture. This estate produced enough rice so that his family was no longer dependent upon the market for it. It was located on the Western Lake outside Sheng-chiang Gate of the city of Wen-chou, with the waters of the lake lapping its shores and with good-looking mountains glimmering in the distance.[3] He grew so fond of this first permanent home that he took for himself the sobriquet Shui-hsin (in the midst of waters), which was also the name of the locality in which his estate was situated.

There is no evidence that Yeh Shih complained of ill health before, although he was not a robust person.[4] Suddenly at about the age of fifty, he was stricken with a serious malady (probably a stroke) with partial paralysis of the back and limbs as well as symptoms of malaria. Undoubtedly, the idyllic life of a farmer had perils for the unsuspecting. The combination of an insalubrious climate and physical over-exertion probably accounted for his affliction. For two or three years, his illness raged. There was nothing the physicians could do.[5] It was not unreasonable for him then to decline an official appointment under these circumstances.

Eventually his condition improved and he was able to lead a more or less normal life, although his back continued to bother him. Unquestionably his illness had a depressing effect on his spirits. Hitherto the shadows of old age had been creeping on him and now they deepened. Time was running out and yet the dark clouds on the political horizon were as threatening as ever, with no prospect of clearing. How many men could keep their faith and retain their self-confidence under these trying circumstances? Old age and adversity have a way of breaking down the most resilient faith. In a particularly despondent mood, he wrote the following poem, entitled "On a Boat on Yen River":[6]

With the towering waves of the River Che all around,
It was as if one were treading on the void.

---

[3] Sun I-yen (1814–1894) who was a native of Jui-an of Wen-chou prefecture, claimed that Shui-hsin Village was located outside of the Lai-fu gate of the city of Wen-chou (*Anecdotes* 8:40b) and also that the name Shui-hsin was still remembered by the natives. He could not, however, identify the Sheng-chiang gate. Nevertheless, he opined that as Lai-fu gate was also popularly known as San-chüeh gate, it was possible that Yeh Shih changed it to the more elegant name of Sheng-chiang.

[4] An example is provided by Yeh Shih's inability to withstand cold. See YSC 13, "Tomb Inscription for the Retired Scholar of Mu-lin".

[5] YSC 15, "Tomb Inscription for Mr. Kao, Former Prefect of Yung-chou".

[6] YSC 6, "On a Boat on Yen River". Apart from the appropriateness of the prevailing mood of this poem, internal evidence also suggests that it pertains to this period of Yeh's life. The couplet, "The Wang youth has no understanding of things. In his trip to and fro on the sampan, what has he learnt from me?" apparently refers to Yeh's disciple Wang Chih. (See ch. 4.)

And the Ching Lake, whipped up by rain and storm,
Was threatening to engulf the sky.
In my solitary wanderings, I arrive at the ancient kingdom of Kou Chien,
Thither a forlorn rivulet meandering flows.
The hidden dragon has now lain itself at the bottom of the ravine,
And the firefly no longer illuminates the rush clusters.
The lowly woodland harbors no great cypresses,
And the heroic ethos is no more to be seen.
Nothing remains but *hao* and *p'eng* grass.
At this time of early winter, before the hard freeze sets in,
Heaven and Earth are patches of bluish grey,
And the day is always on the wane.
Nobody "wades across the river to pluck at the lilies" anymore,[7]
And who lingers to admire the wild daisies on the roadside?
Hungry birds and distant *en*-geese are on my trail.
I hear their sad cries and spy their flight by day,
Chickens and dogs in the village ahead have taken up position before the
    fence [at my approach].
How piteous are their howlings!
Grieving, languishing, my sinews and bones have shrunk;
In my life's journey so far (and I have passed the mid-point of a man's
    alloted span), my constant companions have been long sighs.
The Wang youth has no understanding [of things].
In his trips to and fro on the sampan, what has he learnt [from me]?
Surely I have aspired to be a teacher, preserving culture for a hundred
    years,
But a single sitting [at the spiritual feast] is not enough to sustain me
    through all my trials and tribulations.
Still, in the presence of wine, I can sing a hearty song,
Sages and worthies have their "decrees" (or, Heavenly-ordained fate),
Why should we ordinary mortals begrudge them?

It is not a great poem, but the sentiment is clear. Reality, cold and
harsh, now bore down on him with overwhelming force. He was cut
down to size. No more illusions of personal grandeur. Picking up the
bookcase that contained the manuscripts of his *Wai-kao* one day, he
sighed. The heroic age when everything seemed possible was gone
for good.[8]

The regime of Han T'o-chou was not more corrupt than that of others
such as Ts'ai Ching or Ch'in Kuei, but it was probably more inept.
Han himself might be a master of intrigues but he was not consistently
calculating or ruthless. Without any fixed ideas of his own except to
stay in power, he did not set the tone of his regime. He was more often
the resistance to be moved than the prime mover. This characterization

---

[7] Both the sentiment and the wording of this line are derived from the sixth poem
of the *Ku-shih shih-chiu shou* (Nineteen Ancient Poems) of the *Chao-ming wen-hsüan*.
[8] YSC PC 15:843–844.

perhaps helps to explain some of the major developments during his period of ascendancy.

Han's partisans made use of the "Bogus Learning" issue as an expedient to strike at their enemies. Some of them were more active in exploiting it; they had personal axes to grind. Some, like Hu Hung, were motivated by a desire to settle past scores; he believed himself snubbed by both Chu Hsi and Yeh Shih.[9] It was unlikely that Han T'o-chou himself harbored any inveterate hostility towards the *tao-hsüeh* masters or their learning *per se*. Thus, it was highly probable that the Ch'ing-yüan Proscription decrees, which put the names of fifty-nine men on the black-list and condemned their writings, were only half-heartedly enforced. Most men on the black-list were scholars of repute and the persecution probably enhanced their renown. Their writings were officially banned, but there is no question that they continued to circulate and were read clandestinely.[10] There were even government officials who took considerable risks to keep up correspondences with the proscribed scholars.

Eventually, the anti-*tao-hsüeh* forces waned. The small coterie of men most active in pushing the issue gradually fell out of favor with Han and were removed from office.[11] Han was well entrenched in power and his potential rivals were dead. The political *raison d'etre* for keeping up the anti-*tao-hsüeh* stance vanished. The way was now open for a rapprochement between the establishment and the opposition.

In the funerary inscription which Yeh wrote for Ch'en Ssu-ch'eng (courtesy name, Ching-ssu), who stood in relation to Yeh somewhere between a friend and a disciple, we catch a glimpse of the process of reconciliation. Ch'en was related to Han T'o-chou by matrimonial ties and considered himself a disciple of Chu Hsi. In the exchange of correspondence between him and Chu Hsi, he managed to make the latter admit that he had basically no grudge against Han. This was undoubtedly intended as a mild apology on the part of Chu Hsi for his

---

[9] Hu was reported to have gone to Chu Hsi for instruction but took offense at the simple vegetarian meals that were standard fare which Chu offered to the students. See SSCSPM 80. Hu's grudge against Yeh Shih purportedly originated in a casual encounter between them in the ante-room of a Prefect's yamen. The Prefect deemed it fit to receive Yeh Shih in audience ahead of Hu Hung as he had been highly impressed with Yeh's literary talents. See *Ssu-chao wen-chien lu*, reproduced in *Anecdotes* 8:33b–34a.

[10] The ban was specifically against the style and terminology of the self-righteous *tao-hsüeh* masters. However, Yeh's *Chin-chüan* and Ch'en Fu-liang's *T'ai-yü chi* were also singled out for condemnation. See *Wen-hsien t'ung-kao* 32, p. 302.

[11] The major figures whose departure brought about the effect were Hu Hung, Ho Tan and Ching T'ang. See their respective biographies in SS 394.

previous criticism of Han. Ch'en showed this indirect confession to Han who was then much gratified.[12]

In a preface which Yeh wrote for the poetic works of his disciple, Wu Ta-shou, we learn how the latter strove to mitigate the vengeance with which some of Han's partisans pursued Hsü I. Together with his senior kinsman, Wu Chü, who was a nephew of the Dowager Empress Hsien-sheng, he managed to get her to plead with the outer court to let bygones be bygones and not to engage in further factional struggle.[13] In both these attempts for reconciliation, we may infer at least the indirect influence of Yeh Shih.

Yeh Shih himself was probably reactivated from his retirement some time prior to 1203, for, in that year, we find him returning to the capital after serving two successive provincial posts, namely, as Circuit Fiscal Supervisory Official (*chuan-yün p'an-kuan*) of Hunan and as Administrator of Ch'üan-chou.[14] He submitted a series of three memorials.[15] The second and third of the series dealt with the administrative problems of Hunan and Ch'üan-chou respectively and call for no special comment. But the first of the series was a reverently worded appeal for unity. In very general terms, he wrote of the high priority that the sage-rulers of the past placed on the harmony of government personnel. Harmony was not only the keynote of an orderly administration; it was also the supreme virtue in art and culture, as, for instance, in the art of cuisine. He concluded by saying that he had been seriously ill for a long time and had already surrendered all hope of personal advancement. The whole burden of his efforts was to make known a pious wish that ministers should devote themselves selflessly to the state, leaving their differences behind and looking forward together to the future.

The statement about his prolonged illness appears to have been earnest, although he might have exaggerated its seriousness. What was perhaps not so sincere was his profession of disinterestedness and his claim to have relinquished all hope of personal advancement, in view of the subsequent turn of events. Shortly after submitting these memorials, he was appointed Acting Vice-President of the Board of War,[16] and three other individuals whom he had recommended strongly, Lou Yüeh (1137–1213), Huang Tu and Ch'iu Chung, were all appointed to prefectural administratorships. Whatever Yeh's motivations, obviously his

---

[12] See YSC 18, "Tomb Inscription for the Venerable Mr. Ch'en". In Chu Hsi's collected works, only one letter to Ch'en Ching-ssu is preserved (CWCKWC 59).

[13] YSC 29, "Comments on the Poetry of Cho-chai".

[14] YSC, "Pen-chuan".

[15] YSC 1:1–5.

[16] YSC, "Pen-chuan". Yeh's overture to those in power was also commented upon by the historian Li Hsin-ch'uan in his *Tao-ming lu* reproduced in *Anecdotes* 8:34a.

conciliatory tone helped to remove the residue of intransigence that lingered in the dominant faction in court, and so hastened the end of the anti-*tao-hsüeh* campaign.

The lifting of the ban on *tao-hsüeh* was followed by a conscious drive by Han T'o-chou to rally every segment of public opinion behind him for his grandiose plan to reconquer the North by force. In the early years of the thirteenth century, rumor was rampant that the Chin empire was finally on the verge of disintegration, with the Northern barbarians viciously harassing the frontier and with famine and banditry raging everywhere in the interior. Somebody suggested to Han that the opportunity which Southern Sung had been waiting for a hundred years to avenge the wrongs of the ancestors had arrived at long last and that he ought to act resolutely to win for himself unprecedented renown.[17] This appeal to his vanity was successful, and the sychophants around him were transformed overnight into the hard core of a vociferous war party. A reign title was adopted to intimate that the rulers of the Sung had not forgotten the lost territories in North China. Starting from 1205, this new reign title was changed to K'ai-hsi, combining elements of two previous reigns of Northern Sung, namely K'ai-pao (968–975) and T'ien-hsi (1017–1021).[18] An overall strategy and preparations for war also began in earnest. Commanders of armies on the front were briefed.

However, the war party did not seem to care for the advantages of a sudden blitz. Being unsure of their position, their strategy was to provoke the enemy into taking the initiative in formally breaking the peace so that they themselves would be exonerated in the event the warlike adventure backfired. Troops on the frontier were recruited by new efforts. Lawless elements were encouraged to raid and plunder in enemy territory. Small-scale probing actions were launched to test enemy defenses.

However, the enemy refused to be rushed into hasty actions. Southern Sung therefore had to shoulder the blame for the open rupture which finally occurred towards the middle of 1206. After news of the capture of a number of frontier towns by Sung troops reached the court, it was deemed appropriate to make a formal declaration of war which would bolster morale and facilitate the war efforts. The honor of drafting this declaration of war was offered to Yeh Shih.[19]

Yeh Shih was undoubtedly the ideal man for such an assignment.

---

[17] SSCSPM 83, "Pei-fa keng-meng" (Northern Expedition and the Alteration of the Peace Pact).

[18] *Loc. cit.*

[19] YSC, "Pen-chuan".

With the death of eminent scholars of an earlier generation in rapid succession during the dark years of the anti-*tao-hsüeh* campaign (Lu Chiu-yüan in 1192, Chu Hsi in 1200, and Ch'en Fu-liang in 1203), Yeh Shih was now a recognized leader of the scholarly community.[20] He was one of the few remaining links to the Augustan age of Southern Sung which passed away with Emperor Hsiao-tsung. His political views were well-known and his prestige as an essayist, unsurpassable. The following anecdote eloquently testifies to his stature.

Han T'o-chou, the Grand Preceptor, was at home one day holding consultation with Yeh Shih when a visitor called on him. On the calling card this visitor presented was written "Shui-hsin Yeh Shih". Han was amazed but decided to receive the impostor in good humor. Hoping to expose him as a fraud, Han quizzed him on the contents of *Chin-chüan*, but the visitor knew it perfectly. He did not, however, seem to hold it in high esteem saying that it was the work of his youthful years and that if he was to write it over again, it would be much better. He then recited excerpts of his new version of this work which did appear to be an improvement of the original. Finally, he revealed his own identity, claiming that if he had not impersonated Yeh Shih, he would not have been able to gain a hearing.[21]

The cause of the war party would be immensely strengthened if a man of Yeh's stature gave it his endorsement. However, Yeh declined the honor. Undaunted, the advocates of war got Li Pi (1159–1222), son of Li Tao the historian, to write it, and hostilities soon flared up along the entire Sung-Chin border of two thousand miles.[22]

At first sight, Yeh's refusal to lend his support to the war party is baffling. Throughout his life, he was known to be an ardent champion of the *hui-fu* ideology, and now that the court was finally prepared to make an all-out effort to implement it, why did he turn a cold shoulder to the enterprise? It should be noted that Yeh Shih never held that the goal of *hui-fu* could be achieved by military actions alone. Military actions could be successful only after a substantial program of socio-political and fiscal reforms had borne fruit. His earlier writings were exuberant, spelling out the specific extent of the desired reforms in each area and setting a timetable for such reforms to bear fruit. His later writings were more subdued in tone and less specific in recommend-

<hr />

[20] Wei Liao-weng (1178–1237), one of the most esteemed scholars and statesmen of the Southern Sung, wrote a letter to Yeh Shih in 1206 or 1207 when he was a young men of twenty-eight, recounting his own academic aspirations and requesting guidance. See *Ho-shan hsien-sheng wen-chi* 32, p. 276.

[21] See Pai T'ing's *Chan-yüan ching-yü*, reproduced in *Anecdotes* 8:40a.

[22] SSCSPM 83. Wu Tzu-liang claimed that the text of the declaration was actually written by Yeh Shih's disciple Chou Nan on behalf of Li Pi.

ation. Apparently, his optimism waned. But there was no contradiction in his basic thinking. He consistently condemned flirting with the idea of *hui-fu* without first carrying out a thorough reform of the institutions of the state. A purely military effort would be irresponsible and even suicidal.

The outcome of the war bore him out.[23] There was little co-ordination among the several army commanders. Insufficient supplies, poor training of the troops, bungling by the officers and rivalry between the various army units impaired the effectiveness of the Sung forces. Furthermore, reports about the imminent dissolution of the Chin empire proved greatly exaggerated. The simultaneous advance of the several Sung armies was halted at the first line of Chin defense. The fortified cities held out and presently the invading Sung armies were beaten back and their retreat turned into a rout.

Han T'o-chou and his henchmen were disheartened at the first news of disaster and sought to exonerate themselves by repudiating the action of some of the army commanders. But, the Chin empire launched a counter-offensive, advancing in nine columns under the overall command of the veteran warrior-statesman, P'u-san K'uei.[24] Everywhere the Sung defenses buckled. The main column under the personal command of P'u-san K'uei crossed the middle stream of the Huai River by a ruse and proceeded to drive right up to the banks of the Yangtze River. They then made preparations for crossing the river, thus putting great pressure on the Sung court.

Early in 1207, while the enemy was still encamped North of the Yangtze, Yeh Shih was appointed Governor of Nanking and concurrently Commissioner of Control along the River (*yen-chiang chih-chih shih*).[25] Shortly afterwards, at his own request, the title of his concurrent appointment was changed to that of Commissioner of Control of the Yangtze and Huai Rivers (*Chiang-Huai chih-chih shih*).[26] This title gave him additional power to deploy and co-ordinate Sung forces North of the Yangtze River, making the task of defense a little easier. Thus,

---

[23] Contemporary accounts of the war are widely scattered over the general literature of the time among which probably the most significant is Yüeh K'o's *T'ing-shih*, especially ch. 14. Many of Yeh Shih's literary compositions in his YSC have bearings on this subject, viz, YSC 10, "An Account of the Studio of Yeh-ling"; YSC 20, "Tomb Inscription for the Venerable Mr. Huang"; YSC 20, "Tomb Inscription for the Venerable Mr. Liu, Former Vice-President of the Board of Personnel"; YSC 21, "Tomb Inscription for the Venerable Mr. Hsü, Former Prefect of Lung-hsing"; YSC 22, "Tomb Inscription for Li Ling-wei".

[24] SSCSPM 83. Also, see the biography of P'u-san K'uei in *Chin-shih* 93.

[25] YSC, "Pen-chuan". Also *Sung hui-yao chi-kao*, p. 3157.

[26] YSC 2, "Memorandum to the Secretariat on Measures Taken to Rehabilitate the Liang-Huai Area".

when the chips were down, Yeh Shih was found standing in the breach, doing his utmost for the national war effort. As the governor of a city on the brink of war, his greatest achievement was to calm the panicky population and make them carry on the routine of life.[27] As a military leader, he helped stabilize the war situation, scoring a number of victories in skirmishes and surprise attacks on the enemy.[28] With a view to building a strong defensive posture for the eastern sector of the frontier, he improvised a crash program of rehabilitation for the territories North of the Yangtze which had been ravaged by war. His immediate objective was to establish three strongly fortified settlements on the northern bank of the river which would provide a haven of refuge for the farming population of the vicinity and deny the enemy access to the river over a vital sector of the current frontier.[29]

By the spring of 1207, the war had developed into a stalemate. The impetus of the Chin counter-offensive was spent. The winter of 1206/07 was particularly severe, with abundant snowfall. When the spring thaw came, the lake-studded terrain north of the Yangtze became virtually impassable. The Chin troops, many of them raw recruits, suffered acutely from the inclement weather. Sickness was rampant. Under these circumstances, P'u-san K'uei had no alternative but to pull back his troops to the more congenial climate of the North China Plain. Only a small detachment was left behind at Hao-chou to press for a better bargaining position.[30]

Both sides were now anxious for a rapid end to the futile struggle. But the war went on all the same. The stumbling block to peace was the Chin insistence that the culprit for starting the war be brought to justice and, by that, they meant Han T'o-chou himself.[31] For, in spite of the considerable loss of prestige that the colossal blunder of the war entailed, Han's regime was still unshaken. Almost everybody of consequence was obligated to him. It took a disgruntled empress, acting in conspiracy with a few confidants, to bring him down. Han was taken by surprise and killed by the conspirators before he was fully aware of what was going on.[32] With the main obstacle to peace removed, the two sides rapidly came to terms.

Probably the best-known article of the new peace treaty (1208) was the

[27] YSC, "Pen-chuan". Also YSC 10, "An Account of the Studio at Yeh-ling".
[28] Loc. cit.
[29] YSC 2, "Memorandum on the Three Fortified Settlements, Ting-shan, Kuan-pu and Shih-pa".
[30] YSC 20, "Tomb Inscription for the Venerable Mr. Liu, Former Vice-President of the Board of Personnel".
[31] SSCSPM 83.
[32] SS 414, biography of Shih Mi-yüan.

stipulation that the body of Han T'o-chou be disinterred and beheaded. His head was then preserved in lacquer and presented to the Chin emperor as a perpetual warning to all Southern Sung rulers who presumed to challenge the supremacy of the Chin emperors.[33]

The men who brought Han down from the pinnacle of power next went after his henchmen. This was standard practice. It not only served to consolidate the new faction in power but also helped provide prizes for the victors. Their first target was to remove those who had abetted Han in his resort to military action. The wanton use of military force which involved the death and suffering of hundreds of thousands of people and calamitous results to the dynasty was an unforgivable crime. It was fitting that all those associated with him in this matter should take some of the blame.

Although Yeh Shih declined to draft the declaration of war in 1206, he eventually played an important part in the war effort. In the years when the war was brewing, he submitted a series of three memorials (in his usual vein), calling for a determined effort to change from a weak to a strong posture.[34] Then on the eve of the war, realizing the vulnerability of the Sung defensive setup along the Yangtze River, he urged a stiffening of the position in anticipation of an enemy attack.[35] In both cases, whatever his intention, his words could only be construed as support for the position of the war party. He was therefore considered tainted with Han's crime and was dismissed from all his substantive offices. However, he was still granted a sinecure.[36]

Yeh Shih left Nanking early in 1208 when he was almost sixty years old. As it turned out, his departure from Nanking was his final departure from active political life. Shih Mi-yüan, the man who took the lion's share of the credit for overthrowing Han T'o-chou, was to dominate the political scene for the next twenty years.[37] The times were therefore unfavorable to Yeh Shih. By this time, most of his associates in political life were either dead or had retired. A new generation of men appeared to grapple with the vastly different situation of the post-Han T'o-chou era. Yeh Shih continued to be supported by a succession of sinecure positions for thirteen years. He died in 1223.[38]

The sixteen years of his retirement were truly the most productive of his life. His teaching activity, which had fallen off since his Soochow days, now rose to a new peak. His literary talent, hitherto revealed mainly

[33] *Loc. cit.* Also SSCSPM 83.
[34] YSC 1, "Memorial to Emperor Ning-tsung".
[35] YSC, "Pen-chuan". The text of this memorial has not been preserved.
[36] YSC, "Pen-chuan".
[37] He was Prime Minister during 1208–1232. See his biography in SS 414.
[38] YSC, "Pen-chuan".

in long, expository prose such as his *Chin-chüan* and *Wai-kao* and his various memorials, now found its fullest development in another prose genre — the funerary inscriptions (*mu-chih ming*). A funerary inscription is intended as a literary memorial of the deceased and it is customary to exaggerate the virtues but conceal his faults. Thus it is often written in a stilted and formal style, without much literary merit. Only on rare occasions, at the hands of a real master, does it become a fine piece of creative writing.

Yeh Shih's supreme accomplishment as a writer of funerary inscriptions lay in his ability to transcend the conventional limitations of this kind of prose genre.[39] There was always a backlog of demand for his services and his clients were of diverse background. Each of the hundreds of funerary inscriptions that he wrote bore his unmistakable mark. He was not afraid to infuse himself into such writings. He wanted his readers to rejoice and lament with him. He had the fine art of a biographer and a portrait painter. With a few bold strokes, he delineated the character of his subject vividly. He relied heavily on well-chosen factual details — in what may be called the "principle of concretion" — to achieve general effects. For example, to portray how a man built up a fortune by practising extreme thrift, he wrote, "He used a single fan for ten years, and if he saw a piece of charcoal barely an inch long by the roadside, he would take it home."[40] The literary inscriptions which he wrote abound in such concrete details that they have become a mine of historical information for the early and middle years of the Southern Sung dynasty.[41]

Needless to say, Yeh Shih was dependent upon various sources such as *hsing-chuang* (a detailed biographic account prepared by someone close to the deceased) in writing the literary inscriptions, especially for subjects of whom he had no personal knowledge. However, we can rest assured that he did not indulge in conscious chicanery or suppress unpalatable facts deliberately. In this latter point, he parted company

---

[39] His accomplishment in this genre of writing was duly acknowledged by his contemporaries, e.g., Chen Te-hsiu (1178–1235). See *Hsi-shan hsien-sheng wen-chi* 35, "Colophon for the Tomb Inscription of the Two Mr. Lius". Through the Yüan and Ming period, Yeh's essays continued to be appreciated as models of excellence. His admirers include Liu Hsün of the Yüan dynasty, author of the *Yin-chü t'ung-i*. His most enthusiastic admirer in the Ch'ing period was Sun I-yen who made persistent efforts to retrieve, collate and re-print Yeh's writings. Sun's influence may be detected in his friend, the Governor-general Chang Chih-tung who included Yeh Shih in his select list of eminent *ku-wen* writers. See Chang's *Chang Wen-hsiang kung ch'üan-chi*, Yu-hsien yü.

[40] YSC 14, "Tomb Inscription for Mr. Liu".

[41] The original compiler of Yeh Shih's collected works, his disciple Chao Ju-tang, had this purpose in mind. See YSC, "*Shui-hsin wen-chi* Preface".

with the distinguished Northern Sung scholar Tseng Kung (1019–1083). Tseng maintained that although tomb inscriptions were similar to historical writings, they constituted a separate genre of literature. While the purpose of history was to record events as they transpired, that of tomb inscriptions was to enshrine the memory of the dead. It was therefore permissible to omit facts which showed up the deceased in a poor light. In the tomb inscription Yeh Shih wrote for Wang Po, who was Assistant Councillor of State (*ts'an-chih cheng-shih*) during the time when the strong man prime minister Ch'in Kuei was in power, he stated that Wang took an active part in the deliberation of court policies. By this time, the vilification of Ch'in Kuei was well in progress. Wang Po's descendants therefore requested that Yeh Shih change his phraseology so that their ancestor's prestige would not suffer on account of his close association with Ch'in. Yeh Shih refused adamantly.

Nor would Yeh Shih indulge in unnecessary moralizing. If he had nothing creditable to say, he would say little. The following is a good illustration:[42]

> The younger brother of Hsüeh Ching-shih was named Shan, and styled Jen-ching. He died on the twenty-seventh day of the second month of the seventh year of Chia-ting [8th April, 1214], and was buried on the second day of the fourth month of the ninth year of Chia-ting [20th April, 1216]. His grave is located at Heng-shan of Ting-hai. Mr. [Hsüeh] read the *Book of Changes* frequently, and always kept a copy of it at hand. All through his life, this habit of his remained unchanged. Very often, when spoken to, he did not respond; or, [without a word] he would stand up abruptly, and nobody knew what he wanted.

Yeh Shih thus limited himself to strictly observable facts and made this inscription very short. His reticence perhaps tells us more about the man than any amount of eloquence could. In the concise, matter-of-fact presentation of his observations, Yeh managed to convey the extent of this man's alienation.

The efforts of the last years of his life not only enhanced his stature as a literary figure but also assured him a place in the history of philosophical thought. Although recognized as a leading *tao-hsüeh* master and enjoying a considerable following,[43] Yeh Shih hitherto wrote little on the doctrinal basis of his teachings. The only relevant writings were some sections of *Chin-chüan* written more than thirty years ago. He now decided to make up the deficiency. He undertook a critique of all the major works in the *ssu-pu* classification, viz. *ching* (classics), *shih* (history), *tzu* (philosophers) and *chi* (belles-lettres). The outcome of

---

[42] YSC 29, "Inscription for Hsüen Jen-ching's Tomb".
[43] See note 20 of this chapter and ch. 8 for more information.

this resolve was *Hsi-hsüeh chi-yen hsü-mu* (An Orderly Presentation of Words Jotted Down While Studying), published shortly after his death by one of his disciples, Sun Chih-hung, in fifty *chüan*. The title of this work may sound unpretentious, yet there is no question that this was an ambitious project. According to Sun Chih-hung, Yeh started working on it immediately after he went home from Nanking, kept working on it for the last sixteen years of his life, and discussed his progress and problems with friends as he went along.[44] Perhaps Yeh Shih had an inkling that his long-term historic position as a Confucian scholar was at stake and that he would be judged by posterity primarily on the basis of this work.

An Orderly Presentation of Words must be reckoned as an important source of Southern Sung intellectual thought, providing valuable documentation of the under-currents of intellectual life of which history seldom takes cognizance. The dominant note of the work is iconoclasm, an iconoclasm which appalled his contemporaries as it did posterity. Yeh Shih was breathing fire and fury on almost every page. He was apparently against everything and everybody.[45] As a person, Yeh Shih was known to be amiable and tolerant of differences. How do we account for this pronounced streak of intransigence which amounts to a radical reversal of form? A modern philosopher, Mou Tsung-san, incensed by Yeh's vehement assault on his cherished beliefs, undertook a laborious refutation of his ideas and concluded that only a man of perverse heart and mind could have harbored them.[46] However, to interpret Yeh's iconoclasm as sheer perversity is to miss its contextual significance. As we will see later, Yeh's indiscriminate indictment of others could be the result of an unconscious displacement of an untenable self-indicting situation. It is also possible that Yeh's apparent "perversity" was an over-reaction to the contemporary intellectual milieu and therefore symptomatic of the malaise that gripped Confucian scholarship. We will deal with this subject at greater length in Chapter Eight.

Although Yeh Shih had retired for good from active political service, his heart was probably still in politics. He followed developments in the capital with keen interest and kept up correspondence with promising scholar-officials of a younger generation. Among them, the best known was Wei Liao-weng (1178–1237), one of the most respected men of the

[44] HHCYHM Preface I (by Sun Chih-hung) and HHCYHM 46:14a.

[45] Most commentators on the HHCYHM seemed to have voiced this sentiment, for example, Ch'en Chen-sun (see *Anecdotes* 8:6b) and Liu Hsün (*Anecdotes* 8:26b).

[46] Mou Tsung-san, "Tui-yü Yeh Shui-hsin tsung-lun chiang-hsüeh ta-chih chih heng-ting", originally published in *Min-chu p'ing-lun* in four installments eventually incorporated into his book *Hsin-t'i yü hsing-t'i*, Vol. 1.

late Southern Sung period. It is possible that Yeh had hoped to put his political views into practice via them.[47]

Yeh Shih's sustained interests in affairs of state were linked to an unexpected turn of events. Shortly after the conclusion of the second peace treaty between the Southern Sung and the Chin, the long rumored disintegration of the latter finally occurred.[48] By 1206 the Northern barbarians had been welded into the Mongol nation by Chinggis Khan who then started his world-conquering career. After subduing the Tanggut kingdom of Hsi Hsia in 1209, Chinggis Khan turned southeastwards and made shreds of the Chin defense line. The Mongol invasion triggered widespread rebellions among the remnants of the Khitan people in Manchuria and among the Chinese in Shantung. Unable to resist the Mongols, who had had the Chin capital under seige for a long time, the Chin emperor submitted in 1214, paying a large ransom for the capital city of Chung-tu (present-day Peking). To lessen Mongol pressure on the court, the Chin capital was moved to K'ai-feng the next year. K'ai-feng, however, was too close to the Southern Sung border to be comfortable for either regime. The harassed Chin court, desperately attempting to recoup its fortunes and misled by the spineless showing of the Sung commanders during the previous round of fighting, considered the Sung territories easy prey. By 1217 hostitlites flared up again along the Sung-Chin border.[49] By this time, the Mongols had captured Peking and were in control in the Northern provinces of the Chin empire. Mongol power was on the rise everywhere. Clearly the Southern Sung empire would have to look beyond its immediate problem with the Chin and seek a *modus vivendi* with the Mongols.

Most Southern Sung observers with a sense of history were quick to realize the close parallel of the current situation with that more than a hundred years ago when the Liao empire was in its last gasps. Their primary concern now was not how to bring down the Chin empire. The imperative consideration was how to prevent the repetition of history, i.e., how to avoid falling into the same error that brought the Northern Sung dynasty to grief. The greatest value now was the value of survival.[50]

---

[47] YSC 7, "Wei Hua-fu Ho-shan shu-yüan" (Poem, Commemorating the Ho-shan Academy). This is the only reference Yeh Shih made to Wei Liao-weng in his writings. However, in Wei's *Ho-shan hsien-sheng wen-chi*, several references were made to Yeh Shih indicating that Wei and Yeh kept a fairly close contact with one another.

[48] SSCSPM 85, "Meng-ku ch'in Chin" (The Mongol Invasion of the Chin Empire). For a comprehensive account of the Mongol war with the Chin, see Henry D. Martin, *The Mongol Conquest of North China* (Johns Hopkins University Press: 1950).

[49] SSCSPM 86, "Chin hao chih chüeh" (The Rupture with the Chin).

[50] For a specimen of contemporary views, see the relevant memorials of Chen Te-hsiu, *Hsi-shan hsien-sheng wen-chi* 5, "Chiang-tung tsou lun pien-shih" (Discussing Frontier Affairs from Chiang-tung).

This radical change in the international situation rendered the traditional *hui-fu* ideology completely outdated.

In this light, one of Yeh Shih's essays in his collected works, "Hu Shang-shu tsou-i hsü" (Preface to the Collected Memorials of the Board President Hu) is significant.[51] In it, he quotes a lengthy passage from one of Hu's memorials which compared the condition of the Southern Sung dynasty to a palsied man with half of the body paralyzed. Yeh Shih endorsed this view and went on to say that the only sensible course open to the dynasty was to imitate the well-known physician Ch'ien I,[52] who managed to restrict his palsied condition to his limbs and lived well into his eighties. If the state could do likewise, it would no longer stand in constant dread of the malady penetrating to the viscera of the body politic.

Shortly before Yeh Shih's death in 1223, he was working on a document in which he discussed the external situation and put forth several programs of action in varying degrees of detail to meet the exigency of the times. This document came to be known as *Hou-tsung* (Postscript) which tied together many loose ends in his *ching-shih* ideas.[53] The central theme of *Postscript* was preparedness. As it was impossible to anticipate all contingencies that might develop in the relationship with the barbarian regimes of the Jürchen and the Mongols, security could only be sought by building up a strong posture, which involved: (a) making the Huai River and not the Yangtze River the first line of defense; and (b) reducing taxes by slashing the military budget. Both items were old hat. It was the means that he proposed to achieve them that disclosed new ideas.

Hitherto in Yeh Shih's blueprint for the rejuvenation of the dynasty, i.e., his *Wai-kao* as discussed in Chapter Three, he affirmed the paramount necessity of reducing military expenditure without, however, specifying how reduction was to be brought about. The only suggestions he made in that comprehensive document was the reduction of army size and making the frontier prefectures responsible for the support of the field armies. He did not say how these frontier prefectures were to find the revenue to support them. Now after more than thirty years, Yeh Shih finally came up with an answer in his *Postscript*: the frontier armies were to be self-supporting, in the manner of the T'ang *fu-ping*

---

[51] YSC 12. The Board President is identified as Hu I (1107–1174). See his biography in SS 388. It is impossible to date this essay of Yeh Shih's precisely. However, as Yeh Shih stated that it was far removed from the time of the Board President Hu, we may perhaps assume that it pertained to the post-Han T'o-chou period.

[52] See his biography in SS 462.

[53] YSC PC 16.

militia: they were to exploit the abundant wasteland along the frontier.

He did not spell out the detailed arrangements for making the army self-sufficient. His interests in frontier defense at this juncture were pre-empted by the need to cope with the chaotic conditions in the Liang-Huai region due to frequent Jürchen incursions. Inhabitants of the region had been fleeing *en masse* to the relative security South of the Yangtze River. Those who could not get away sought protection from the ravages of war in the traditional manner by banding together and by taking shelter behind advantageous locations. Yeh Shih's plan for stabilizing the Huai frontier called for systematic mobilization of the self-help potential of the people. The population along the entire length of the Huai River was to be organized into self-sufficient communities, given training in the use of arms and provided with places of refuge in the event of enemy attack. In Yeh Shih's plan, these places of refuge were built at regular intervals, protected by deep moats and high ramparts so that they could stand up against the initial onslaughts of the enemy. These fortified strongholds, strung along the entire Huai River area, afforded security not only to the people but also should serve as an effective barrier against enemy troop movement.

One of the most astounding ingredients of his *Postscript* is an un-abashed appeal to racism. Yeh Shih suggested that it was not necessary for the Sung dynasty to resort to military power to subdue the enemy (probably referring both to the Jürchen and the Mongols). What it should do, he maintained, was to issue a proclamation to the people of North China to cease serving in the armies of the enemy. Moreover, the Sung government should make known to all the people that it would pay a bonus of five hundred strings of cash for each head of a *bona fide* barbarian (*hu-jen*) killed. A specific sum of money would be made available for this purpose, sufficient to pay for all the enemy heads that were to be decapitated. In this way, he claimed, the enemy would be forced to leave Chinese territory and to withdraw to his homeland.

In offering a price for the head of each barbarian killed, Yeh was acting on the inveterate assumption that men would do anything if sufficient inducements were offered. Cowards have been transformed into brave men under the enticements of liberal rewards. For instance, the second emperor of the Sung dynasty, T'ai-tsung (reigned 976–997), after his humiliating defeat by the Khitan, was known to have said that when he had accumulated ten million strings of cash, he could have exchanged them for all the Khitan heads.[54] The same strategy was used

[54] See SS 179 (Shih-huo) in connection with the establishment of the *nei-tsang* treasury.

by the imperial commissioner Lin Tse-hsü (1785–1850) in his dealings with the trouble-making British sailors before the outbreak of the Opium War (1839–1842).

Yeh was correct in assuming that there was a reservoir of hostile feeling among the Northern Chinese against their Jürchen and Mongol conquerors, although he over-estimated their ability to act upon their feelings. The amorphous populace of the countryside, unarmed and unorganized, had little chance against the well-disciplined armies of their barbarian rulers. The intense anti-foreign feeling that Yeh Shih exhibited here was frankly based on racial grounds. In Chapter Seven, we will have a chance to discuss some of the cultural connotations of this anti-foreign attitude.

The second half of his *Postscript* is devoted to his land acquisition plan for the prefecture of Wen-chou. In view of the fact that he had taken pains to work out the detailed guidelines of the plan, he obviously considered it feasible. It was in fact intended as a pilot project, which he hoped would be eventually applied to the entire empire.

The pilot project visualized the creation of public estates of arable land so that their rental income would meet the cost of the prefectual army. These estates were to be created by a process of land appropriation in the environs of the prefectural city, within a radius of thirty *li*. Yeh Shih's guideline called for buying up one half of all the landholdings of any individual household in excess of thirty *mou*. The land was to be bought at a uniform rate amounting to about ten times the average ground rent. He probably had access to the tax register of Wen-chou, for he was able to locate the households with excess land in each administrative village (*hsiang* and *tu*). The total acreage to be acquired were 98,125 *mou* which would cost the government 2,943,750 strings of cash.[55] The government treasury, however, was not to be depleted by this amount. The purchase was to be financed in the customary way, namely, the sale of monks' certificates (*tu-t'ieh*) and official ranks.

There is no question that this contemplated acquisition of land, as in all other schemes of appropriation by the state, involved a certain amount of inequity. Within a radius of thirty *li* there could be tremendous variations in the productivity of land often involving enormous differentials in capital investment. Moreover, even the stipulated rate of indemnification was not to be accepted on face value. The monk's certificates and the patents of official ranks with which Yeh Shih proposed to finance the land purchase could hardly be unloaded at actual market conditions. It is doubtful that the dubious prerogatives asso-

[55] Figures for total acreage and purchase price are based on data supplied by Yeh Shih in *Hou-tsung*.

ciated with lowly official ranks offered for sale or those conferred by monkish status were sufficient inducement for the level-headed men of wealth to part with their money or their land.

In spite of the fact that the terms of indemnification amounted to sheer confiscation in some cases, the land appropriation plan was not motivated by a desire to hurt the powerful landowning class in Southern Sung China. Yeh Shih was quick to point out that land acquisition was limited to within the thirty *li* radius so that the major part of the prefecture, stretching to over a hundred *li* in either direction from the prefectural city, would not be affected in any way except to enjoy the benefit of lower taxation.[56] The policy in question was essentially justified on grounds of expediency and cannot be explained apart from the worsening financial situation of the dynasty.

The abortive Northern Expedition of Han T'o-chou put a severe strain on government finances. The subsequent resumption of hostilities following the move of the Chin capital to K'ai-feng further boosted war expenditure. To make up for revenue deficiency, government printing presses turned out enormous quantities of greatly depreciated paper currency. Inflation got out of hand, which further dislocated the economy.[57]

Yeh Shih's re-organization plan for the army and his land purchase project were inspired by a desire to dampen inflation by reducing the military budget, undoubtedly the main item of government expenditure. If his plans were implemented, neither the frontier army nor that of the interior would have been a charge on government treasuries. It is unlikely that they could be implemented as they rested on an untenable principle, viz. the frontier armies, despite the fact that they were expected to bear the brunt of the fighting, were required to produce their own food, whereas armies of the interior, unlikely to see much action, were to be comfortably supported by the revenue of the public estates.

The historic significance of Yeh's land-purchasing scheme lay in the fact that it could be regarded as the precursor of the land reform which was eventually put into effect around 1264 by the last powerful prime minister of the Southern Sung, Chia Ssu-tao (1213–1275), more than

---

[56]Information on economic geography and fiscal history of Wen-chou in Sung times may be gleaned from the collected works of Sung authors, e.g., Wu Yung who was Prefect of Wen-chou during the reign of Emperor Li-tsung. See *Ho-lin chi* 23, "Yu Ma Kuang-tsu hu tsou chuang" (Memorial in Rebuttal to that of Ma Kuang-tsu). From information supplied by Wu, we learn that Wen-chou produced more rice than it consumed and the surplus was regularly shipped upstream to Chü-chou.

[57] For inflation due to the resumption of hostilities, see Ch'üan Han-sheng, *op. cit.*

forty years after Yeh's death.[58] There is no solid evidence that Chia or his advisors were aware of Yeh's scheme. Yet, the points of similarity between Yeh's blueprint and the system implemented under Chia were striking. To illustrate: Yeh would take one half of the land in excess of an absolute amount, viz., 30 *mou*, whereas Chia took one third of all holdings in excess of the statutory limit as permitted to individuals in accordance with their official ranks. Both based their compensation on a flat rate and both schemes were to be financed by the forced sale of monks' certificates and patents of official rank. Chia's scheme offered a wider range of ranks and titles, aimed at both prospective men and women buyers. In both cases, the price of patents and titles were jacked up to an exceedingly high level, with Chia charging three times more than Yeh recommended for a corresponding rank to compensate for the greatly depreciated currency.[59]

Chia's land reform was undertaken at a time when the Southern Sung dynasty was already near its end, with the rich province of Szechwan chopped off and the invading Mongol armies closing in from the North and West. Although the economic center of the empire, Chekiang, and the neighboring provinces, were still intact, it was precisely in these provinces that the practice of tax evasion had been most rampant. This was undoubtedly due to the fact that the imperial government had always been dominated by men from these provinces who used their official positions to expand their landholdings and to thwart the tax-collectors.

Under these circumstances, the only way for the dynasty to sustain the Mongol war of attrition and carry on the struggle for survival was to tap the rich resources of these hitherto under-taxed provinces. Chia Ssu-tao's land reform was a desperate measure. However, the malady which had been gnawing at the vitals of the dynasty for so long was too far gone to be cured by this drastic remedy. The haste and excesses with which the reform was carried out created a reservoir of resentment against the dynasty among influential segments of the people of Chekiang and the nearby provinces which undoubtedly contributed to the rapid collapse of the Sung defense efforts.[60]

Yeh Shih's land-purchasing scheme was addressed to the same malady in the body politic of the dynasty which finally provoked Chia to action. However, he had a forty year head-start over Chia which means

[58] SSCSPM 98, "Kung-t'ien chih-chih" (The Establishment of Public Estates).

[59] For the rank of *ch'eng-chieh lang*, Chia would charge 30,000 strings of cash or their equivalent in paper money.

[60] This is the view of Herbert Franke, in his article, "Chia Ssu-tao, Last Bad Minister", published in Arthur Wright, ed., *Confucian Personalities* (Stanford University Press: 1962).

that the malady was at a less advanced stage and probably still curable. It may be argued that if Yeh Shih lived and were empowered to implement his pilot project, he would have been able to discern some of the built-in inequities in his blueprint and to cope with the difficulties as they arose.

We will close out the biographical section of this study of Yeh Shih by raising the following question. As he approached the end of his life, what were his thoughts on himself and on his life-work? How did he measure up to his own yardstick? An essay on a Buddhist shrine which he helped renovate gave him away on this point:[61]

Alas! I am now old, sick and frail. Indolent, without ambition. I am not unaware of the fact that I should pattern myself on the great men of antiquity, yet I drift along aimlessly and waste myself on the learning of the foreign lands. There are those who, dreading the end of the day, rush hither and thither in delirium and yet turn back now and anon to gaze at the declining sun. I write this not only to warn myself but also to laugh at myself.

Obviously Yeh Shih's mood during the last days of his life was very different from that of the author of the famous boast "I have fought the good fight; I have finished the course; I have kept the faith."[62] Unlike the Apostle Paul, the serenity and peace of mind that came with a self-approving attitude were not his to enjoy. He could not rest on his laurels; he had to push forward. He was unable to derive much satisfaction from his Confucian studies and his statesmanlike efforts: hence his continuing interest in Buddhism. Nevertheless, he was not totally disenchanted. The realization that he was unintentionally straying from the chosen path provoked him to redouble his efforts. It was doubtless in this frame of mind that he wrote his *Postscript* and his *Orderly Presentation of Words*.

[61] YSC 9, "Su-chüeh an chi" (Essay on the Su-chüeh Shrine).
[62] Timothy II, 4:7.

CHAPTER SIX

Yeh Shih and the Dynastic Cycle

I

IN RETROSPECT, we may say that Yeh Shih's pilot project for Wen-chou and Chia Ssu-tao's land procurement policy were prompted by the necessity to do something about the phenomenon of dynastic decline. Chia's policy came too late to be effective. Yeh Shih had a forty year headstart and as we surmised in the last chapter, the maladies of the body politic which eventually proved fatal might still have been curable in his time. Whether Yeh Shih could have succeeded in curing the maladies depended, of course, not only on his gaining the confidence of the rulers but also on his providing the proper diagnosis of the problems.

In his major works of political commentary, viz. *Chin-chüan* and *Wai-kao*, Yeh Shih appraised the basic institutions of the dynasty from a specific point of view, namely, their bearing on the dynastic goal of *hui-fu* (complete recovery of lost territories). His comprehensive reform plan was predicated on the premise that *hui-fu* could not be attained without a process of dynastic rejuvenation, substituting a polity of strength for one of weakness, as he called it. It goes without saying that dynastic rejuvenation was a formidable task that could not be accomplished without first coming to grips with the causes of dynastic decline. In Chapter Three we dismissed his blueprint for dynastic rejuvenation on the ground that his analysis of the needs of the dynasty was based on an anachronistic view of the Sung monarchy. It may be desirable to reconsider the issue and approach it from a different angle. Is it possible that his failure to provide a viable program of reform was due to his inability to comprehend the real causes of dynastic decline?

It is a truism that Yeh Shih was cognizant of the fact of dynastic decline. Southern Sung scholar-officials seemed to have accepted the increasing degradation of the "times" as an axiom of thought. We have already alluded to the *tsun Yao* mentality in Chapter One. To men of the early Southern Sung, i.e. of the reigns of Kao-tsung (1127–

1162) and Hsiao-tsung (1163–1189), the good old days were the days of the ancestors, namely, that of the Northern Sung. Some fifty or sixty years later, reflecting on the axiomatic acceptance of the increasing degradation of the times, the days of Kao-tsung and Hsiao-tsung were in turn looked up to with envy by men of the reign of Emperor Li-tsung (1225–1264).[1]

This axiomatic acceptance of the fact of dynastic decline, however, was normally not accompanied by a heightened awareness of its mechanisms or causes. If scholar-officials commented upon the cause of decline, they usually dwelt on the morality and talent (*jen-ts'ai*) of the ministers of state during the successive stages of the dynasty.[2] This is the moralistic approach characteristic of Confucian political thought which placed a premium on the human factor in government. Decline in the morality or talent of the ministers of state is not easily quantifiable nor is it acceptable as an adequate explanation of dynastic decline even if empirically proved to be true, for we will then be confronted with a new question, "What is the cause of the observable decline in morality and talent?" To locate the dynamics of dynastic decline, we will have to look elsewhere.

Modern scholars, under the influence of the materialistic conception of history of the Marxian school, have focused on the changing economic basis of the ruling elite as the "real stuff of history". The Northern Sung struggle between the Conservatives and the Reformers, for instance, has been interpreted by some Japanese scholars as the struggle for supremacy between two identifiable economic interests, namely, between the big landed interests of North China well entrenched in government service and the new men connected with the burgeoning commercial interests of the Southeast who were pressing for greater participation in the political life of the empire.[3] By the same token, the shifting policy decisions on war and peace as well as the cultural, ideological complexion of the Southern Sung dynasty has been linked by some scholars to the changing balance of power between two groups

[1] This attitude is understandable because the reign of Li-tsung was characterized by almost continuous warfare first with the Jürchen then with the Mongols, causing considerable dislocation to the economic and political life of the Southern Sung empire. For a general discussion of the traditional attitudes and expectations of the behavior of dynasties, see Lien-sheng Yang, "Towards a Study of Dynastic Configurations in Chinese History", in *Studies in Chinese Institutional History* (Harvard University Press: 1961).

[2] A good example is supplied by Wu Yung. See *Ho-lin chi* 17, "Lun Yüan-yu, Chien-chung, Chia-ting chi chin-jih keng-hua su" (On the Turning-points during the Reigns of Yüan-yu etc.).

[3] For a systematic treatment of Japanese scholarship on this subject, see James T.C. Liu, *Reform in Sung China*, ch. 2, "Problems of Interpretation".

of landed interests, namely, between the indigenous landlords of the South and the new landlords who came into existence with the establishment of the Southern Sung regime in Hangchow.[4] For our purpose here, it is not necessary to concur with their interpretations nor trace the intricacies of their arguments. Suffice it to say that the researches of Japanese scholars have enhanced our appreciation of the role of land in the economic foundation of the Sung dynasty.

The emergence of a class of large landlords was a concomitant of the development process that transformed China from the institutional pattern of the T'ang to that of the Sung. Under the *chün-t'ien* system of land grant prevalent during the T'ang, peasants were entitled to an allotment of land under tenures which restricted their sale on the market.[5] The *men-fa* aristocracy consisted of families of honorable lineage who were secure in their entrenched position and did not need to bolster their position by engaging in aggrandizing activities in the economic sphere.[6] The elite of the Sung dynasty, on the other hand, lived in a society where social status was not inherent in one's lineage but dependent on the criterion of achievement, especially that of passing the civil service examination. As the examination was open to all people, without reference to their occupation or background, no single class had a monopoly of the avenues of social advancement.[7] The members of the official class therefore had to make an effort to perpetuate their position. The most effective way to do this was to acquire large landed estates which guaranteed a steady income so that their offsprings could be spared the necessity of making a living and could devote themselves to a life of preparation for the examination. Since wealth was the prerequisite of leisure and, through the latter, of academic and political success, it became itself a criterion of social status. This was especially the case when the sumptuary laws governing the life styles of the different social classes were allowed to lapse in the early years of the dynasty.[8] Members of the official class were joined in

[4] See Yamauchi Masahiro, "Nansō seiken no sui-i", in *Sekai rekishi*, Chusei 3 (1971).

[5] On the *chün-t'ien* system, see Denis Twitchett, *Financial Administration of the T'ang dynasty*, ch. 1.

[6] The classic study on the T'ang *men-fa* aristocracy was by Ch'en Yin-ko; see his *Sui T'ang chih-tu yüan-yüan lun-lüeh.*

[7] Edward Kracke Jr. has made a statistical study of the social background of the successful candidates of the metropolitan examinations for the beginning and for the end of the Southern Sung period. He is of the opinion that through success at the examination, the official class was able to perpetuate itself to a considerable extent. See his article, "Region, Family and Individuals in the Examination System", in J.K. Fairbank, ed., *Chinese Thought and Institutions.*

[8] See Edward Kracke, Jr., "Change within Tradition", in *Far Eastern Quarterly* 14 (1954–1955), pp. 479–488.

land-grabbing by the big merchants who also desired social advancement and considered land a safer investment than commerce or usury.

The rise of landlordism and its correlate, tenancy, was inimical to the interests of the state. Being officials themselves or related to officials, the landlords were likely to be classified as *kuan-hu* (official households) and hence exempted from the corveé and other onerous labor services. Official status did not in theory confer tax-immunity on their landholdings. However, as they were men of influence in the communities and as they were related through a ramifying network of kinship, matrimonial and friendship ties to the empire-wide ruling elite, it was not difficult for them to evade their fair share of the land taxes.[9] The consequence was a serious reduction to the resource base of the dynasty.

To compensate for this reduction of the resource base, the state was compelled to raise the tax rate on land still liable to taxation and to impose a multitude of revenue-yielding, indirect taxes. This increasing tax burden had a tragic effect on the independent cultivators, known in official sources as *chu-hu* (principal households). Unable to meet their obligations, some abandoned their land to join the ranks of the urban proletariat or sought relief by commending themselves to the local magnates, becoming the latter's tenants or hired hands and were classified in the tax and census registers as *ke-hu* or *tien-hu* (guest households). As such they were shielded from the extortionate practices of the state and its local agents. In either case, they were no longer contributing their share of the agricultural taxes and the resource base of the dynasty was accordingly diminished. Their removal from the tax rolls further piled up pressure on those who remained on them. A vicious circle was thus set in motion with a steadily diminishing resource base and an increasingly heavy burden for the tax-paying people. The circle, when permitted to run its course, led to an extreme polarization of the population until the dispossessed, pauperized multitude took the law into their own hands, recovered their land and brought about a more equitable socio-economic order.[10]

The process described above gathered momentum during the early years of the Southern Sung period. In addition to the tangible loss of territories in North China, the attrition of the resource base due to

[9] Sudō Yoshiyuki, the prolific Japanese scholar, has made the economic history of Medieval China a life-long study. His books and articles published over the last thirty years deal with the rise of the landed estates, landlord-tenant relationship, agricultural technology etc. For a concise statement of the privileges enjoyed by official households, see McKnight, *op. cit.*, pp. 109–120

[10] The classic study of the land tax in relation to the dynastic cycle is by Wang Yü-chuan; see his article, "The Rise of the Land Tax and the Fall of Dynasties", in *Pacific Affairs* IX, pp. 201–220.

landlordism also proceeded rapidly. A significant proportion of the refugees from North China were men of wealth and of offical status. Settling down in the relative security of Szechwan, Kiangnan, and Chekiang, they began to build up landed estates of their own. An increased demand for land provided the incentive for large-scale reclamation of lakeshore, coastal and hilly land. These projects were generally sponsored by powerful families as they alone possessed the material resources, organizational ability and political influence to implement the projects and enjoy the fruits of their labor.

Population growth and the increasing commercialization of agriculture which were notable during the Southern Sung period also favored the growth of large estates at the expense of the small owner-cultivators.

It is conceivable that the vigorous expansion of the large estates had an impact on contemporary social and political thought. Most references to the subject in the general literature of the time, however, dealt with unscrupulous practices in the acquisition of land or operational details in the management of these estates and were not concerned with the justice or overall socio-economic consequences of the system. It is difficult to find any man who denounced the system of large landed estates in unequivocal terms. This is to be expected because the only people who could make themselves heard across the barriers of time were the literati or scholar-officials who were, for the most part, beneficiaries of the system. Nevertheless it is possible to discern considerable hostility towards the aggrandizing activity of the landlords not only from the hapless peasants but also from elements more capable of articulating their sentiments. Beyond doubt there were some prefectural or sub-prefectural officials who placed their role as bureaucrats and functionaries of the state above other considerations. They hated to bend the law and conduct their official business largely for the benefit of what they call the *hao-min* (men of wealth and influence). In addition, hostility may also stem from the yamen clerks (*hsü-li*). The latter is generally thought to be men without scruples working in collusion with the local men of wealth and influence to victimize the peasants. However, this co-operative attitude may easily give way to one of vehement opposition if the clerks perceived that their vested interests in the local power structure were being encroached upon. From these elements came demands for special legislation for curbing the so-called plutocrats (*chien-ping chih chia*).[11]

---

[11] Yeh Shih, as we will see later on in this chapter, in arguing for a *laissez-faire* policy, alleged that the run-of-the-mill functionaries (*su-li*) were hostile towards the men of wealth. Included in his category of *su-li* were probably the yamen clerks. The early Southern Sung official Wu Ching was more specific. He recognized the clerks

II

THERE is considerable disparity between the two major works of Yeh Shih's political commentary. *Chin-chüan*, though occasionally showing flashes of insight into the nature of Chinese state and society, does not have the coherence and sustained analysis that characterizes *Wai-kao*. Written by a man who had yet to cross the threshold into officialdom, it was understandably suffused with generalities masquerading for knowledge. Nevertheless we must draw upon it to reconstruct Yeh Shih's response to the erosion of the dynasty's resource base as *Wai-kao* was almost totally silent on the subject.

In *Chin-chüan*, Yeh Shih showed a consistently conservative attitude on the land question. He saw no viable alternative to the *status quo* and counseled a *laissez-faire* state policy. In defense of his conservative position, he dealt with the following issues which, no doubt, represented the terms in which the contemporary discussion on the land question was carried on.

Firstly, the utopian approach to the land question, the restoration of the *ching-t'ien* system that allegedly prevailed during the feudal past. The classic exposition of the system envisions an agricultural society divided into self-help communities of eight families each.[12] These eight families, each with its own plot of agricultural land, grouped around a communal plot cultivated in common for the state, were distributed in the manner of the Chinese character for "well" (井 *ching*); hence the name *ching-t'ien*, meaning well-field. In addition to providing an adequate means of livelihood for the peasants, the chief appeal of the system was the emphasis on the value of neighborliness — families in the same octave unit learned to watch out for one another and pool their resources in times of hardship, an antidote to the unseemly competitiveness that existed in contemporary Sung society.[13]

In proposals to revive the system, minor variations of detail are

---

(*hsü-li*) as a counterweight to the local men of influence and wealth (*hao-min*). His formula for achieving peace consisted in playing off the clerks against the men of wealth and influence. See *Wu Wen-su kung chi* 3:5a, "Simple Speech". For a scholarly presentation of the varying relationship (in opposition as well as in collusion) between the *hsü-li* and the *hao-min*, see Fukuzawa Yokuro, "Sōdai chiho seiji ni kansuru ichi kanken", *Tohōgaku* 19 (1957), pp. 63–76.

[12] The earliest reference to the Well-field System is to be found in *Mencius* (James Legge's translation, Bk. 31, ch. 3). For a statement of its controversial nature and the pertinent literature, see Cho-yün Hsü, *Ancient China in Transition*, pp. 195–196, note 15.

[13] T'ao Hsi-sheng, in an article, "Pei-Sung chi-ko ta ssu-hsiang chia ti ching-t'ien lun", *Shih-huo* 2:6, marshalls together utterances of a few outstanding scholars of the Northern Sung period on the Well-field System. His overt Marxist sympathies, however, seem to have detracted from the value of his analysis.

discernible. Chang Tsai, the well-known *tao-hsüeh* master, in trying to prove the feasibility of the system for contemporary Sung society, sought to accommodate to the vested interest of the class of large landlords. To win the latter's support for the *ching-t'ien* system, he proposed making them hereditary fief-owners, on the premise that a feudal form of government would have to accompany the implementation of the *ching-t'ien* system. Another scholar, Lin Hsün, approached the *ching-t'ien* system from a different point of view. During the early years of the Southern Sung period, before the regime at Hangchow was consolidated, the dynasty was often in dire financial straits. In 1130, in his capacity as a professor in the prefectural school of Canton, he submitted a plan to the throne in which he envisioned a redistribution of the land of the whole empire, saying that if each adult male was granted fifty *mou* of arable land and taxed at a given rate, the revenue from this source alone would be more than sufficient to cover the expenditures of the government so that all commercial taxes and state monopolies could be dispensed with.[14]

However, most Sung scholar-officials took pride in being realists and ruled out the feasibility of the *ching-t'ien* system. In maintaining its infeasibility, the argument most often advanced is the immense difficulty of converting to the ancient system involving a redrawing of the boundary lines of the fields, a rerouting of the irrigation canals, and a redistribution of the peasant dwellings to conform to the grid-iron pattern of the *ching-t'ien* system of settlement. The cumbersome *ching-t'ien* system, according to Su Hsün, a keen commentator on socio-political problems, was not created by the sage-rulers of antiquity, as was commonly believed, but was the product of historic evolution in response to the physical environment and technology of the ancients. He was of the opinion that even Confucius and the Duke of Chou, should they rise again, would not advocate a return to the system.[15]

Yeh Shih joined the chorus of the realists. Elaborating on the theme already adumbrated by Chang Tsai that *ching-t'ien* and feudalism were interdependent systems, he argued that the former could not be resuscitated without the country reverting to a genuinely feudal system of government. In addition, he advanced the argument of intrinsic value. The rectilinear pattern of boundary lines and irrigation ditches associated with the *ching-t'ien* system did not contribute to increased productivity. It was in fact a sheer waste of time and money.[16]

A more potent threat to the *status quo* was Wang An-shih's legacy

---

[14] SS 173 (Shih-huo): 5a-b.
[15] Su Hsün, *Chia-yu chi* 5:8a–9b.
[16] YSC PC 2, "Min-shih san" (Civil Affairs, section 3).

of reformism, as symbolized in the reform measure setting up a system of farm credit known as *ch'ing-miao* (green sprouts). *Ch'ing-miao* was beyond doubt the most vilified of Wang's "New Policies" because it epitomized a conception of the state which threatened the economic base of the Sung ruling elite. By making cash and crop advances to the needy peasants, which was what the reform measure purported to accomplish, the state undercut the position of the local power structure — needy peasants no longer had to rely exclusively on the local magnates for credit. Bearing in mind the latent hostility towards the aggrandizing activities of the landlords, it is easy to understand why the scholar-officials continued to fulminate against *ch'ing-miao* at a time when Wang An-shih's legacy was in complete disgrace — it provided a historic precedent as well as ideological sanction for the restrictive legislation demanded by anti-landlord sentiments.[17]

To combat this undesirable legacy, Southern Sung conservatives produced an *exposé* literature, demonstrating that *ch'ing-miao* was not what it purported to be, a benefit to the people, but a cunning device of Wang An-shih and his partisans to make a profit at the expense of the people. Apart from denouncing the rapacity of Wang An-shih, Yeh Shih also sought to prove that the basic idea of *ch'ing-miao* was theoretically unsound.[18] His approach was to examine the appropriateness of the sanction that Wang An-shih claimed for it, namely, the *ch'üan-fu* (circulating treasury) institution as described in the *Chou-li*, which was traditionally regarded as the handbook of government which the Duke of Chou wrote for the young King Ch'eng, son of King Wu. According to the *Chou-li*, *ch'üan-fu* was one of the treasuries of the king and among its many functions was that of regulating the market. When there was a glut in the market so that prices fell, *ch'üan-fu* authorities would make large-scale purchases to bolster up the price level. They would also extend loans to people in need. Commenting on this institution, Yeh Shih argued that while it was laudable for the Duke of Chou to do these things it would be reprehensible for Wang An-shih and his partisans to do the same. This is because they lived in different "times". The Duke of Chou lived in a society consisting of *ch'i-min* (people of uniform status or wealth). There were no particularly wealthy people. Under these circumstances, if the state did not provide succor to people in need, nobody else would. The "times" were now different. The society

---

[17] See note 42, ch. 1.

[18] YSC PC 2, "Ts'ai-chi I" (Monetary and Fiscal Policy). A significant portion of Yeh's phraseology is directly taken from the *Chou-li*. The only translation of this classic in a Western language is that by Edouard Biot, *Le Tcheou-Li ou Rites des Tscheou* (1851).

of *ch'i-min* had given way to one in which inequality was prevalent. Control of the economic processes of production and distribution had devolved upon the men of wealth. This had been the practice for ages. It would have been unfair for the state to change the situation overnight. Yet by instituting the *ch'ing-miao* measure, the state was undermining the position of the men of wealth.

By itself, Yeh Shih's argument was not convincing, being an argument of the type "Whatever is, is right". However, he did manage to find a better rationalization for the *status quo*. In voicing his opposition to the restrictive laws which enemies of the big landlords wanted to slap on them, he wrote:[19]

It is unfortunate that the state has lost the power to provide for the livelihood of the people. This power devolved upon the men of wealth long before our life time. People who have no land rent it from rich men. Without the means to put the land into cultivation, they take loans from rich men. In case of emergency, they seek help from rich men. Destitute people attach themselves as domestic servants to rich men. Idlers, tramps, acrobats and actors subsist on rich men. Furthermore, rich men discharge their obligations to the state and submit to innumerable levies. Even the officials themselves, in the event of unforeseen demands from superior authorities, and failing to meet them from their own resources, turn to rich men for support. Thus rich men constitute the mainstay of local communities on whom both the superior and inferior [classes] have to depend. In view of the fact that they help government support the people and provide revenue for the state we should not begrudge them their handsome remuneration which is what their painstaking efforts deserve.

Somewhere at the beginning of this exposition, Yeh Shih brought about a subtle change of emphasis. Instead of arguing against anti-plutocratic legislation, it became a vindication of the social and economic function of wealth. Plutocracy is a term with bad connotation. Generally it signifies gobbling up the substance of the helpless by force or economic pressure. A straightforward apology for plutocracy is therefore impossible and Yeh Shih did make due concessions to popular sentiments by agreeing that overt plutocratic tendencies should be curbed. What he opposed was the attempt to enact legislation against the men of wealth. In the event such laws were passed, it was usually the honest, law-abiding and humanitarian-minded landlords who would be ruined while the cunning and ruthless plutocrats would still find loopholes to exploit. A vindication of rich men was necessary to protect them from unwarranted governmental encroachment.

[19] YSC PC 2, "Min-shih san" (Civil Affairs, section 3). This section has been translated by Dunn Li, in his *The Essence of Chinese Civilization* (V. Nostrand: 1967), ch. 13.

Plutocrats or good and responsible members of the community were usually two sides of the same coin for the thousands of large estate-owners who dominated Southern China at that time. It is impossible to determine whether they were plutocrats first or the other way round. These two roles were probably related structurally. Yeh Shih played up the responsible aspect and, in this regard, provided a rationalization for the existing social and economic structure. By attributing social and economic value to wealth, he added the normative aspect to the descriptive in his approach to social realities. Borrowing a phrase from Hegel, the real is rational and by inference, the rational becomes real.[20]

Yeh Shih of *Chin-chüan* was, of course, not entirely complacent on social and economic issues. There was a crying need for action in areas of grave concern to the dynasty. The greatest challenge to the dynasty, as he saw it, was rapid population growth. The pace of growth was such that although the present regime had but half of the territory of the Sung empire at its height, its population almost equalled the latter. This phenomenal growth was particularly concentrated in the South-eastern circuits close to the metropolitan area of Hangchow. To feed the teeming millions, every inch of land was brought under cultivation and other natural resources (fisheries, forests, mines) intensively ex-ploited. This sustained exploitation which made no allowance for the equilibrium of nature was rapidly depleting the productive capacity of the land. In emphatic terms, Yeh Shih warned of the danger to come:[21]

People go on multiplying. Already the price of land has skyrocketted. With continuous, intensive cultivation, giving the land no respite, the productive capacity of the soil will ultimately be exhausted. What will happen in twenty or thirty years' time is inconceivable. The already keen struggle for survival will become keener and the ingredients of an explosive situation are ac-cumulating day by day.

In showing the consequences of over-population, Yeh Shih described a phenomenon which in a slightly different form has cropped up all over the developing countries — the influx of people from the countryside to the cities. People flock to the cities because they are displaced by population pressure or advancing technology, or because they are

[20] The enthusiasm with which Yeh Shih vindicated the role of the wealthy may be compared with the more subdued tone of Hu T'ai-ch'u; see *Tsou-lien hsü-lun* 14, "Shih-li pien" (Recognizing the Realities).

[21] YSC PC 2, "Min-shih erh" (Civil Affairs, section 2). For study of Sung popula-tion, see Kato Shigeru, *Shina keizai shi kōshō* (Tōyō Bunka: 1952–53), ch. 2. Also, Yuan Chen, "Sung-tai hu-k'ou", in *Li-shih yen-chiu* 3 (1957).

attracted by the prospect of a better life in the cities. Unable to be absorbed into the modern economy at once, the immigrants fester in ghetto areas where despair, poverty and crimes of violence reign supreme. In Southern Sung China, without the benefit of modern industries to give employment to thousands of people, the displaced peasants from the villages had little chance of being integrated into the urban economy. Yeh Shih described them as an amorphous riff-raff. Eking out a pre-carious existence in good years, they succumbed with the first onslaught of adverse times, becoming a liability and source of danger to the dynasty.

Yeh Shih's solution of this problem was simple: large-scale transplant-ing of the excess population from the congested areas of the South-east to the under-populated Ching-Hu area in present-day Hupei. Ching-Hu in former times was a prosperous province of great strategic importance particularly during periods of disunion when rival factions were con-tending for supremacy in China. The decline of the area started during the T'ang dynasty, and continued into the Sung. The strategic import-ance of the area, right in the center of the Chinese world, however, did not diminish with socio-economic decline. Ching-Hu, therefore, featured prominently in the plans for military reconquest of the North submitted by *hui-fu* enthusiasts. Ch'en Liang, for instance, advocated moving the capital of the dynasty there.[22]

Yeh Shih did not specify how the large-scale transplantation of people to Ching-Hu was to be accomplished. He made his position clear and emphasized the imperative necessity of the proposed action. Anticipating conservative critics who habitually opposed large-scale changes of any kind on the ground that unforeseen complications might arise and the resultant fluid situation might be tempting to fomentors of sedition, he alleged that in view of the high stakes involved, a prudent man should not hesitate to take the risk.

In view of the foregoing account, it cannot be said that Yeh Shih was blind to the socio-economic processes of the dynastic cycle. His analysis of the effect of the growing population on the worsening economy, though oversimplified, was essentially correct. His dire predictions of the future were also largely borne out by history. The bankruptcy of rural economy accelerated, sending the dispossessed to the cities. Hang-chow was bursting at its seams just before the Mongol conquest of the city in 1276.[23]

Yeh Shih, however, omitted a crucial ingredient in his diagnosis of

---

[22] SSCSPM 79, "Ch'en Liang hui-fu chih i".

[23] The enormous influx of people into Hangchow and the problems of rural im-poverishment have been discussed by J. Gernet, see *Daily Life in China on the Eve of the Mongol Invasion*, chs. 1 and 6.

the impending disaster — the exploitative role of the landlords. In the context of Southern Sung, the latter, despite Yeh Shih's apology, must be regarded as a parasitic class. It is unlikely that their contribution to the economic life of the country could balance their drain on the economy due to their expensive habits. Not many landlords were involved in providing for the supportive services of agriculture such as land reclamation, embankment and dyke building, and the maintenance of irrigation systems. Fewer still were innovative farmers themselves, experimenting with crop rotation, seed selection, etc. The majority were interested only in collecting their rent. Many of them were in fact absentee landlords permanently domiciled in Hangchow and the other metropolitan centers, leaving their country estates to the management of land bailiffs or stewards. As landlords were usually adepts at tax evasion, the peasants were saddled with two crushing burdens, namely, supporting the state structure and supporting the parasitic landlords. The payment of taxes and rent thus represented a permanent drain on the rural economy. No economy, however strong, could stand the cumulative effect of a continuous drain. There could be no ultimate solution of the fiscal difficulties of the state unless this fact was squarely faced up to.

In this light, it is easy to perceive the rationale of Yeh Shih's position on tax reduction and the poignancy with which he presented his argument. The strained rural economy was due to the dual stresses of taxation and exploitation by landlords. To reduce the strain on the economy, one could either reduce the excessive taxation or the excessive exploitation by landlords. Without going against the interests of the social class to which he belonged, he had to put the blame entirely on unwarranted tax increases. If state taxes could be rolled back to an acceptable extent, the plight of the people would be considerably lessened. The proliferation of taxation and the increase of tax rate, however, were not isolated developments but facets of a complex phenomenon involving fundamental changes in the character of the political regime as it went through the cycle of maturity, decline and dissolution. To vindicate the feasibility of tax reduction Yeh Shih could not avoid coming to grips with this cycle which pertained to the institutional setup and administrative practices of the dynasty.

III

MODERN scholars dealing with the phenomenon of the dynastic cycle in Chinese history usually recognize the importance of the "administrative component" in the cycle.[24] Undoubtedly, the fortune of a dynasty is linked to the efficiency of its administrative bureaucracy which collects taxes, administers justice and keeps the country under control. The administrative bureaucracy, nevertheless, owes its existence and its development to the conscious planning of the ruling elite of the dynasty. At the beginning of the dynasty, administrative efficiency is usually low but rises rapidly as the regime is consolidated and the main structures of the administrative machinery are set up. Refinement of administrative procedures and techniques further raises efficiency. The rise in efficiency eventually levels off, and before long a downward trend may be perceptible. To explain the reduced efficiency of an administrative bureaucracy as a dynasty advances in age, we may posit the existence of a force of inertia which, after the bureaucracy has attained a certain size and complexity, operates as a powerful deterrent against change so that the dynasty no longer has the flexibility to assess and cope with new problems. Under this circumstance, some of the basic institutions of a dynasty, devised to cope with specific problems in the past, may become dysfunctional when the socio-economic reality changes.

From the point of view of Chinese institutional history, the Sung dynasty is notable for its extent of centralization.[25] Centralization was a persistent trend observable in the evolution of the fiscal, territorial and military administrations. As is to be expected, centralization in Sung China spawned a mammoth bureaucracy, operating on the basis of impersonal rules and regulations. The rationale for a vast bureaucracy in a centralized polity is easy to comprehend. Having removed the power of appointing subordinate officials from the prefectural administrators, for instance, the state needed to have a large staff for the selection and evaluation of the thousands of state functionaries in the capital and in the provinces. Similarly, when the state reduced the fiscal autonomy of the prefectures by removing from their jurisdiction miscellaneous resources such as the Ever-normal Granaries, mining and minting, and maritime customs, it had to institute a host of intendancies to administer them. All these offices of the state could only operate within the operational guidelines established by the state. The

---

[24] The existence of an administrative component is presumed by most scholars dealing with the phenomenon of Chinese dynasties. For example, Lien-sheng Yang, *op. cit.*; Wang Yü-chuan, *op. cit.*; Hans Bielenstein, "The Census of China during the Period 2–742 A.D.", *Bulletin of the Museum of Far Eastern Antiquities* XIX (1947), pp. 125–163; Ch'ao-ting Ch'i, *Key Economic Areas in Chinese History* (London, Allen and Unwin: 1936).

[25] The standard work on Sung government is that by Edward Kracke, Jr., *Civil Service in Early Sung China*. For a concise account of the forces shaping the dynasty, see chapter 2 of the above cited work. For a discussion of the process of centralization, see James T.C. Liu, *Reform in Sung China*, ch. 5.

proliferation of rules and regulations thus proceeded apace as the dynasty continued the course of centralization.

The trauma of the Northern Sung debacle did not produce any noticeable change in the political orientation of the dynasty. After the initial dislocation brought about by the Jürchen invasion, every effort was made to restore the established practice in the administration of the empire. Edict after edict was promulgated, affirming the regulations which had been in force before the debacle. It may be conceded that the considerable destruction of central government archives which the dynasty sustained during the years of the Jürchen invasion could have threatened the administrative continuity of the dynasty as, in the absence of written records, officials could not be sure of the precise scope and application of the thousands of regulations that governed every phase of bureaucratic operations. However, as the archives of many provincial centers remained intact, it was not difficult to retrieve the relevant dynastic statutes.[26] From the perspective of history, we may therefore presume a high degree of administrative continuity and take the Southern Sung period as the descendant phase of the administrative cycle.

In view of the fact that in his major work of political commentary, the *Wai-kao*, Yeh Shih discussed the Southern Sung institutions precisely in terms of the administrative cycle, his arguments will be presented at length here. In keeping with the general format of his *Wai-kao*, he wrote a long prefatory essay on his understanding of the nature of political institutions (*fa-tu*).[27] Political institutions could not be visualized apart from the totality that gave them meaning, the dynasty. Speaking in general terms, he explored the patterns of the rise and fall of dynasties. They did not rise and fall by chance. There was a specific reason why a dynasty rose at one time and fell at another. But since each case was unique, it would be futile to take precautions against the evils that brought down a previous dynasty. The vitality of a regime was not to be sought in negative or preventive measures, but in positive, life-giving ones. Yeh Shih posited the concept of a "life-principle" (*i*): dynasties rose and were sustained in power because their "life-principle" was strong and healthy. They fell because it became diseased. "Life-principle" was an organic quality and could not be faked or called into existence arbitrarily.

---

[26] The retrieval of government statutes owed a great deal to the initiative of the Fiscal Staff Supervisor of Kwangtung, Chang Chieh. During his tenure of office, he had a copy made of dynastic regulations promulgated by successive Northern Sung emperors and kept in the office of the Fiscal Intendancy. Returning to the capital at the expiration of his tenure of office, he presented this copy, consisting of 1018 *chüan*, to the court. See Li Hsin-ch'uan, *Chronicles*, p. 2411.

[27] YSC PC 12, "Fa-tu tsung-lun" (Overall Views on Institutions).

The burden of Yeh Shih's discourse was that hitherto the Sung dynasty had been operating on false premises, being obsessed with negative measures instead of trusting in its own "life-principle". This negative attitude of mounting guard against the abuse-prone institutions of the Five Dynasties and the Late T'ang was responsible for the discomfiture of the current dynasty. He asserted that Sung institutions were not informed by any positive principle and deviated from the norm of centralized bureaucratic empires:

Both the political institutions and the public opinion of our dynasty are based upon an unchanging premise; namely, the imperative need to guard against the blunders of the Late T'ang and the Five Dynasties. For this reason, regulations become more minute and more comprehensive, so that every movement of the hand and foot has to conform to the prescribed pattern. . . . By the time of Emperor Jen-tsung (reigned 1022–1063) which was already far removed from that of the Five Dynasties, there was no abatement in the obsession of guarding against the blunders of the Five Dynasties. Even after the events of Ching-k'ang (1126), with immense changes overtaking our dynasty (the Northern Sung debacle), and with our calamities equalling those of the Late T'ang and the Five Dynasties, who can say that the desire to guard against the evils of the Late T'ang and the Five Dynasties does not remain the basis of our policy-decisions? Thus, in a state which has been in existence for over two hundred years, the guiding policy is to combat the imaginary evils that plagued its predecessors, and little attention is paid to the pressing concerns of the present reality. . . .[28]

No wonder under the influence of this anachronistic system, government operations were hamstrung and endless evils cropped up.

Whenever any project is launched, it is believed that the project would be conducive to a desired end, but the consequence is inevitably the defeat of this purpose. Whenever any law is enacted, it is because the law is intended to be beneficial; however, it inevitably turns out to be harmful.[29]

Yeh Shih believed that the essence of this anachronistic system was control intended to take power away from the officials and concentrate it in the emperor. It found expression in minute regulations of every act the official was called upon to perform. As the years went by, the tightening of control by rules increased. Completely deprived of the ability to take the initiative, the official resigned himself to regimentation by giving himself up to fulfilling the letter of the law. The situation thus fostered a climate of opinion which looked favorably on a self-effacing, non-assertive attitude for officials, interpreting such an attitude as magnanimity and decorum. It was rare for an official to try to go beyond the call of duty because whatever he did, he was likely to

[28] *Ibid.*, p. 789.
[29] *Loc. cit.*

run into a prohibition or penalty for exceeding his authority. It was natural that the morale of officials deteriorated under these circumstances.

Yeh's claim that the Sung dynasty overemphasized measures to prevent a recrudescence of the evils of the Late T'ang and Five Dynasties was not entirely original. The idea of "over-shooting the mark in correcting a previous bias" (*chiao-wang kuo-cheng*) is proverbial. This same idea found its way early into the arsenal of history commentators. Su Che, for instance, alludes to it:[30]

There is no constant source of trouble for the empire. Peace is secured only when evils are combated wherever they appear and good principles of government perpetuated regardless of their derivation. The unenlightened statesman, seeing evil issue from the east, directs all his efforts towards the east, and forgets about the west; seeing it issue from the center, directs all his effort towards the center and forgets the exterior. Thus calamity arises unexpectedly and cannot be averted.

Su Che then singled out Sung army policy for comment, alleging that when the evil of insubordinate army commanders had been averted, the evil of an undisciplined army arose instead.

IV

HAVING exposed the underlying malaise of Sung institutions in his prefatory essay, Yeh Shih went on to discuss individual institutions. He did not seek in each instance to relate the unsatisfactory functioning of an institution to the basic dynastic position. The only conspicuous example in which his view of the dynastic position had an immediate bearing on his analysis was in his treatment of circuit intendants (*chieh-tu-ssu*).

The vehemence of his observations in connection with the circuit intendants no doubt stemmed from his own frustrating experience — he wrote *Wai-kao* during his tenure as an Assistant to the Judicial Intendant (*kan pan kung shih*) of Che-hsi. He was particularly bitter about the stringent regulations governing the relation between circuit intendants and the prefectural officials. Circuit intendants, he charged, were prohibited from making unannounced or random inspection trips. They had to adhere to a fixed schedule, and were not permitted to stay

---

[30] Su Che, *Luan-ch'eng ying-chao chi* 42, "Ch'en-shih" (Affairs of Ministers, Pt. I, section 4).

in any one locality in the course of their inspection tours for more than three days, unless a specified, valid reason warranted it.[31]

He alleged that the original purpose of setting up the circuit intendants was to bring the prefectural and sub-prefectural levels of government under closer surveillance. The prefectures and sub-prefectures were units of government which implemented the law; the intendants were the agents of the central government who made sure that the prefectures and sub-prefectures implemented the law. Nevertheless, since the central government denied the intendants any discretionary power and prescribed a rigid procedure of operation, it is plain that the primary concern of the central government was fear and distrust of the latter. It stood firmly on guard against the intendants so that the latter could hardly exercise their surveillance function over the prefectural and sub-prefectural governments.[32]

With the foregoing exception, Yeh Shih did not explicitly spell out the effect of the basic premises of the body politic on the development of individual institutions. Instead, he launched a devastating attack on bureaucratic red tape and unreasoning and rigid adherence to the prescribed procedure in the operation of government institutions. We might call the prevailing attitude which Yeh sought to demolish the "fetishism of law". The word "law" is to be taken in a broad sense here, signifying not only civil and criminal law but also organic and administrative law as well as all established ways of doing things sanctioned either by imperial decrees or by tradition.

Yeh believed that the source of this fetishism was a false faith in the potentialities of the law. This faith was symbolized in the domineering position of the administration manual, popularly known as *Hsin-shu* (new book). This manual was composed of the organic law of the government, administrative and penal codes, together with imperial directives, enactments, and precedents, and was issued periodically under the

---

[31] The restrictions on the freedom of movement of the *chien-ssu* that Yeh Shih alleged are corroborated by provisions in the *Ch'ing-yüan t'iao-fa shih-lei* 4:14, 21, 29b. For the signification of the term *t'iao-fa shih-lei*, see note 33.

[32] The perfunctory nature of the inspection tours of the intendants is attested in contemporary literature. For instance, see the statement by Wang Shih-p'eng, *Mei-ch'i Wang hsien-sheng wen-chi*, hou chi 25, "Yu Chüeh t'i-hsing" (Letter to the Judicial Intendant Chüeh). To remedy the situation, Yeh Shih proposed that the authority of the fiscal intendants who used to have overall surveillence over fiscal and personnel matters of the circuits be strengthened. The contention of Yeh Shih that the authority of the fiscal intendants had been diminished is supported by the findings of Ide Tatsuro who claims that during the Southern Sung period the function of the fiscal intendants was limited to that of the *ts'ao-ch'en* (officer in charge of provisioning the army). See his article, "Nansō jidai no hatsu'unshi oyobi ten'unshi", *Tōyō shigaku ronshu*, vol. 3 (1954).

name of the current reign title.[33] Yeh claimed that the *Hsin-shu* was what held the court and the bureaucracy together because all their operations had to conform to provisions in the book.

This exclusive reliance on the *Hsin-shu* was certainly untenable. It was bound to give rise to grave difficulties. Yeh Shih enumerated three of these.[34] The first and third actually referred to the same thing, namely, the deleterious effects on governmental personnel. As a consequence of the faith that *Hsin-shu* was all inclusive and that it provided for every contingency, the intelligence of the tens of thousands of officials was not permitted to transcend the limitations of the book. Initiative and fresh ways of dealing with problems were discouraged. This bureaucratic inertia was responsible for the development of a perverse, self-deceiving frame of mind, which was Yeh Shih's second point. Knowing the law to be ineffectual, this frame of mind nevertheless refused to see the truth, holding to the traditional forms of operation in an ostrich-like world of make-believe.

Yeh Shih's discourse on governmental institutions in his *Wai-kao* was characterized by a forceful, straightforward style. Metaphysical language and analogical reasoning were kept down to an irreducible minimum. The use of appropriate analogies could be very enlightening. Chang Lai (1054–1114), a Northern Sung scholar,[35] for instance, compared a political regime to the life history of a man. In the administration of the affairs of the state or in the management of the affairs of a man, minute regulations (*fa*) were not necessary as long as affairs were under control. Rules were devised to cope with problems which would not otherwise yield a solution. The proliferation of rules was thus a symptom of weakness. For, if a man had to observe strict rules of diet and hours of sleep, he was, in all probability, old and decrepit. By the same token, a political regime which had to operate on the basis of elaborate regulations was precariously balanced between conflicting interests. A strong

---

[33] The *Hsin-shu* is known under the technical name of *Ch'ih-ling ke-shih*. The signification of this name is given by the treatise on punishment (Hsing-fa) of the *Sung-shih* (SS 199): Interdictions prior to [the offending actions] are known as *ch'ih*; interdictions after [the offending actions had occurred] are known as *ling*; [standards of reward or promotion] set up in anticipation of those who can meet them are known as *ke*; models for the emulation of men are known as *shih*. A redaction of the *Hsin-shu* is often known as a *t'iao-fa shih-lei* (statutes, laws and precedents). Of the four categories, i.e. *ch'ih, ling, ke* and *shih*, the first two categories obviously pertain to the realm of criminal law whereas the two latter deal with matters of personnel policy. A description of the mechanism and the principles for the revision of the *Hsin-shu* may be found in Wang Ta-yü's *hsing-chuang* (draft biography for the deceased), see *Kung-ku'ei chi* 88:14b.

[34] YSC PC 14:806, "Hsin-shu".

[35] See Chang Lai, *K'o-shan chi* 32, p. 383, "Lun fa shang" (On the Law, first section).

man or a vigorous political regime could never be confined by the straitjacket of minute regulations.

In a succinct statement, Yeh set forth his understanding of the true nature of law:

> The book (i.e., the *Hsin-shu*) provides for the letter (*wen*) and not for the actuality (*shih*); it provides for the simulacrum (*ssu*) and not for the real (*chen*).[36]

Thus he seems to imply that in the nature of the case, it is impossible to have legislation which fits individual cases exactly. This is not due to any lack of insight or industriousness but to the nature of things. Perhaps Yeh subscribed to a nominalist philosophy so that to him there was no universal essence which underlay discrete objects of the same name. In any case, the law dwells on the level of the universal, the abstract, whereas individual cases to which the law is applied pertain to the world of particular, empirical existence. The gap between the universal and the particular can only be bridged through the mediation of the mind. In enforcing laws, the administrator does not act in a mechanical manner. He considers the degree of conformity or deviation of a particular case compared with a hypothetical one provided by law.[37] This view of law makes the service of the administrator indispensable. It supplies a rational explanation for the Confucianist dictum that the law cannot enforce itself, that it must be enforced by men. This view also tends to destroy the magic power of law. No amount of perfect legislation can guarantee the desired result; much would depend on the caliber of the men who administer these laws.

An apt analogy for the relationship between the administrator and the law is that supplied by his friend Ch'en Fu-liang. Laws, Ch'en said, were like ancient writings on military strategy, while administrators were like generals planning a campaign. Campaigns were not won by following slavishly the instructions of ancient military writings, for such writings only dealt with basic principles and needed to be applied judiciously by generals.[38]

The development of a perverse mentality as a consequence of the exclusive reliance on law is amply illustrated in Yeh's treatment of *ch'üan-hsüan* (merit evaluation) and *chien-chü* (sponsorship) systems.[39]

[36] YSC PC 14, "Hsin-shu", p. 807.

[37] In Sung practice of jurisprudence, precedents (*li*) were of crucial importance. The treatise on punishments of *Sung-shih* claims that often a law (*fa*) is rendered inoperative for lack of suitable precedents. Nevertheless, the entrenched position of precedents does not detract from the validity of this principle as it is impossible to find an exactly fitting precedent.

[38] Ch'en Fu-liang, *Eight Cutting Edges* 3:9b.

[39] YSC PC 12, "Ch'üan-hsüan"; 13, "Chien-chü".

In both cases, he showed how the reality of these institutions was at variance with the ostensible rationale.

The ostensible purpose of merit evaluation procedures was to single out worthy men and promote them to high positions. However, the actual manner of operation of this institution gave the impression that the laws were deliberately drawn up to make it impossible for the worthy to be distinguished from the worthless. Yeh pointed out that the anomaly of the situation was nowhere more obvious than in the presumed and actual functions of the top echelon officials of the Board of Personnel (*li-pu*). Confucianist principles of statecraft to which the Southern Sung regime still paid lip-service required that these officials be entrusted with the task of advancing the worthy and keeping back those without merit. However, in actual practice, they were not permitted to do so. Yeh dramatized his point by putting the following words into the mouth of the sovereign:[40]

I do not trust you in the slightest; you are not supposed to trust yourselves in the slightest.

Thus it was a matter of utter indifference whether the ministers themselves were men of ability and virtue or whether the men they promoted or demoted were worthy or unworthy. Everything was supposed to have been taken care of by law.

Yeh intensified his attack on the fetishism of law in his treatment of the sponsorship system, originally designed to speed up the promotion of exceptionally talented men. However, promotion by sponsorship was soon routinized and came to be accepted as the recognized procedure for regular advance through the lower echelons of the official hierarchy. The original purpose was thus defeated. Commenting on the irrationality of the situation, Yeh wrote:[41]

Those in positions of authority do not have confidence in the sponsors; the sponsors do not have confidence in those seeking recommendations; those seeking recommendations do not have confidence in themselves. Their explanation is, "It is impossible to know whether this [the alleged merits of the sponsorship system] is so or not. However, since this has been the law of the court, the selection of personnel has to come by this route." Similarly, the court would rationalize: "Since our legislation has been such, we cannot but tolerate this development." Thus in dealings between superiors and subordinates, everything hinges upon this "impossible".

[40] YSC PC 12, "Ch'üan-hsüan".
[41] YSC PC 13:795.

V

IN THE MILIEU of Southern Sung China, Yeh's denunciation of the all-encompassing regimentation of law was remarkable not only for its vehemence but also for its unconventionality. The prevailing trend was towards greater stringency in the enforcement of law. The demand for tightening up law enforcement was understandable in view of the overall laxity and rampant corruption of Southern Sung politics. A succession of self-seeking, power-grabbing prime ministers such as Ch'in Kuei, Han T'o-chou, Shih Mi-yüan and Chia Ssu-tao packed the court and important positions in the provinces with their protégés. The only way for upright men in high positions to combat the evils of favoritism was to insist on the rigorous application of the law. This was especially the case with officials charged with censorial duties.

It might be argued that Yeh Shih and the advocates of stringent law-enforcement were not talking about the same thing, and that the two apparently contradictory stances were actually compatible. This supposition was borne out in the writings of Yang Wan-li, who, in his celebrated *Ch'ien-lü ts'e* (A Thousand Deliberations), a work similar in nature and in scope to Yeh's *Chin-chüan*, called for stricter law enforcement and simultaneously condemned the regimenting influence of rigid adherence to the prescribed procedures in the merit evaluation system.[42] Presumably, Yeh Shih and Yang Wan-li favored an extension of discretionary power to the heads of other government agencies within their areas of jurisdiction.

Modern theories of bureaucracy may shed light on our discussion.[43] It is generally assumed that explicit rules of procedure and well-defined areas of competence are fundamental to any organization beyond a certain complexity. To those in positions of command, these elements assure a certain predictability in the performance of their subordinates. They guarantee a continuity in the output of services and provide reliable machinery for the implementation of new objectives. To those in subordinate positions, the existence of clearly defined rules is even more necessary. Rules enable them to escape from personal subjection, transform their relation to their superiors into an impersonal one, and afford them a sense of security. It is perhaps mainly for these reasons

[42] The cycle of essays known as *Ch'ien-lü ts'e* is included in Yang Wan-li's collected works.
[43] One of the most succinct observer of this phenomenon in its diverse ramification is the French sociologist, Michel Crozier. See his book, *The Bureaucratic Phenomenon* (University of Chicago Press: 1964). The relationship between the regime of routinization (impersonal rules) and that of discretionary powers is explored at great length in Pt. III, "Bureaucracy as an Organizational System".

that in complex organizations, rules have a tendency to proliferate. The proliferation of rules is commonly referred to as "the bureaucratic phenomenon".

When the bureaucratic phenomenon reaches an advanced stage, the efficiency of an organization declines. It becomes a slave of its own rules, bound to the treadmill of routinization. Rules are a two-edged weapon: they enable a superior to control his subordinates; they also enable the subordinates to control their superior. Whatever is covered by the rules is no longer under the personal, direct control of the superior; it is routinized, and as long as the subordinate takes shelter under the rules, the superior can do nothing about him. The superior has no choice but to sanction routine arrangements in conformity with the rules. His behavior is altogether predictable. There is no need for the subordinate to be in awe of his high position because he has no power. Power consists in freedom to do what the wielder of power wills. The decision of the wielder of power is not predictable. Power can only be propitiated, not controlled. Thus the wielder of power can compel obedience and exact a high level of endeavor from those placed under the power. For an organization to achieve maximum efficiency, it is necessary to strike an optimal balance between the area of routinization and the area of discretionary power.

In the light of the foregoing analysis of the bureaucratic phenomenon, Yeh Shih's stance is immediately understandable. He was combating the expansive tendency of routinization and sought to restore the proper balance between routinization and discretionary power. The position of the advocates of stringent law-enforcement warrants more discussion.

In Hegelian dialectics, a state of being (thesis) tends to call into existence its opposite (antithesis). By the same token, as the ever-increasing proliferation of rules reaches a point when no one can keep track of them, their sovereign power to bind and to loose comes to an end. They become a dead letter. Long before things come to such a pass, energetic men who have felt the cramping effects of routinization seek to get things done outside regular channels by developing extra-legal procedures. The latter eventually develop into the focus of real power. The impulse to expand the area of discretionary power by bypassing the regularly instituted channels could originate with the emperor, if he was determined to rule as well as to reign. He had his ready-made machinery to implement his objective, namely, his household and palace servants personally obligated to him, constituting what came to be known as the "inner court". Under the emperor's blessing, the offices of the inner court could be entrusted with wide-ranging responsibilities and came into active competition with the regular bureaucracy, the outer court.

The impulse for breaking out of routinization also came from ambitious ministers. They did not have ready-made machinery to achieve their purpose but could improvise it. The bureaucratic milieu was a hotbed of factionalism. Cemented by ties of mutual help and motivated by thoughts of gain, factions were formed, amalgamated and split up. Rival factions struggling for supremacy or for a share of the patronage generated the dynamics of the bureaucratic process.

The position of the upright scholar-official, conscious of the cherished ideals of his profession, was undermined by the self-aggrandizing tendency of the emperor as well as by the factional alignments of career-minded bureaucrats. The only way for him to remain loyal to his ideals was to oppose any deviation from the customary or statutorily prescribed norms of operation and to take shelter within the area of routinization. He took his stand on the laws of the dynasty which had become the strongest bulwark of his dignity and his reason of existence. This explains his persistent pleading with the emperor to refrain from confiding important business to the denizens of the inner court at the expense of the outer court, and also explains his vehement denunciation of collusion and mutual protection among officials.

Assailed by the twin evils of the regimentation of law and subversion of bureaucratic procedures by extra-legal actions, most idealistic scholar-officials chose to combat the latter as the greater menace to their position. Yeh Shih, on the other hand, fixed his attention on the deleterious effects of the former. However, it is doubtful that he had fully grasped the nature and the sources of routinization.

From the foregoing account we gain the impression that he assigned a passive role to the officials themselves in this development of over-routinization.[44] Closer scrutiny shows that he did not hold this opinion and that he would probably concur with the view that the officials themselves constituted the principal source of routinization. However, he was not really interested in the processes or agencies that brought about this phenomenon. This non-concern detracted a great deal from his analysis of the problem.

His primary concern was how to undo the harm that over-routinization involved. To this end, he addressed the following appeal to the emperor:[45]

Your Majesty is in full possession of *ming-ch'i* (sovereign prerogatives) with which you could mobilize the multitude and control the empire by

[44] For example, his statement in YSC PC 12:794.
[45] YSC PC 12:794.

tightening or loosening the reins. Why is it that you allow yourself to be saddled with the moribund laws, which are the cumulative debris of centuries?

Reflecting his implicit belief in the unlimited power of the emperor in moulding the bureaucratic machinery, he unfolded a plan for dealing with the *hsü-li* problem. The clerks were a crucial element in the regime of routinization. As the literati usually had no formal training in the statutes and regulations of the ruling dynasty, and as they were shifted about from post to post, they were often reduced to utter dependency on the clerks for supplying vital knowledge about governmental affairs. The clerks were firmly entrenched in the central and provincial governments. Yeh quoted a prevalent saying, "For officials, there is no feudalism; for clerks, there is feudalism."[46]

Yeh's suggestion for reform was drastic. He would be satisfied with nothing less than the total abolition of this category of government personnel, symbol of the perennial enslavement of the officials. Not even Wang An-shih, for all his reforming zeal, dared go so far. Wang sought only to check their rapacity and bring them under closer control.[47] Yeh maintained that the functions hitherto performed by the clerks could be discharged by regular members of the civil service at the start of their official careers. There were several advantages in this arrangement. For one thing, it would greatly relieve the pressure of the scramble for posts by opening up this immense field with its almost inexhaustible demand for personnel. Secondly, it would enable future officials to serve a period of apprenticeship where they would learn the actual techniques and procedures of administration so that they would eventually become competent, well-informed officials. Their educational background and their aspirations for promotions would restrain them from nefarious dealings which might compromise their prospects.

Obviously Yeh Shih's denunciation of the government clerks was impractical; but his approach to reform in this area may also be rooted in China's tradition of political thought. Confucianism and Legalism indeed had different orders of priorities, but they agreed on one vital point, namely, on the emperor as the center of attention. Both wanted to show the emperor the proper way to rule. From this perspective, the Confucian emphasis on virtue and the Legalist emphasis on law had the same function, that is, as instruments of imperial rule.

Classical Legalist concepts of *shu* (techniques) and *shih* (position)

---

[46] YSC PC 14, "Li-hsü".
[47] See James T.C. Liu, *Reform in Sung China*, ch. 6. Also James T.C. Liu, "The Sung Views on the Control of Government Clerks", *Journal of Economic and Social History of the Orient*, Vol. 10, No. 2–3 (1967).

attributed to Shen Tao and Shen Pu-hai (died 337 B.C.) respectively had anticipated some of the modern theories of bureaucracy. These classical concepts were usually at the back of Sung observations of the bureaucratic process. The following passage by Ch'en Fu-liang is noteworthy:[48]

The [secret of the] sage in ruling the empire lies with his ability in making other men do what he wants, whereas other men cannot make him do what they want. . . . If he can get what he wants from other men, power rests with him. If other men can get what they want from him, power rests with them. Power is the instrument that restrains people from wrong-doing and spurs them towards laudable endeavors. If this instrument is given to other men, those who desire wealth will become wealthy, and those who desire honor will become honorable, as if they were [coupon-]holders demanding the equivalent value [in commodities or cash]. It would be impossible to deny their demands. If it is impossible to deny their demands, chaos and disaffection will ensue, because there is not enough wealth and honored position in the empire to satiate their insatiable greed. . . .

For all his sophistication, Ch'en Fu-liang had not transcended the traditional concerns. The bureaucratic phenomenon was investigated exclusively from the point of view of the ruler, not in terms of its own dynamics. Against this background, Yeh Shih's preoccupation with the role of the ruler is readily understandable.

As Yeh Shih grew older and wiser, he came to have a better appreciation of the intricacies of the bureaucratic process. For instance, while commenting on the failure of the abortive reform attempt of Fan Chung-yen, he pointed out the indiscretion of the reformers in first tackling the question of unearned merit (the triennial *mo-k'an* and the *yin* privilege), thus helping to crystallize the forces of opposition. Yeh observed that under-estimation of the obstructionist potential of the establishment — or of the resilience of routinization — had time and again proved the nemesis of would-be reformers.[49]

However, this pertinent remark was tucked away in his prosaic commentary on the *Sung wen-chien*, itself part of his *Orderly Presentation of Words*, amid a mass of irrelevant material. The happy conjunction of historical and psychological circumstances that eventuated in the production of the *Chin-chuan* and *Wai-kao* could not be duplicated. The urge to present his ideas in a sustained systematic exposition had vanished. Consequently, the insights and considered opinion of the mature person were consigned to oblivion, whereas it was the fury and enthusiasm of youth in its quest for recognition that was propagated for posterity.

[48] Ch'en Fu-liang, *Eight Cutting Edges* 3:9b.
[49] HHCYHM 48:6a.

CHAPTER SEVEN

The Blind Alley of Historical Studies

I

YEH Shih's inability to grasp the dynamics of the fiscal-administrative cycle was obviously culturally conditioned. It should not be difficult to explain, in our post-Freudian era, that a man has no direct access to reality except through the medium of his "culture". Consequently only those aspects of reality consistent with his cultural values are readily perceived; facts that contradict these values are usually not permitted to reach the level of consciousness.[1] An investigation into Yeh Shih's cultural values is therefore in order.

We may classify the values by which an individual or a culture lives into two categories, depending on their respective modes of genesis, viz. (a) values which partake of the character of eternal truths and owe their existence to divine revelations, and (b) values which are historically evolved representing the traditional or customary ways of thinking. A good illustration of this dichotomy is provided by the Roman Catholic Church. Like other Christian churches, it subscribes to the view that the Bible is divinely inspired. However, unlike most Protestant denominations which consider the Bible as the infallible and adequate guide to Christian truth, the Roman Church takes the position that as the source of Christian doctrines, the Bible has to be supplemented by "Tradition", representing the teaching of the apostles and the Church Fathers and handed down through the ages by the "Unbroken

---

[1] A good example of this line of reasoning is provided by Erich Fromm. He postulates the existence of a social filter which suppresses experiences incompatible with the way society perceives and conceptualizes reality. Schematically an experience has to meet three conditions before it can be elevated from the unconscious to the conscious level. Firstly, the availability of language. Only those phenomena for which words designating them exist can be grasped by the mind. Secondly, the formal patterns of thought and reason. Western thought is dominated by Aristotelian logic based on the principles of identity, contradiction and excluded middle. The mind steeped in this rationalist climate would have difficulty grasping phenomenon which seems to contradict these canons of thought. Thirdly, the inhibitive effects of social taboos which declare certain ideas and feelings to be improper, forbidden. See Erich Fromm, *Escape from Freedom* (Routledge and Kegan Paul: 1961).

Apostolic Succession" of the Church.[2]

The Confucian classics did not purport to be based on divine revelation. Nevertheless, in so far as they were pressed into providing the textual sanction for doctrines presented as absolute truths, their position was not much different from that of the Bible in the Christian lands. By the same token, although *tao-hsüeh* values were not divinely inspired, they resembled Christian dogmas in that their legitimation did not depend on tradition but on the claim of *tao-hsüeh* masters to have rediscovered the *tao*, a process not dissimilar to the prophetic phenomenon in the Judaeo-Christian tradition. The Chinese equivalent to the Roman Church was the Confucian monarchy which could boast of a similar longevity and continuity.[3] Consequently, the written record of this massive tradition, that is, the official histories, could be regarded as the repositories of the historically evolved values.

Yeh Shih's propensity for historical studies is well attested to in contemporary records. We have, for instance, the testimony of Ch'en Fu-liang. Ch'en submitted a proposal in 1195 for reorganizing the historiographical offices of the dynasty and recommended two men, the most accomplished historians of the time, to do the job.[4] The men he recommended were Chu Hsi and Yeh Shih.

In view of this pronounced historical orientation, it may be justifiable to assume that historically evolved values played a crucial role in Yeh Shih's world view. During the *Chin-chüan* phase of his life, his approach to history was strongly utilitarian. This is to be expected in view of the *hui-fu* fervor he exhibited. This utilitarian approach is also manifest in his attitude towards the Confucian classics. He dealt with the latter not as authentic records of the sayings and doings of the ancient sages but as possible instruments for efficient government. Judged by the criterion of utility, the classics lost a great deal of the mystique built up by generations of scholars. The paramount question for Yeh Shih, so far as the classics were concerned, was whether they could be relied upon to produce orderly government for the empire. He was of the opinion that they could not:[5]

In antiquity, the administration of the ruler (*ch'ih*) was worthy of being made the subject-matter of the classics but did not depend upon the classics

---

[2] See *New Catholic Encyclopedia*, ed. by Catholic University of America (McGraw Hill: 1967), Vol. 14, pp. 225–228, "Tradition".

[3] The sociologist Max Weber characterized the Chinese monarchy as "Caesaropapist". For an imaginative treatment of the nature of this monarchy during the Han period, see E.R. Hughes, *Two Poets, Vignettes of Han Life* (Princeton University Press: 1960). At a more prosaic level, see Tjan Tjoe Som, *Po Hu T'ung*.

[4] *Chih-chai hsien-sheng wen-chi* 27, "First and Second Pleas for being Relieved the Appointment as Co-compiler of the Bureau of Veritable Records".

[5] YSC PC 5, "Tsung-i" (General Discussion of the Classics), p. 693.

for its success. Later generations depend on the classics for the [success] of the administration and therefore the administration cannot transcend [the limitation of] the classics. Alas! Sages are no longer born so that what the empire depends on [for the success of] the administration are the mere words of the classics.

The same concern with utility also dictated his canons of historiography. Times of peace and tranquility (*ch'ih*) in Chinese history were usually thought to depend on two factors, namely, a responsible and efficient government and a good social order supporting a contented, law-abiding people. Good administrators were always depicted as making strenuous efforts in promoting a desirable social order and in stamping out pernicious influences. Yeh Shih took Ssu-ma Ch'ien, author of the pace-setting *Historical Records* (*Shih-chi*), severely to task for violating this engrained political precept:[6]

The men of the Warring States period (*circa* 400–220 B.C.) extolled treachery and were altogether without principles. They violated the heavenly ordained canons of behavior between sovereign and ministers in order to gratify their transient whims. The events [that were alleged to have transpired] during the struggle between the Ch'u and the Han were of a vulgar, unedifying character and not always worthy of credence. If a sage were placed in the situation of Ssu-ma Ch'ien, he would certainly refrain from reporting them. Even if he did report them, he would not make his account complete. Why? This is because events that have transpired will not be forgotten if only one man records them in historical writings. What [Ssu-ma Ch'ien did] was depict with all his literary powers the deeds of the merchant princes, the villains, the assassins and even the lowly entertainers and diviners. . . . In their biographies are to be found all the techniques for swindling the people and perverting the government.

It is obvious that the function of history for Yeh Shih was a didactic one, teaching by historic example. Events that could not be fitted into the preconceived framework would be arbitrarily suppressed. History was not the window that opened into vistas of reality but the tinted glasses through which one looked at a familiar landscape.[7]

The tinted glasses, to continue the analogy, did not remain of constant hue but took on a slightly different coloration with the accession of each generation of historians. It may be rash to say that the Chinese recognized the universal validity of the statement that each generation of people rewrites history to accord with its own historical perspectives. But the same pressures that make modern historians rewrite the past were also operative on Sung China with its vast social and economic

[6] YSC PC 6, "Shih-chi" (Historical Records), p. 721.

[7] For an account of the various facets of China's historiographic tradition, see Beaseley and Pulleyblank, ed., *Historians of China and Japan*, particularly, ch. 2, "The Ancient Chinese Chronicles and the Growth of Historical Ideals", by P. Van der Loon; ch. 4, "The Organization of Chinese Official Historiography", by Lien-sheng Yang; ch. 6, "L'Histoire Comme Guide de la Pratique Bureaucratique".

changes.[8] Beyond doubt, new perspectives did impose themselves on Sung historians' vision of the past. One example where contemporary realities modified traditional attitudes may be found in Yeh Shih's handling of the barbarian question.

One of the abiding elements in the Chinese world view was the dichotomy between the Chinese people (*hua-hsia*) who are coterminous with civilization and the barbarians (*i-ti*) comprising all who are not Chinese. The great T'ang statesman and institutional historian, Tu Yu (735-812), author of China's first political science encyclopedia *T'ung-t'ien*, accounted for China's superiority in naturalistic terms. According to Tu Yu, China was at the center of the world, nurtured by the pure ethers of Heaven and Earth so that it was capable of supporting the five grains and giving birth to sages with their transforming power generation after generation. [9] Undoubtedly, the majority of Sung scholars would have concurred with him. However, Yeh Shih maintained that the traditional notion of the barbarian had long been obsolete. The barbarians who submitted to the moral leadership of the sage-rulers during the Three Dynasties were entirely different from what were called barbarians in later ages. In his words:[10]

The foundation of the state consists of "propriety" (*i*), "proper definitions" (*ming*), and "expediency" (*ch'üan*). It is in accordance with "propriety" that China does not rule over the barbarians. It is in accordance with "proper definitions" that China remains China and the barbarians remain barbarians. Having possessed these conditions, if the barbarians come raiding, we fight them; and if they come with a view to submission, we receive them with cordiality—dealing with them as circumstances demand—this is "expediency". ... At the time of [Emperors] Yao and Shun, there were barbarians along the seashore and in deep valleys, and, wherever civilized governments did not extend, as far south as the Huai river and the ancient province of Hsü, and as far east as the [ancient] province of Ch'ing. They lived together with the Chinese. They were not like the barbarians of later ages who were limited to the Hsien-yün and the Hsün-yü [areas], living beyond the Great Wall several thousand *li* away and virtually impossible to pacify.

The territories of Yao and Shun were exceedingly cramped and they had no sharp weapons, crack troops, or crafty stratagems. It was because they were in possession of "propriety", "proper definitions", and "expediency" that the barbarians could not prevail against them. Surely, the reason why China was China was due to these [principles]. Later on, these means to sure victory were abandoned, and relying on cunning and on brute force, China was transformed into a state of barbarians. Certainly, it was no matter of surprise that strife and confusion ensued.

---

[8] The conception of the historian's function as "reliving the past" has been a prominent theme of Western historiography since the middle of the 19th century. See H.S. Hughes, *Consciousness and Society* (New York, Knopf: 1958).

[9] *T'ung-tien*, "Tsung-hsü" (General Preface).

[10] YSC PC 4, "Wai-lun" (External Discourse I), pp. 684-685.

From the onset of the Warring States period, for three hundred years the people of Ch'in were the most powerful. Petty states were annihilated one by one, or annexed into the expanding territories [of Ch'in and] the Six States. Ch'in in turn annihilated the Six States, uniting the whole [Chinese] world and taking possession of it. Furthermore, Ch'in sought to seize [the nation of the] Hsiung-nu as well so that the tyranny of Ch'in was worse than that of the Hsiung-nu. The founder of Han was a commoner who rose to contend for supremacy and in a few years occupied the original homeland of the Ch'in people. [In his rise to power,] do we see his [superior] morality, benevolence and righteousness so that he was worthy of the allegiance of the people? [That being the way the Han came to power,] why do we begrudge Mao Tun (the Hsiung-nu chief) his domination of the frontier with several hundred thousand archers [under his command] and his penetration into China as far as T'ai-yüan and Chin-yang? It is obvious that since that time, all these three principles have vanished and there are no more [intrinsic] distinctions between China and the barbarians. They are only to be differentiated with regard to the terrain of the land and their relative geographical positions.

This is an astounding statement and in the milieu of Confucian China, a declaration tantamount to the renunciation of cultural superiority. By debunking the myth of the China-Barbarian dichotomy, Yeh Shih managed to see Sung-Chin relation on a realistic basis. The Jürchen people of the Chin empire were not barbarians; they constituted a rival state which had done wrong to the Sung dynasty. The wrong called for vengeance. By refusing to allow morality and sentimentality to cloud the issue, Yeh Shih was in a better position to come to grips with it. The ultimate development of this attitude was his appeal to the racism of the Chinese of North China to rise in open revolt against their alien rulers. Thus, within the microcosm of Yeh Shih's mind, Confucian cultural universalism had to be dethroned before militant nationalism could hold sway.

Can we assume that the dethronement was more than a transitory phenomenon and that under the impact of the *hui-fu* ideology Yeh Shih could usher in a type of historical scholarship untrammelled by ideological considerations and capable of showing a way out of the present predicament for the Southern Sung dynasty?

II

IN CHAPTER One we noted that both Wang An-shih and the *tao-hsüeh* masters had a deprecatory attitude towards the imperial dynasties. History was not a source of edification for them. It may surprise us to find Yeh Shih of *Chin-chüan* sharing the same attitude. In the "Chün-te" (Virtue of the Prince) section of this work, he arranged the outstanding

emperors of the past in types.[11] Emperor Wu-ti of the Han was assigned
to the same category as Ch'in Shih-huang-ti, exemplifying the autocrat
who stopped at nothing in his lust for power and military conquest.
Emperor T'ai-tsung of the T'ang exemplified the artful dissembler
exacting services unrelentingly from his subordinates without appearing
to be ruthless.

Yeh Shih's attitude on the Han and the T'ang dynasties was thus
diametrically opposed to that of his close associate, Ch'en Liang, who
set forth his daring views in a well-known debate with Chu Hsi.[12]
Chu Hsi took the tao-hsüeh line that the rule of the Three Dynasties was
based exclusively on "Heavenly Principles" (t'ien-li), whereas all
subsequent dynasties were founded on "Human Lusts" (jen-yü). In
reply, Ch'en Liang repudiated the customary way of thinking which
viewed ideals as having an autonomous existence apart from tangible
realities. For him, "Heavenly Principles" were nothing but the sub-
limation of "Human Lusts". For this reason, if the Han and the T'ang
dynasties fell short of the standard of the Three Dynasties, it was not
because they were governed exclusively by "Human Lusts" but because
they were not yet successful in sublimating their baser motives. By the
same token, if the Han and the T'ang had been more prosperous than
other dynasties since the dawn of the imperial era ("caught more game
birds", in the picturesque language of Ch'en Liang), it was because
they made greater headway towards the truth. The obvious implication
of Ch'en Liang's position was that history provides models of achievement to emulate and pitfalls to avoid.

Ch'en Liang's articulate exposition failed to convince Chu Hsi, nor
did it seem to have any immediate effect on Yeh Shih who undoubtedly
was aware of the views of his friend.[13] As far as can be determined
from his later writings, for example his Orderly Presentation of Words,
Yeh Shih did not budge from his early position. He remained as critical
of the regimes of Han Wu-ti and T'ang T'ai-tsung, convinced that
they had been unduly glamorized by historians. A critical attitude does
not detract from a historian's greatness; on the other hand, it may be
argued that it is an essential equipment of all great historians. The
reconstruction of the past which is the function of the historian is
analogous to reconstructing a homicide in a court of law. The historian
(like the counsel for the prosecution) cannot expect to get at the truth

---

[11] YSC PC 1, "Chün-te" (Virtue of the Prince).

[12] Carson Chang devotes a whole chapter to this famous debate between Chu Hsi
and Ch'en Liang. See his The Development of Neo-Confucianism, Vol. 1, ch. 14.

[13] In the following chapter, I will follow a line of reasoning linking Ch'en Liang's
unorthodox views on the T'ang and the Han dynasties to changes in Yeh Shih's
ideological orientation.

if he allows sentimental attachment to his subject to stand in the way of his judgment.

Yeh Shih's critical attitude, when applied to the study of Chinese history, for instance that of the T'ang period, resulted in a number of significant discoveries. The T'ang dynasty not only formed the immediate background to the Sung but was also popularly reckoned as one of the most exemplary periods of imperial rule. There was a definite mystique which pervaded all T'ang practices and institutions. This mystique Yeh Shih seemed to have taken upon himself to destroy: he challenged all established notions. Of the two official histories of the T'ang dynasty of his time, it was the *Hsin T'ang-shu* (A New History of the T'ang) that bore the brunt of his attack.

The T'ang mystique was epitomized in the reign of Emperor T'ai-tsung under the reign title of Chen-kuan (627–649), a veritable golden age in the popular mind so far as the well-being of the people was concerned. The *Hsin T'ang-shu* attributed the success of the reign to the emperor implementing a "rule of benevolence" (*jen-cheng*) at the recommendation of his minister Wei Cheng (580–643). Against this conventional view, Yeh Shih marshalled a number of concrete facts, culled from the annals and the biographies, indicating the existence of widespread misery of both man-made and natural origin.[14] He referred, for instance, to the extensive flooding and desolation in the center of the empire well into the reign. He also pointed out the mental anguish and physical privation of the conscript army setting out or returning from campaigns. The implication was clear; these things could not have happened in a truly golden age presided over by a truly benevolent ruler. Yeh Shih further criticized the authors of *Hsin T'ang-shu* for implying that benevolence was all that was required for an orderly, successful administration.[15]

Among the cluster of early T'ang institutions, the *fu-ping* militia system was one of the most idolized in later times. The author of the "Treatise on War" of the *Hsin T'ang-shu* for instance, proudly stated that with this institution, the early T'ang reverted to the system of the ancients, namely, a citizen soldiery whereby the farmers doubled up as soldiers when called up for service. The "Treatise on War" also claimed that the great victories of Emperors Kao-tsu and T'ai-tsung were won primarily with the *fu-ping* troops. In questioning the validity of these views, Yeh Shih dwelt on the historic antecedents of the T'ang system. He showed that the regimes of the Northern Chou

---

[14] HHCYHM 40:8b.

[15] *Ibid.*, 40:8a. Wang Ying-lin, in his *K'un-hsüeh chi-wen* 14:1b, also took exception to the view of the authors of the *Hsin T'ang-shu* on this matter.

and the Sui, predecessors of the T'ang, owed their successes in war to a similar militia system. The excellent performance of the *fu-ping* army in campaigns in and out of China during early T'ang could not be attributed entirely to the sagacity of the Emperors Kao-tsu and T'ai-tsung. They were not innovators but beneficiaries of a military system evolved over a long period of time.[16]

Yeh Shih also castigated the authors of the "Treatise on War" for failing to discern the true nature of the *fu-ping* system. His contention was that under the T'ang system, there was no exact reversion to the practices of the ancients in which the roles of the soldier and the farmer were combined in the same person. The T'ang system gave a semblance of this merging of roles but was in fact the institutionalized beginning of the separation of roles. Yeh Shih's contention is obviously based on the consideration that military service under the *fu-ping* system was not universally required of all the farming population but only a small minority whose names were entered in the registers of the local draft boards.

The historian in Yeh Shih found fulfilment not only in evaluating works of historiography but also in passing judgment on non-historical writings by well-known authors which could have influenced popular historical attitudes. A good example is his note on Su Shih's rebuttal of Mencius. Mencius was alleged to have said that it had never been known that a man who was not benevolent could have gained the empire. Seizing this naïve statement, Su Shih retorted, "What about Ssu-ma I and Yang Chien (reigned 589–604)?" These two men were known for their craftiness and yet they gained the empire. Ssu-ma I laid the foundation for his grandson's usurpation of the Wei throne and Yang Chien personally usurped the Northern Chou throne. In Mencius's defence, Yeh Shih alleged that Mencius was living at a time when powerful states were contending for supremacy and the unification of China was finally in sight. Mencius hoped that the rulers of states would adopt his doctrine of benevolence and so spare the people unnecessary turmoil and war. It is unfortunate that his utterance was not borne out by history. Thus from Yeh Shih's point of view, words, like deeds, could not be judged out of context. The utterance of Mencius must be recognized for what it was, namely, ideology, not statement of fact.[17]

In his *Orderly Presentation of Words*, Yeh shih did not seem to have toned down his criticism of Ssu-ma Ch'ien. Nevertheless, there is a subtle shift of ground on which he based his criticism. He was no

[16] HHCYHM 39:10a–11a.
[17] *Ibid.*, 36:1b.

longer needling the "Grand Historian" for covering harmful and frivolous matters. Instead he indicted him for his inability to reach the underlying reality behind the surface phenomenon of history. Ssu-ma Ch'ien was likened to a clever artificer who fashioned out of diverse materials an amazingly life-like statue. The pity of it was that there was no real life in it. The statue remained an inanimate object. This was a severe indictment.[18]

It is doubtful that Yeh Shih could substantiate his charges. Most of his comments on the *Historical Records* of Ssu-ma Ch'ien were concerned with the author's handling of specific historic episodes. We may dismiss most of them which were concerned with obscure details and suffused with a casuistic, fault-finding spirit. Nevertheless, some of the points he raised were valid.

For instance, his treatment of Ssu-ma Ch'ien's account of the Hsiung-nu is pertinent. He dealt with only one small point, namely, the origin of the Hsiung-nu. Ssu-ma Ch'ien had perfunctorily traced the descent of the Hsiung-nu people, linking them to the major groups of barbarians known to the Chinese since remote antiquity.[19] To Yeh Shih, with his strong views on the differences between barbarians of the dawn of history and those of the Ch'in and Han era, this lumping together of all barbarian peoples without trying to disentangle the historic realities was sufficient ground for condemnation. Another of Yeh Shih's valid criticisms dealt with Ssu-ma Ch'ien's treatment of T'ao-chu Kung, a minister of Kou-chien, king of the state of Yüeh, who later became a millionaire businessman. Since the "Grand Historian" was unsure of what happened to T'ao-chu Kung during the last phase of his life, he gave a number of variant versions which were all admittedly hearsay. Yeh Shih took him to task for this abdication of responsibility in ascertaining the truth.[20]

The paragon of historiography for Yeh Shih was the annalistic *Ch'un-ch'iu* (Spring and Autumn Annals). He was of the opinion that the *Ch'un-ch'iu* and other historical writings of antiquity such as the

[18] *Ibid.*, 21:13b. H. Creel, in connection with his study of Confucius, brought out some of Ssu-ma Ch'ien's flaws as a historian. It is interesting to observe that his principal charge against Ssu-ma Ch'ien is similar to the indictment leveled by Yeh Shih, for instance, the following statement from his book, *Confucius, the Man and the Myth* (New York, John Day: 1949), p. 245: "The biography of Confucius is, by contrast, a slipshod performance. There is little motivation and almost no development of a consistent character for Confucius. It consists, in fact, of a series of incidents gathered from Confucian, Taoist, Legalist sources, thrown together in what is alleged to be a chronological order with little criticism or harmonization. The result is that Confucius moves through the story like a puppet."
[19] HHCYHM 20:8b.
[20] *Ibid.*, 19:12a.

Shu-ching were concerned primarily with the moral import of historic events. The emphasis on the moral import, however, was usually accompanied by an indifference to the contingent facts of history such as the exact dates, place names, etc. This indifference to facts was a serious drawback in ancient works of historiography as it made them more vulnerable to the conscious manipulations of unscrupulous men who could interpolate where there was no verifiable chronology or historic context to thwart their design. The historicity of accounts in ancient works of historiography was therefore open to question.[21] On the other hand, Yeh Shih believed that later works of historiography were usually meticulous in presenting the contingent facts of history but negligent in pointing out the moral import of events. He was therefore of the opinion that reform of Chinese historiography consisted of combining the merits of both types of historiography and avoiding their weaknesses. Nevertheless, in spite of the apparent soundness of his programmatic views, he never produced anything in the conventional sense of history.

A question may be raised here: in what sense can a man who has written no history be considered a historian? It may be observed that under the category of *shih* (history) the Ch'ing compilers of *Ssu-k'u ch'üan-shu* (Complete Library of the Four Treasuries) had a sub-category *shih-p'ing* (historical criticism). Modern bibliographers in turn sub-divided the latter into two sections, viz. *i-fa* (methodology) and *shih-i* (commentary on historical events and personalities).[22] The first is concerned with the more abiding features of history such as the format of the different genres of history, the principles governing the recognition of legitimate dynasties, and the choice of diction to accord with the historian's function of praise and blame. The second deals with the more transitory, contingent facts of history, namely, historic figures and episodes. Although some of Yeh Shih's comments in his *Orderly Presentation of Words* bore on the principles of historiography, in the main he was more concerned with concrete situations and individuals. Consequently his book could be classified in the *shih-i* section of historical criticism, were it not for the fact that it also deals with miscellaneous, non-historical subjects.

As a scholar who specialized in historical criticism, Yeh Shih was probably superior to many others who indulged in this exercise. It is unlikely that the compilers of *Critical Notes of the Ssu-k'u ch'üan-shu* could describe *Orderly Presentation of Words* in the language in which they characterized *Tu-shih kuan-chien* (Some Limited Views from

---

[21] *Ibid.*, 21:1a.
[22] A good example is *Chung-kuo ts'ung-shu tsung-lu*.

Reading History) by the celebrated scholar Hu Yin (1098–1156):[23]

With regard to people, it (Hu Yin's book) expected every one to be like Confucius, Yen Yüan, Tzu-ssu or Mencius. With regard to human affairs, it measured everything by the yardstick of the dynasties of Yü, Hsia, Shang, and Chou.

Still it must be said that like the above evaluation of Hu Yin's work, Yeh Shih's *Orderly Presentation of Words* was characterized by a negative tone. It lacked an element of utopian make believe which alone transforms the reading of history from a dreary exercise into a heart-warming experience. Truly great historical literature could not be produced without an all-consuming passion. For some historians, the quest for immortal fame was a powerful drive. However, it alone did not suffice. The great historian had to be convinced of the value of the enterprise that he proposed to embark upon. In writing the *Historical Records*, Ssu-ma Ch'ien was deploring the passing of the socio-political order he adored and, by preserving the memory in his writings, he hoped to contribute to its eventual return.[24] Ssu-ma Kuang's purpose in compiling the *Tzu-ch'ih t'ung-chien* was expressed in the title of the work which means "A comprehensive mirror in aid of government". Ou-yang Hsiu wrote his *Hsin T'ang-shu* because of his admiration for the heroic quality of T'ang life. For these men the researching and writing of history was more than a literary exercise. It was the very fulfilment of their ideals.

Yeh Shih was barred from taking the same course due to the strength of his inhibiting ideas. Against the latter, his *hui-fu* fervor and his desire for the rejuvenation of the dynasty were all of no avail. He spurned the model of government most often cited by history-minded statesmen, the Han and the T'ang dynasties because he perceived the sordid reality behind their brilliant facade. Moreover, he spurned them because they were embodiments of the autocratic, absolutist principle and as such ran counter to his cherished Mencian principle of the primacy of the people.

It is obvious that historically evolved values played only a limited role in Yeh Shih's motivational pattern. The limits were set by ideas which pertained to the realm of absolute values.

---

[23] *Ssu-k'u ch'üan-shu tsung-mu* 89:4b–6a.
[24] See Frank Algerton Kierman, *Ssu-ma Ch'ien's Historiographical Attitudes as Reflected in Four Warring States Biographies* (Studies on Asia, Far Eastern and Russian Institute, University of Washington: 1962).

CHAPTER EIGHT

The Possibility of an Alternative to *Tao-hsüeh*

I

IN a recent paper, Professor James T.C. Liu traces the vicissitudes that Southern Sung *tao-hsüeh* went through before it attained the position of state orthodoxy under Emperor Li-tsung (reigned 1125-1264).[1] With his sharp, analytical mind, he deals with its rise as a historic event and reveals the changing pattern of relationship between it and the state. In his view, the state championed the *tao-hsüeh* cause under Emperor Li-tsung because it had need of added ideological sanction to bolster its claim to legitimacy vis à vis the emerging Mongol empire which, acting on the advice of Yelü Chu-ts'ai (1189-1243) was beginning to take on the trappings of a Confucian state. No matter what happened in the superficially sinicised Mongol state of the North, the Southern Sung claimed to be the legitimate government of China, for it was in Southern Sung territory that the teaching of the sages (the *tao-t'ung* succession) was passed down.

While acknowledging my indebtedness to Prof. Liu for his insight into this historic phenomenon, I will endeavor in the following pages to present a different, though not antagonistic, view of the same phenomenon. Instead of focussing primarily on the interaction between the state and the bearers of *tao-hsüeh* learning, I will approach the subject primarily from the viewpoint of the internal development of *tao-hsüeh* itself. The latter approach, among other things, makes it possible to account for the phenomenon of informed protest exemplified by Yeh Shih.

It may be observed that *tao-hsüeh* scholars of the Northern Sung had an ambivalent attitude towards official service—a feeling of alienation towards the establishment, as Prof. Liu puts it. Not unexpectedly, this negative attitude called forth a similarly negative response from the state.

[1] James T.C. Liu, "The Road to Neo-Confucian Orthodoxy: An Interpretation", paper delivered at Sung Conference II, Cambridge, England, 1972, later published in *Philosophies, East and West* 23.4 (1973), pp. 483-506.

To explain the mutual estrangement, we will have to start with a central element in the propagation of *tao-hsüeh*, namely, its self-image. In so far as the propagation of *tao-hsüeh* values may be regarded as a movement, the matter of self-image is of paramount importance. Suffice it to say that a viable self-image is indispensable to all historic movements; it is the cement that binds leaders and followers together and motivates them to strive towards a single objective. To illustrate: Judaism could not have survived if the idea of the "elect of God" had not been deeply implanted in the consciousness of the Jewish people nor would Marxism have triumphed in Russia if the Communist Party had not conceived itself as the "vanguard of the proletariat".

To reconstruct the *tao-hsüeh* self-image, we may recall the celebrated quatrain of Chang Tsai:[2]

To ascertain the mind of Heaven and Earth,
To make [true] life possible for myriad ages.
To revive the learning of the former sages which has become extinct,
To establish perpetual peace for ten thousand generations.

The foregoing is no doubt an admirable summation of *tao-hsüeh* aspiration but is not an adequate statement of *tao-hsüeh* self-image, for it leaves out the one thing which in the propagation of the movement generates the self-confidence to match its aspirations, namely, the *tao-t'ung* succession. *Tao-hsüeh* scholars dared to proclaim their ideal world order which, like the utterances of the Old Testament prophet, was often an indictment of the inadequacies of the present regime, because in their self-image as the legitimate bearers of *tao* they had a monopoly of truth. Their claim to ideological authority was resented by the Confucian state which recognized no limits to its own omnipotence. Therefore, as long as *tao-hsüeh* scholars maintained this self-image unabated, a rapprochement between them and the state was unlikely.

After a movement has been under way for some time and especially after the original founders have passed away, the maintenance of its self-image is often a problem. Objective circumstances may have changed, necessitating a change in its perception of reality. Strains may then show up between its self-image and its perception of reality. To ease the strains, a process of accommodation usually follows, resulting commonly in a "revision" of its self-image. This revisionism generally indicates a mellowing of the movement with a noticeable reduction in its militancy.

It is reasonable to expect a mellowing of the *tao-hsüeh* movement as the generation of the Northern Sung pioneers passed away. As original

---

[2] *Chang-tzu ch'üan-shu*, "Yü-lu", 2:6b.

founders of the movement, they obviously had no difficulty in advocating the *tao-hsüeh* self-image. They were men of uncommon attainments, each a trail-blazer in his own right. As such they probably saw nothing extraordinary in their claim to a monopoly of truth on which the *tao-hsüeh* self-image depended. By the very nature of things, however, their attainment was non-duplicable. Ch'eng I's rediscovery of *tao*, for instance, was regarded by himself and by his associates as a unique event in history making him the legitimate bearer of the *tao-t'ung* succession. Their disciples were consequently under considerable strain when they inherited the *tao-hsüeh* self-image. Without the credentials of their masters, their claim to a monopoly of truth lacked an authentic ring.

Contrary to our expectations, the *tao-hsüeh* movement did not seem to mellow during the greater part of the Southern Sung period. It maintained its self-image with considerable success and the intransigence with which leading *tao-hsüeh* scholars stood the ground led to repeated clashes with the state. How do we account for this apparently anomalous phenomenon?

To account for the particularly strong showing of Southern Sung *tao-hsüeh*, I will attempt to draw a parallel between it and the great historic movements which shaped Western civilization. We may for instance trace the rise of Christianity or Marxism back to an original mind, the founder-prophet who proclaimed a new vision for mankind. A founder-prophet, however, was normally a visionary, not a practical man so that he was generally unable to come to grips with the mundane problems that his movement encountered. The movement initiated by him, therefore, did not make much headway until its leadership passed to men of a more pragmatic bent, such as the apostle Paul or the revolutionist Lenin. The great achievement of this new breed of leaders was their ability to make the lofty ideals of the founder-prophet relevant by devising a concrete code of conduct for the "true believers" and defining their position vis à vis the "infidels" with regard to all mundane situations in which they might be involved. They acquired status and immortality as a result of having solved these basic problems which paved the way for the eventual triumph of their movements.

The analogies of Christianity and Marxism thus throw light on the upsurge of ideological authority that characterized the heyday of the Southern Sung *tao-hsüeh* movement. Men like Chu Hsi and Lu Chiu-yüan may be seen playing a role in the propagation of *tao-hsüeh* similar to that of St. Paul or Lenin. Applying the vision of *tao-hsüeh* pioneers, and following particularly the work of Ch'eng I, they perfected the techniques of moral instruction, devised a code for practical living (reform of the rituals, promotion of clan solidarity, etc.) and defined the *tao-hsüeh* position rigorously vis à vis the entirety of China's cultural heritage (annotation of the classics, interpretation of history, refutation of heterodox philosophers etc.).[3]

The labors of Chu Hsi, Lu Chiu-yüan and their colleagues laid the indispensable ground work for the eventual triumph of the *tao-hsüeh* movement: the patron saints of the movement, viz. Chou Tun-i, Chang Tsai, the Ch'eng brothers and Chu Hsi were installed in the Confucian temple and their commentaries on the classics officially promulgated by the state.

In the same process, however, they destroyed the viability of the *tao-hsüeh* self-image. All that was essential to the implementation of the *tao-hsüeh* ideal was now made known by these great scholars in their lectures and writings accessible to all who cared to learn. Under these circumstances it would be ludicrous for their disciples to keep up the pretense that they alone possessed a monopoly of truth. The *tao-hsüeh* self-image was no longer viable. With the dissolution of its self-image, the propagation of *tao-hsüeh* as a militant movement potentially capable of challenging the ideological authority of the state may be said to have ended. As *tao-hsüeh* values were no longer the exclusive legacy of a few conceited scholars, they could be easily appropriated by the state and harnessed for purposes of ideological control in the same way as the teaching of Wang An-shih or that of Confucius and Mencius had been previously harnessed.

As indicated in Chapter One, the vogue of *tao-hsüeh* in Southern Sung society was largely due to the absence of competition. Being the only coherent, intellectually satisfying approach to China's cultural heritage, it attracted a great number of adherents. This mass adherence to *tao-hsüeh*, like the mass conversion to Christianity in Roman times was accompanied by serious abuses. For many mediocre students, participation in the *tao-hsüeh* movement became a badge of sophistication.

Like other historic movements, *tao-hsüeh* developed a self-consciousness as the movement matured. Having won a considerable degree of social and academic acceptance, protagonists of the movement could

---

[3] The encyclopedic scope of Chu Hsi's efforts needs no elaboration. For an enumeration of the books written or edited by him, see Carson Chang, *op. cit.*, ch. 12. Lu Chiu-yüan is generally remembered on the basis of his idealistic philosophy. His teaching, nevertheless, had considerable effect on practical living, attributable in part to his own example of living in harmony with his kinsmen. The Lu clan of Chin-ch'i, to which Lu Chiu-yüan belonged, was commended by his contemporaries for its ability to reconcile considerations of clannish solidarity with incentives for individual advancement. See SYHA 57.

afford to look at it in a more objective light, trying to see what it really was instead of what they wished it to be.[4] It is in this light that we appraise the activity of Yeh Shih as a *tao-hsüeh* scholar.

II

ALTHOUGH Yeh Shih was not reckoned in the front line of the Southern Sung *tao-hsüeh* movement, there was no question that he made a considerable contribution to the cause. The strongholds of *tao-hsüeh* sentiments in Southern Sung China were the private institutions of learning centered around various charismatic teachers.[5] Yeh Shih was one of the most dynamic teachers of the day. He was closely associated with Lü Tsu-ch'ien and Cheng Po-hsiung, both stalwarts in the *tao-hsüeh* camp. He had spoken out in defense of Chu Hsi, the recognized leader of the *tao-hsüeh* scholars. Yeh Shih's credentials in the *tao-hsüeh* camp was so impressive that the young Wei Liao-weng (1178–1237), who eventually was to become one of the greatest champions of the cause, addressed Yeh Shih as the "Dean of *tao-hsüeh* scholars".[6]

And yet, this man was responsible for probably the most scathing indictment of the *tao-hsüeh* movement during the Sung period. The chastisement was all the more telling because it came not from a foe but from a friend. Yeh Shih was not simply condemning the excesses of some *tao-hsüeh* scholars; he was in fact taking up the entire *tao-hsüeh* phenomenon, examining its intellectual antecedents and evaluating the direction in which it was evolving. In the process, he came up with a penetrating critique that shed light not only on the *tao-hsüeh* movement but also on China's cultural heritage.

His critique of *tao-hsüeh* was obviously anchored in his own personal experiences. He was brought up in an academic atmosphere saturated with *tao-hsüeh* values. Although the focus of his learning was the political sciences, the proper ordering of state and society, his basic intellectual orientation remained that of the *tao-hsüeh* scholar. This orientation is time and again revealed in his early writings, as for instance, when he

[4] An example of this growing consciousness is the changing attitude towards Buddhism. To stake out a claim for the universal validity of their learning, the first generation of *tao-hsüeh* scholars took a militant stance, focusing on Buddhism as their main target of attack. With the lapse of time and with the place of *tao-hsüeh* in the academic community secured, the conscious hostility towards Buddhism declined. Many *tao-hsüeh* scholars were prepared to concede a measure of validity to Buddhist teaching. Among the most well-known examples were Yu Tso and Lü Hsi-che; see *I-lo yuan-yuan lu* 9, p. 93 and *ibid.* 7, pp. 66–67 respectively.

[5] See Carson Chang, *op. cit.*, ch. 3 "Institutions according to the School of Reason".

[6] *Ho-shan hsien-shen wen-chi* 32, "Letter to Yeh Shih".

assigned the sage the role of sustaining the social order[7] or when he asserted that people did not understand the message of Confucius until the advent of the Northern Sung masters made it manifest.[8]

Nevertheless, interspersed in these early writings were remarks which foreshadowed his devastating critique of the *tao-hsüeh* movement. He castigated the vogue of *hsing-ming* learning, saying that ignorant men made a fetish out of the abstruse concepts of nature and destiny.[9] The vogue of speculation on high-sounding words could not be blamed entirely on the *tao-hsüeh* movement, as we have seen in Chapter One. However, *tao-hsüeh* scholars were no doubt responsible for it to a great extent.

Of the diverse forces molding Yeh Shih's intellectual environment, the phenomenon of Lu Chiu-yüan was of crucial significance.[10] Blessed with an original mind and a forceful personality, Lu was rapidly building up a reputation as a great teacher during the formative years of Yeh Shih's life. Lu's ideas were making a stir throughout the academic world. His impact on Yeh Shih was further heightened by the meeting at Goose Lake, arranged by his mentor Lü Tsu-ch'ien, in which the two foremost scholars of the land, Chu Hsi and Lu Chiu-yüan, had an opportunity to thrash out their differences.[11] Yeh was probably not present at the meeting, but he seemed to have followed the proceedings with keen interest.

The differences between Chu and Lu which they sought to resolve at the Goose Lake meeting pertained not to their value systems but to their epistemology and pedagogy. Both were committed to the typical *tao-hsüeh* quest of sagehood. It was not the end but the means of the quest that set them apart.

Of the two, the position of Chu Hsi was more moderate. In his view, the attainment of sagehood was a long and gradual process, involving both the intellect and the will.[12] In technical language, this dual approach is known as "the honoring of virtue" and "following the path of study" (*tsun te hsing, tao wen hsüeh*). Although Chu Hsi himself claimed that both approaches were equally important in his system, to an

---

[7] YSC PC 5, "I" (Book of Changes).

[8] YSC PC 5, "Tsung-i" (General Discussion of the Classics).

[9] YSC PC 3, "Shih-hsüeh hsia" (Education of Scholars, section 2).

[10] For the life and thought of Lu Chiu-yüan, see Huang Hsiu-chi, *Lu Hsiang-shan, Neglected Rival of Chu Hsi* (New Haven, American Oriental Society: 1944). Also, Carson Chang, *op. cit.*, ch. 13, "The Debate between Chu Hsi and Lu Chiu-yüan".

[11] The impact of the meeting at Goose Lake on Yeh Shih is attested in HHCYHM 8:4b. See also his account in his letter to Lin Yuan-hsiu, YSC 27.

[12] For the system of Chu Hsi, see Carson Chang, *op. cit.*, chs. 12, 13, 14. Also Fung Yu-lan, *History of Chinese Philosophy* (Princeton University Press: 1953), trans. by Derk Bodde, vol. 2, ch. 13.

impartial observer, his emphasis seems to fall on the second approach. His epistemology was dominated by the concept of *ke-wu* (investigation of things). The saving knowledge of truth was attained when the mind was directed to things (*wu*) and comprehended their principle (*li*). Investigating one thing today, another tomorrow; or understanding one principle today, another principle tomorrow, and persisting unceasingly for a long time, Chu alleged, would eventually lead to the kind of knowledge which was the essence of the sage. Theoretically, sagehood was attainable for anybody; in actual fact, considering the extent of self-discipline required, the chances of ordinary mortals attaining it were remote. For pedagogical purposes, therefore, he set a more realistic goal for his students, namely, that of *pien-hua ch'i-chih* (transformation of the physical endowments of men through a process of study and self-discipline).

Lu Chiu-yüan, on the other hand, took the opposite approach and advocated the discipline not of knowledge but of the knowing mind. The basis of this philosophy of sagehood was a monistic idealism. He denied the customary notion of the dichotomy of the subject and object, the knowing mind and the object to be known. This monistic position was illustrated in his celebrated saying: "The universe is my mind; my mind is the universe." As the mind is identical with the principles of things to be known, it was not necessary to look beyond the self for the saving knowledge of truth. Ordinary men, however, were so accustomed to being governed by externally imposed standards that they no longer recognized the light within. The task of philosophers was to awaken them to the inner light. When a man succeeded in perceiving the inner light, he was said to have achieved enlightenment (*wu*). *Wu* (Japanese, *satori*) was always a sudden, abrupt experience. It admitted of no gradations or intermediate steps. Some men were known to have attained *wu* instantaneously while on their feet listening to Lu's lectures.[13] Others, such as his disciple Yang Chien, had to struggle mightily with their doubts and then it dawned on them suddenly that they had been struggling in vain.[14] Still others, in compliance with Lu's suggestions, practised protracted meditation in seclusion and experienced *wu* upon emerging from their lengthy seclusion.[15]

Part of the magnetism of Lu Chiu-yüan lay in his eloquence. He had a gift for felicitous expressions. His extant writings indicate his ability to sustain a line of argument with great cogency. However, his striving

[13] Yeh Shih attested to it; see YSC 17, "Tomb Inscription of Hu Chung-li".
[14] For Yang Chien, see SYHA 74, "Tz'u-hu hsüeh-an".
[15] For an example of enlightenment that comes after long periods of meditation, see the biographical note on Chan Fo-min, in SYHA 77.

for *wu* was essentially the striving for a mystical experience. Like all forms of mysticism, the state of *wu* was verbally indescribable. The man who had attained it could not communicate and share his experience with others who had not yet attained it. Nor was it amenable to intellectual analysis. The mystical approach was essentially a form of anti-intellectualism. Not a few of Lu's disciples, with the mystical experience looming large in their lives, downgraded the intellectual aspect of learning. They not only discouraged book-learning but also refrained from extensive deliberation of their doctrines. Verbal communication was unprofitable; the only viable form of communication was silence.[16]

For some unexplored reason, Lu Chiu-yüan's teaching found an exceptionally favorable reception in Eastern Chekiang. The best known of his disciples, for example, were the so-called "Four Masters of Ssu-ming" because they all hailed from the prefecture of Ssu-ming, also known as Yueh-chou, corresponding to present-day Ningpo area. They were all dynamic teachers, fully capable of carrying on the tradition of their mentor. In addition, there were some scholars who, though not reckoned as disciples of Lu Chiu-yüan, were spiritually akin to him. There were, for example, Hsu I of P'ing-yang[17] (in Yung-chia prefecture) and Ch'en Kuei of Chu-chou prefecture,[18] whose learning was described by Yeh Shih as oriented to the concept of *wu*. Through these men, the anti-intellectualist form of *tao-hsüeh* must have made a considerable impact on the younger scholars of Chekiang.

To the action-oriented, pragmatic young Yeh Shih who prized utilitarian knowledge (*ching-shih* scholarship), the mysticism of this Lu Chiu-yüan brand of *tao-hsüeh* was anathema. He seems to have attracted students who likewise had a revulsion against this approach to learning. To establish his credentials as a teacher, he had to counter the mystical vogue of scholarship with a viable alternative. The alternative he offered was the discipline of knowledge. However, unlike Chu Hsi, Yeh Shih relegated the quest for sagehood to the background. The goal of learning was to master the world of harsh realities and empirical facts; or, as

[16] Yeh Shih provided a good description of this type of learning in the tomb inscription of Sung Chiu-fu, YSC 25, p. 490, "At that time, Confucian scholars regarded vacuity, silence and examination of the mind as the essence of learning. They merely stood in a reverent posture, staring ahead in silence but could not expound [their learning]. Obscurantly they said, 'the tao has already come into our possession.'" There are indications that the phenomenon of non-verbal communication among *tao-hsüeh* scholars was not limited to the school of Lu Chiu-yüan but was in fact quite widespread. Ch'in Hsün, the son of Ch'in Kuei, condemned the school of Ch'eng I among other things, for this claim of non-verbal communication. See Li Hsin-ch'uan, *Chronicles*, p. 5305.

[17] YSC 21, "Tomb Inscription of the Prefect of Lung-hsing Mr. Hsü".

[18] YSC 17, "Tomb Inscription of Ch'en shu-hsiang".

he put it, "taking the myriad phenomena of the world in one's stride, linking up the past with the present."[19]

There were two noticeable peaks in Yeh Shih's teaching career. The first peak, occurring in the 1180's, coincided with the period of maximum impact of Lu Chiu-yüan on the intellectual world. Next to Lu, there were a host of eminent scholar-teachers, most of whom were staunch members of the *tao-hsüeh* camp, such as Chu Hsi, Lü Tsu-ch'ien, Chang Shih, and Ch'en Fu-liang. In the midst of this august company, the young Yeh Shih had to assume a radical posture to command a hearing.

His friend Ch'en Liang, in a similar predicament, made a name for himself in the annals of Chinese intellectual history by taking on the greatest exponent of *tao-hsüeh* ideology of Southern Sung China, Chu Hsi. The points at issue were ostensibly their varying interpretations of the character of the regimes of Han and T'ang, the greatest of the imperial dynasties. In disputing the assertion of Chu Hsi that the emperors of Han and T'ang were solely motivated by selfish desires (i.e. contrary to *tao*), Ch'en Liang was in fact assailing the inner citadel of *tao-hsüeh* orthodoxy, viz., the contention that *tao* had been in abeyance for more than a thousand years since the death of Mencius and was rediscovered by the *tao-hsüeh* masters of the Northern Sung.[20]

The debate between Ch'en Liang and Chu Hsi was carried on in an exchange of letters over a number of years; as such, it did not have the impact of a public debate. However, the repercussions of this debate were obviously felt by those close to the contestants. Ch'en Liang, as we have pointed out previously, wrote to his friend Ch'en Fu-liang, hoping that the latter would endorse his philosophic position. It is not known whether he also called upon Yeh Shih for moral support. However, in view of the generally close relationship between them, it is unlikely that Yeh Shih would be uninformed of the issues involved when the controversy was in progress. Years later, after Ch'en Liang's death, Yeh Shih probably had a chance to review the highlights of the debate: he was Ch'en Liang's literary executor responsible for the editing and publishing of his collected works known as *Lung-ch'uan chi*.[21] Undoubtedly Yeh Shih found much inspiration going over the letters in which Ch'en Liang fought the running battle with the *tao-hsüeh* orthodoxy.

[19] YSC 10, "Wen-chou hsin hsiu hsüeh chi". In this essay Yeh Shih analysed the dominant influences that shaped the academic tradition of Wenchou into the Chou Hsing-chi–Cheng Po-hsiung school which stood for moral perfection and the Hsüeh Chi-hsüen–Ch'en Fu-liang school which stood for practical learning. While Yeh Shih aspired to a synthesis of the two, his accent obviously fell on the latter.

[20] See Carson Chang, *op. cit.*, ch. 14.

[21] See YSC 12, "Lung-ch'uan chi hsü".

By the time of the second peak of Yeh Shih's teaching career, after his permenent retirement from official service in 1208, the academic community was not what it used to be. The great masters of a former era were all dead. Few of their immediate disciples had as yet acquired sufficient stature to stand out above the crowd of mediocrities. In the absence of scholars of established reputation, Yeh Shih emerged as a leading teacher of the time.[22] The situation was thus markedly different from that of Yeh's early teaching career when, as a young, budding scholar, he was overshadowed by a host of truly great scholars. The time had come for him to make a determined bid for leadership of the academic community and reset the course of China's intellectual development.

In his bid for leadership of the academic community, he was not without competition. In fact, he had to wage an up-hill fight.

Two of the foremost masters active during the reign of Emperor Hsiao-tsung, Lü Tsu-ch'ien and Chang Shih, died in their early forties. Their disciples probably gravitated into the orbit of Chu Hsi, Lu Chiu-yüan, or other masters. Chu Hsi died in 1200. He was the dominant personality of his age and has remained a major influence in Chinese culture ever since. However, his towering stature and longevity probably had an inhibitive effect on the growth of his disciples. Overawed by his incomparable achievements and amazing versatility, they learned to defer to his judgment in all matters. They were thus perpetual wards, and when the master died, no one was big enough to step into his shoes.[23] Huang Kan (1152–1221), Chu's son-in-law and presumed successor, fared poorly as a leader. Dissension and disputes on the legacy of the master were rampant among the disciples and Huang was powerless to stop them. It was with a view to reasserting his authority as legitimate interpreter of the master that he wrote in 1221 his definitive version of the master's *hsing-chuang* (basic draft biography). He died in the same year.[24]

In comparison with Chu Hsi, Lu Chiu-yüan died fairly young in his

[22] Yeh Shih's eminence in the academic community of the post-Han T'o-chou period was emphasized by Ch'üan Tsu-wang, one of the compilers of the SYHA. See his opening remarks on "Shui-hsin hsüeh-an", SYHA 54. Among Yeh Shih's contemporaries, the testimony of Liu Tsai may be cited; see *Man-t'ang chi* 19, "Sung Huang Chu-chien hsü" (On Sending Huang Chu-chien Off) and *Man-t'ang chi* 10 "T'ung Wei Shih-lang" (Letter to Wei Liao-weng). In both instances, Liu Tsai mentioned Yeh Shih in the same breath with Yang Chien, indicating that he esteemed them equally.

[23] For the decline in the ranks of Chu Hsi's disciples, see the statement by Huang Kan, *Huang Mien-chai hsien-sheng wen-chi* 4, "Letter in Reply to Li Kuan-chih, the Minister of War". The same statement also enumerates the surviving disciples in different parts of the empire.

[24] See Huang Kan, *op. cit.*, preface to the *hsing-chuang* he wrote for Chu Hsi.

mid-fifties in 1192. Perhaps partly for this reason and partly because of the mystical nature of his philosophy, his disciples were more successful in carrying on his tradition after his death. Of his disciples, we have already alluded to the "Four masters of Ssu-ming" who scrupulously upheld the legacy of their mentor. The stiffest competition to Yeh Shih was to come from this group.

Among the "Four masters", the one who had the greatest impact on his contemporaries was Yang Chien, popularly known as the "Master of Tz'u-hu" (Compassionate Lake). Yang was a more thoroughgoing idealist than his professed mentor, Lu Chiu-yüan.[25] His conversion to Lu's central doctrine of the unity of the mind and the universe was accompanied by vivid personal experiences. The memory of the brief blessed moments when he suddenly perceived the truth was made the goal of his system of pedagogy. It was to this goal of instantaneous enlightenment that he recommended his students to direct their efforts. Judged by this criterion, his teaching was highly successful. Towards the end of his career, he was able to declare triumphantly: "In the past ten or twenty years, more than a hundred persons have attained enlightenment. It is a feat unheard of even in ancient times. Our tao has indeed prospered."[26] He counted many men in prominent official positions among his students, including the powerful prime minister, Shih Mi-yüan.

As in the case of Yeh Shih, Yang's rise to prominence was assisted by the fact that he outlived most of the leading scholars who might have caused competition (including Yeh Shih). He lived to a ripe, venerable age, over eighty, remaining active and alert almost to the very end of his life. His prestige as a teacher was such that at the time of his death, there was considerable talk that he be given a state burial in recognition of this contribution to the way of the sages.

Hitherto, Yeh Shih had an ambivalent attitude towards the tao-hsüeh phenomenon. Although he was opposed to some of its manifestations, his outlook was too much conditioned by his upbringing to permit a total break from tao-hsüeh influence. Under the necessity of girding up for the battle against the extreme idealism of Yang Chien, he had to define his own ideological position more precisely. The consequence was his conscious secession from the tao-hsüeh camp. To combat the extreme manifestations of tao-hsüeh effectively, he had to tackle it at the source—the tao-hsüeh phenomenon itself.

[25] Carson Chang, op. cit., ch. 15 gives a good account of the philosophy of Yang Chien.
[26] The source of this statement is Huang Tsung-hsi. It occurs in the revised (abbreviated) version of the SYHA, p. 863 but has been omitted from the expanded version.

This survey of the academic scene should enable us to look at Yeh Shih's efforts during the second peak of his teaching career in proper perspective. His masterpiece, the *Orderly Presentation* was in the form of a bibliographic survey of the major categories of traditional Chinese literature. In fact, it was a sustained assault on his opponents in his bid for the intellectual leadership of the academic world. To make sure that his principal argument would not be obscured by a mass of irrelevant remarks, he provided a "Tsung-lun chiang-hsüeh ta-chih" (A Summary Account of His Teaching) at the end of his survey.

However, apart from the structure provided in this bibliographic survey, Yeh Shih's critique of *tao-hsüeh* was unstructured, being dispersed throughout his work. He availed himself of every opportunity to lash out at what he thought were *tao-hsüeh* fallacies. Some of his central ideas were nevertheless discernible. We will deal first with his perception of the external characteristics of the *tao-hsüeh* phenomenon.

III

STEMMING from the cosmological concerns of the Northern Sung masters, the *tao-hsüeh* movement of the Southern Sung displayed a strong metaphysical bent. The strength of this orientation may be seen in the fact that in compiling the *Chin-ssu lu* (Reflections of Things at Hand), Chu Hsi, with the collaboration of Lü Tsu-ch'ien, placed the chapter on the "Tao-t'i" (Substance of the Way) at the very beginning of the compilation. The first line of this chapter reads:[27]

Master Lien-hsi (Chou Tun-i) said, "The Ultimate of Non-Being (*wu-chi*) and also the Great Ultimate (*t'ai-chi*)."

Yeh Shih sought to explain this persistent concern with metaphysical ideas. He believed it explicable in terms of the pernicious influence of Buddhism. His argument started with Fan Yu, who, as disciple of Chang Tsai, contended that a desire to combat the intellectual appeal of Buddhism was one of the primary motives of his master in writing *Cheng-meng*.[28] In addition, Yeh Shih alleged that both Chou Tun-i and the Ch'eng brothers were anxious to cross swords with the Buddhists. These *tao-hsüeh* scholars, he alleged, proceeded on the assumption that Buddhism had nothing significant to teach Confucian scholars, and that the sophisticated Buddhist concepts on cosmology had all

---

[27] See Wing-tsit Chan's translation of the *Chin-ssu lu* (rendered by him as *Reflections on Things at Hand*), Columbia University Press: 1967, p. 5.
[28] HHCYHM 49:9a.

been anticipated by the ancient sages, particularly the group of commentaries attributed to Confucius on *I-ching* known as the "Ten Wings" (*shih-i*).[29] They did not realize that Confucius had nothing to do with the "Ten Wings". Under the indirect influence of Buddhism, *tao-hsüeh* scholars came to venerate ideas such as the Great Ultimate and the Two Modes (*liang-i*), which were alien to the teaching of Confucius.

The question whether *tao-hsüeh* ideas on cosmology were in accord with the teaching of Confucius or not can be answered only if we can agree on the original teaching of Confucius. In the course of history, scholarly opinion on the teaching of Confucius has varied greatly. The Confucius of the apocryphal texts (*wei* or *chan wei*), for instance, was very different from that of the canonical texts.[30] One can even argue for two different Confuciuses on the basis of the *Analects*, the most trustworthy of the classical texts purporting to relate the sayings and deeds of the Master, namely, Confucius the rationalist and Confucius the empiricist.[31]

Confucius the rationalist was a philosopher who sought to comprehend the unifying principles or patterns that underlay the myriad affairs of the phenomenal world. He was the man who sought, as he himself put it, "a unity all pervading."[32] His thinking was deductive. He expected his disciples to make use of their rational faculty. The most esteemed of his disciples was one who, having been shown the truth of one thing, would be able to grasp the truth of ten other things.[33]

On the other hand, Confucius the empiricist sought to set limits to deductive reasoning. The learning he cherished was empirical knowledge, particularly knowledge of the laws and institutions of the former kings who presided over the golden age of Chinese history. The mission of Confucius was not to innovate but to preserve. As he himself put it, "I am not a creator but a transmitter."[34]

Undoubtedly, Yeh Shih favored the empiricist view of Confucius. He argued that to Confucius, truth was inseparable from the empirical situation in which it was embodied. The way of learning was not abstract reasoning or contemplation but unremitting attention to concrete facts, both natural and man-made. Yeh Shih did not seem to have developed a sophisticated epistemology to support his argument.

---

[29] HHCYHM 49:12b–13a.
[30] For the image of Confucius in the apocryphal texts, see *Po Hu T'ung*, pp. 100–120.
[31] H. Creel, who has written an excellent biography of Confucius, uses the same two terms to refer to the self-image of Confucius. See H. Creel, *Confucius, the Man and the Myth*, p. 136.
[32] Legge, *The Chinese Classics*, vol. 1. *Analects*, Bk. XV, ch. 5, p. 295.
[33] *Ibid.*, *Analects*, Bk. V, ch. 8, p. 176.
[34] *Ibid.*, *Analects*, Bk. VII, ch. 1, p. 195.

He fell back on the sensation psychology of the pre-Ch'in scholars: sense perception was the starting point of all knowledge.[35] The ancient sages, he alleged, achieved great deeds because they depended not only on their mind but also made judicious use of their sense organs, the eye and the ear.[36] There was no secret to their *tao* (i.e. their prescription for success) other than their unceasing effort in solving the problems of the world.

Yeh Shih was of the opinion that for Confucius, as for the ancient sages, the word *tao* did not denote a specific system of teaching or an abstract principle. It was simply a word indicating what was appropriate and desirable:[37]

Confucius was particularly notable for his discourses on the *tao*. However, he never defined what *tao* was. Is it possible that what the ancients referred to as *tao* was known to the [rulers] above and the [ruled] below, and that their only worry was they might fall short of it in conduct?

The first man to part company with the pragmatic spirit of the ancient sages, Yeh Shih charged, was Lao-tzu, the author of *Tao-te ching*. Lao-tzu made a supreme effort to define what *tao* was.[38] The consequence was that scholars began to venerate abstractions which bore no relation to the concrete realities of the world. This trend of development culminated in the practice of contemporary scholars, who, expatiating on their concept of the "Ultimate of Non-Being" and the "Great Ultimate", had in mind a *tao* which pre-dated even Heaven and Earth.

The *tao-hsüeh* masters of the Northern Sung period, Yeh Shih claimed, turned to the teachings of Tzu-ssu and Mencius to find sanctions for their metaphysical propensities.[39] This sanction they found in Tzu-ssu's doctrine of "sincerity" (*ch'eng*). "Sincerity" came with acting in accordance with one's nature. The man who was completely sincere, i.e. the sage, formed a trinity with Heaven and Earth. They also found it in the Mencian doctrine of the original goodness of human nature.

---

[35] For the sensation psychology of the pre-Ch'in scholars, see a succinct treatment of the subject by Frederick Mote, "The Problem of Knowledge" in his book *Intellectual Foundations of China* (New York, Alfred A. Knopf: 1971), ch. 6.

[36] For a discussion of the "Ten Wings", see Creel, *op. cit.*, ch. XII, "From Myth to Myth".

[37] For Yeh Shih's emphasis on perception as the starting point of knowledge, see HHCYHM 14:9. In this passage, he particularly laid emphasis on the interaction between the inner (mind) and the outer (visual-audio images perceived by the mind).

[38] HHCYHM 7:2b.

[39] HHCYHM 49:13b–14a. Yeh Shih probably judged Tzu-ssu on the basis of the *Doctrine of the Mean*. He was nevertheless aware that it contained materials not written by Tzu-ssu (HHCYHM 8:12a). For a critical analysis of the source of this work, see E.R. Hughes, *op. cit.*, ch. 4.

The logic of his doctrine committed Mencius to an extreme view of innate human power. The man who had recovered his original goodness and taken proper care to nurture it, Mencius claimed, did not lack anything — such as wisdom, benevolence and courage. He was complete in himself (*wan-wu chieh pei yü wo*). As a consequence of this Mencian attitude, Yeh Shih asserted, all the well-established methods whereby the ancients advanced their learning were abolished; attention was concentrated on the mind (or heart) as the sovereign ruler. Commenting on the significance of Tzu-ssu and Mencius as forerunners of the *tao-hsüeh* penchant for abstractions, Yeh Shih wrote:[40]

When the ancients refered to *tao*, they meant the culmination of their lifelong quest for virtue. When people nowadays refer to *tao*, they mean something which they expect to apprehend right away. Those who made *tao* the culmination of their lifelong quest were the Duke of Chou and Confucius. Those who sought to apprehend *tao* right away were Tzu-ssu and Mencius.

Yeh Shih was undoubtedly right in tracing the *tao-hsüeh* penchant for abstractions to Tzu-ssu and Mencius. Both were notable for the streak of mysticism in their teachings.[41] Tzu-ssu's doctrine of sincerity and Mencius' idea of *hao-jan chih-ch'i* (vast, flowing passion nature) which pervaded Heaven and Earth offered scholars the possibilities of participating in a more meaningful existence, transcending the petty distinctions of ephermeral, individual lives. As such, Tzu-ssu and Mencius may be considered Confucian counterparts to Lao-tzu and Chuang-tzu. Originating in a time of crisis, when Chou feudal society was rapidly disintegrating, they addressed themselves to the most pressing problem of the time, namely, man's quest for meaning. Thoughtful men, cut off from their familiar moorings because of the crumbling feudal institutions, were looking desperately for a new pattern and rationale of life. Tzu-ssu and Mencius, like Lao-tzu and Chuang-tzu, satisfied this craving for meaning by providing a new basis of total integration, involving not only individual people but also the physical nature in a cosmic scheme of harmony. As these teachers sought an ultimate solution to human problems, there was a marked

---

[40] HHCYHM 44:10b. The prominence given by Yeh Shih to Tzu-ssu and Mencius in his indictment of the intellectual roots of *tao-hsüeh* seems to lend support to Mou Tsung-san's hypothesis. According to the latter (see his *Hsin-ti yü hsing-ti*, Pt. I, ch. 1, section 4), the mainstream of Sung and Ming Neo-Confucianism is not represented by the Ch'eng-Chu school as is usually assumed but by that which included Chou Tun-i, Chang Tsai, Ch'eng Hao, Hu An-kuo, Lu Chiu-yüan, and Wang Yang-ming among others. The source of inspiration of the members of this school comprised of the *Doctrine of the Mean* and the book *Mencius*.

[41] For the streak of mysticism in the thought of Tzu-ssu and Mencius, see Fung Yu-lang, *History of Chinese Philosophy*, vol. 1, ch. 6, "Mencius and His School of Confucianism".

militancy in their attitude. Repudiating conventional wisdom and putting down rival teachings, they promoted their own *tao* as the ultimate teaching. Under the necessity of justifying their doctrine as the ultimate teaching, (against the counter-claim of Buddhism, for example,) *tao-hsüeh* scholars could not dispense with their metaphysical abstractions. It is easy to understand why they saw the mysticism of Tzu-ssu and Mencius, which was the first step towards an intellectually satisfying cosmology, as the pattern and legitimation of their own efforts.

The redirection of effort away from the world of empirical facts to the *tao*, which was above forms and shapes, from the outer sphere of concrete realities to the inner sphere of mental abstractions, found expression in another *tao-hsüeh* characteristic, namely, an intense cultivation of moral sensibilities. For the majority of *tao-hsüeh* scholars who came under the influence of the Ch'eng-Chu school, this heightened sensibility was a major stage in the striving for sagehood, denoted by the formula *"pien-hua ch'i-chih"* (transformation of the physical endowment).

In placing their emphasis on the cultivation of moral sensibilities, *tao-hsüeh* scholars were conscious of their affinity to Tseng-tzu, the moralist par excellence among Confucius' disciples. As a moral rigorist, Tseng-tzu was not satisfied with the mere performance of culturally sanctioned acts such as providing the support which grown-up sons owed their parents. He was concerned with the moral quality of actions. Emphasis was not on the moral act but on the person who performed the act, i.e. on his motives and sensibilities. A culturally sanctioned act performed for ulterior reasons had little merit. A man who was not genuinely filial but went through the motion in order to project the image of a filial son in the community did not deserve to be called a virtuous man. In his system of ethics, the maintenance of the proper frame of mind was therefore a matter of utmost importance. He was known to have practised self-examination three times a day to make sure that none of his hidden faults remain undetected.[42] On his death-bed, his parting words to his good friend, Meng Ching-tzu, were:[43]

There are three principles of conduct which the man of high rank should consider specially important: that in deportment and manner he keeps from violence and heedlessness, that in regulating his countenance, he keeps near to sincerity, and that in his words and tone, he keeps far from lowness and impropriety. As to such matter as attending to the sacrificial vessels, there are the proper officers for them.

Tseng-tzu's legacy, however, was liable to abuse. His preoccupation

---

[42] Legge, *op. cit.*, *Analects*, Bk. I, ch. 4, p. 139.
[43] *Ibid.*, Bk. VIII, ch. 4, p. 209.

with moral sensibilities could lead to the undermining of the institutional basis of society. Viable societies are not held together entirely by the spontaneous goodwill of their members. They need an element of compulsion; members of the same society, in so far as they want to communicate with one another, are bound by the values and symbolism current in that society. The element of compulsion in primitive societies is naturally greater. Unlike more advanced societies where inter-personal relations fall increasingly under the domain of contract, life in primitive societies is dominated by the force of tradition, enshrined in rituals. In ancient China, as in other primitive societies, the magical potency of ritual, that is, what the Chinese referred to as *li* (ritual or rules of propriety) and *yüeh* (music), was an axiom of thought; cosmic and human orders were sustained by the appropriate performance of the ritual of sacrifice, burial, marriages.[44] With so much at stake, the fulfillment of ritual obligations was not left to individual whims; it was enforced by the vigilance of public opinion and backed by the sanction of the state.

The rise of civilizations usually entails an increasing emphasis on a more rationalistic view of the universe and a corresponding de-emphasis on the magical potency of rituals. Confucius of the *Analects* was definitely moving in this direction. He justified the "Three Years Mourning", for example, not on the ground that such a lengthy period of mourning was necessary to purge the mourner who had been contaminated by contact with the dead person, but on the ground that it provided an appropriate outlet for human sentiments.[45] It was probably with a view to reminding his listeners of the human dimension behind the external aspects of *li* and *yüeh* that Confucius made the following remark:[46]

The Master said, " 'It is according to the rules of propriety,' they say— 'It is according to the rules of propriety,' they say. Are gems and silk all that is meant by propriety? 'It is music,' they say—'It is music,' they say. Are bells and drums all that is meant by music?"

Tseng-tzu, Yeh Shih argued, in taking over this legacy of the master, went too far. In Tseng-tzu's system of ethics, externally imposed norms of behavior, *li*, were pushed to the background and the center of attention was shifted to the self. The preoccupation with the self as

[44] For an account of the ancient Chinese attitude towards ritual, see Arthur Waley, *The Analects of Confucius*, "Introduction", particularly sections entitled, "The Magical Efficacy of Rituals", "Music and Dancing", pp. 64-69.
[45] See Confucius' retort to his disciple Tsai Wo, Legge, *Analects*, Bk. XVII, ch. 21, p. 327.
[46] Legge, *Analects*, Bk. XVII, ch. 11, p. 327.

a yardstick of morality is clearly brought out in Tseng-tzu's attempt to define the legacy of Confucius:[47]

The doctrine of our master, he said, "is to be true to the principles of our nature (*chung*) and the benevolent exercise of them to others (*shu*)—these and no more."

The traditional interpretation of the concept of *chung*, based on the etymology of the word, "is duty-doing, on a consideration, or from the impulse of one's own self; *shu* is duty-doing, on the principle of reciprocity."[48] The self, needless to say, is not infallible. The history of the world abounds with men who, acting on their convictions, wreaked untold havoc on their fellow-men because of their excessive zeal for what they regarded as noble causes. The world would surely be out of joint if everybody insisted on the sovereign authority of his inner light and disregarded the externally imposed norms of behavior.[49] The deterrent effect of *li* and *yüeh* could not be slighted. Yet the logical consequence of Tseng-tzu's teaching which counseled exclusive concern with moral sensibility and indifference to the external aspects of rituals was precisely the erosion of the deterrent effect of *li* and *yüeh*. The external form of *li* and *yüeh*, for example, the three hundred minutiae of ritual (*ch'ü-li*), are just as indispensable as the inner spirit.[50] To redress the imbalance brought about by Tseng-tzu, Yeh Shih commented on the previously cited remarks of Confucius on "gems and silk, bells and drums":[51]

But can one have rules of propriety without gems and silk? And can one talk of music without bells and drums?

For Yeh Shih, the perils of a self-centered moralism were not idle fears but concrete realities. The influence of the Lu Chiu-yüan–Yang Chien brand of *tao-hsüeh* was on the rise. The quest for enlightenment in this system of philosophy was essentially the quest for a particular state of mind, the striving for the mystical experience. Lu Chiu-yüan had often been accused of being a Ch'an Buddhist in disguise because of the importance he attached to the mystical approach. His disciples were subject to the same reproach. Their efforts in learning were often so pre-empted by the quest for the mystical experience that they did not have time for anything else. They were men who were ignorant

---

[47] *Ibid.*, Bk. IV, ch. 15, pp. 169–170.

[48] Legge, *Analects*, his annotation to the text.

[49] Yeh Shih expressed this idea by saying that the self is not necessarily right, society is not necessarily wrong. HHCYHM 13:11a.

[50] HHCYHM 8:1.

[51] *Ibid.*, 8:8b–9a.

and yet thought they knew everything of importance because of their mystical experience. The proliferation of this description of men could only spell trouble for the world. Yeh Shih clearly alluded to this peril when he wrote the following:[52]

Why is it that the learning of the Buddha and of Lao-tzu should not be admitted into the tao of Confucius and of the Duke of Chou? This is because the tao of Confucius and the Duke of Chou is based on performance of virtuous deeds and manifests itself in unpretentious but untiring [efforts for the betterment of the world.] It is therefore immutable, being coeval with Heaven and Earth; it does not consist merely in a man's transient state of mind.

Even without the complication of the Lu-Yang brand of philosophy, Southern Sung tao-hsüeh ran into a common problem which plagued all successful movement: fellow-travelers and unsavory characters climbed on to its bandwagon. Ch'en Liang brought this point out in his battle against tao-hsüeh:[53]

In recent years, there arises a philosophy which centers around discussions of such topics as tao, virtue, human nature, heavenly decree. Only those who are good for nothing belong to this school. They appear earnest, silent and profound; they walk slowly and their speech is careful. They behave as if they are subtle and mysterious; but that is only to disguise their being good for nothing. They do not consider knowledge and skill as a worthy part of the tao of the sages.

The phenomenon that Ch'en Liang castigated was no doubt a perversion of the tao-hsüeh movement. Yeh Shih was of the opinion that tao-hsüeh was vulnerable to this perversion because of the legacy of Tseng-tzu. In the latter's system of ethics, the three things which a gentleman considered as important, viz., appropriate countenance, deportment, and tone of voice were probably intended as the external expression of an inner piety.[54] However, the phraseology of the crucial

---

[52] Ibid., 50:7.

[53] Carson Chang, op. cit., p. 313. Similar criticism of the superficiality and pharisaical display of tao-hsüeh scholars had been voiced by other Sung scholars, for example the following statement by Chou Mi (see Li-tai pi-chi hsiao-shuo hsüan, p. 635): In addition, there are some shallow scholars who realize that they do not have the qualifications for advancement in the normal manner. Therefore they attach themselves to the tao-hsüeh [movement]. They wear long robes with broad belts; they sit in a dignified attitude and walk with large strides. Citing yü-lu excerpts of tao-hsüeh masters, they launch into highsounding discourses; keeping their eyes closed, they claim to be engaged in meditations. However, if [you put] their learning to the test, [you will find] that they know nothing about the affairs of ancient and modern times. If you look closely at their personal conduct, [you will find] that they know nothing about the distinction between propriety and self-seeking. These men are the big offenders among the followers of the sages.

[54] This interpretation is in agreement with Ch'eng I's view. When the question, "What is the characteristic mark (ch'i-hsiang) of the sages?" was put to him, he replied,

passage in the *Analects* is such that it implied that Tseng-tzu assigned priority to the external expression. Syntactically, the passage may be analysed as follows:[55]

There are three things which a gentleman prizes:
He maintains a proper deportment so that ...
He regulates his countenance so that ...
He speaks with the proper tone and diction so that ...

Little wonder shallow-minded men regarded their self-conscious mannerisms as in the best tradition of Tseng-tzu.

The position of Tseng-tzu, Tzu-ssu, and Mencius in the *tao-hsüeh* movement was virtually unassailable, by virtue of their being in the main line of the *tao-t'ung* tradition. To prove the unviability of their teachings, Yeh Shih had to demolish the rationale of the *tao-t'ung* tradition. He did not seem to dispute the notion that a succession of sages represented the orthodoxy or desirable norm in Chinese culture. He merely objected to the inclusion of Tseng-tzu and Tsu-ssu in the list of sages coming after Confucius. Yeh Shih established two points to support this argument: (*a*) the nature of Confucius' legacy and (*b*) Confucius could not have intended Tseng-tzu to succeed him.

In line with his own empiricist orientation, Yeh believed that the supreme historic mission of Confucius was one of conservation:[56]

... It may be observed that, from the time of Yao and Shun to the Duke of Chou, there were indeed [sages] who created but none who transmitted. Although the affairs of the world are infinite, the principles that govern them are not. For this reason, it is the inability to transmit in later times that is a matter of serious concern; there is no room for creation.

Also:[57]

In as much as Confucius turned away from creation to transmission, he inaugurated a new era — that of preservation. He made it possible for the achievements of Yao and Shun and the Three Dynasties to live in the re-membrance of posterity so that men could take them as norms for their feelings and aspirations. [If the task of transmission was neglected] and [ambitious men] vied with one another exclusively in creation, established traditions would be discarded in an endless pursuit of novelty. If there were no attempt to preserve [what was worthwhile in the old, civilization would

---

"We may know them by their speech." See *Erh-Ch'eng ch'üan-shu*, "Ts'ui-yen" (Pure Words) 1:24a. For other similar utterances by the same author, see *op. cit.*, "I-shu" (Posthumous Works) 18:7, 18:20.

[55] The crucial word is *ssu* which is obviously a connecting particle in this context; see Matthew's *Chinese-English Dictionary*, no. 5574a.

[56] HHCYHM 13:7.

[57] *Ibid.*, 13:10.

retrogress] so that human society eventually becomes [as inhospitable as] the realm of the ghosts and [as primitive as] the time of [Fu-]hsi and [Huang-]ti.

This uncompromisingly conservative interpretation of Confucius provided Yeh Shih with valuable ammunition in his assault on the *tao-t'ung* tradition. Invoking the name of Confucius, Yeh Shih laid down the law: the process of innovation did not belong to the post-Confucian epoch and was therefore condemned *ipso facto*. The great developments in the Confucian school associated with the name of Tseng-tzu, Tzu-ssu, Mencius and Hsun-tzu were therefore no more than perversions. Confucius did not discourse on human nature and the way of Heaven, while Tzu-ssu, Mencius and Hsun-tzu were fond of discoursing on them. The latter, therefore, were guilty of innovation.

In seeking to establish the credentials of Tseng-tzu as the successor of Confucius in the transmission of the *tao*, *tao-hsüeh* scholars resorted to the concept of *hsin-ch'uan* (transmission of the mind). As proof of this *hsin-ch'uan*, they pointed to the fact that when Confucius addressed his cryptic remark about his seeking an all-pervading unity to Tseng-tzu, the latter understood it immediately, and was able to render a creditable account of his understanding:[58]

The teaching of our Master consists of *chung* and *shu*, and no more.

The doctrine of *hsin-ch'uan* did not impress Yeh Shih. *Tao* to him was not a mystical entity that could be perceived or experienced in its entirety; it was but the collective name of moral principles.[59] There could be no transmission of *tao* apart from verbal communication in speech or in writing.[60] In this regard, there was no indication that Tseng-tzu had received special instruction from Confucius so that he came to have a more penetrating understanding of the teaching of the Master. His celebrated dictum on *chung* and *shu* as the essence of Confucian teaching, though impressive, was of doubtful validity, for it was not ratified by the Master.[61]

If Confucius did intend his *tao* to be transmitted through Tseng-tzu, Yeh Shih contended, it is reasonable to expect that he should have expressed his approbation of Tseng-tzu in a more tangible manner.

[58] *Ibid.*, 13:10b.
[59] *Ibid.*, 13:14. Yeh Shih alleged that even Yen Yüan, with his superior intelligence, had to pursue the subject of benevolence (*jen*) beyond its ontological essence (*ch'üan-ti*) to its concrete manifestations (*mu*). Ontological essence took on meaning only in conjunction with concrete manifestations.
[60] HHCYHM 13:17. Yeh Shih claimed that even Confucius received the *tao* from the ancient sages not directly but via the written records.
[61] *Ibid.*, 13:3b.

There are, however, no statements in the *Analects* which can be construed specifically as showing the Master's appreciation of Tseng-tzu.
On the other hand, evidence may be marshalled to support a contrary
point of view, namely, that Tseng-tzu was not held in high esteem
by the Master. He was, for instance, omitted from the list in which
Confucius commended his disciples for their achievements in various
fields.[62] He did get included in another list, that in which Confucius
lamented the shortcomings of his students: "Chai is simple; Shan
(Tseng-tzu) is dull; Shih is specious; Yu is coarse."

It may further be argued that if Confucius did intend Tseng-tzu
to be his successor, the majority of the Master's disciples should not
have been completely unaware of it. Upon the death of Confucius, looking for someone to assume the mantle of the Master, the disciples
turned not to Tseng-tzu but to Yu Jo, and, when the latter declined
the offer, the disciples finally learned to stand on their own feet.[63]
Their uncoordinated propagation of the teaching of the Master gave rise
to a number of Confucian schools, for example, those of Tzu-hsia,
Tzu-chang and Tseng-tzu. There is no indication that the school of
Tseng-tzu was accorded a shadow of superiority. The conclusion that
Yeh Shih drew from these considerations was:[64]

It is permitted to say that Tseng-tzu transmitted his own doctrines; it is
not permissible to say that he was the sole transmitter of the doctrine of
Confucius.

By the same token, Yeh Shih intimated, the credentials of Tzu-ssu,
the next link in the *tao-t'ung* tradition, also could not bear close scrutiny.
The latter was indeed the grandson of Confucius and it stands to
reason that in the familial ethic of feudal China, Confucius might have
reserved some peculiarly significant message for members of his family.
This supposition, however, was not borne out by the facts. Confucius's
son, Li, when questioned by a disciple of the Master whether he had
learned anything unknown to the disciples, answered in the negative.
Thus, as far as Li was concerned, the special relationship to the Master
did not amount to very much.[65] There is no reason to believe that in
the case of Tzu-ssu, who was at another remove from the Master, this
special relation ought to carry more weight.

Yeh Shih further adduced evidence to prove that the descendants of
the Master had been woefully negligent in preserving the family heritage.

[62] *Ibid.*, 49:11, 13:13. Legge, *Analects*, Bk. X, ch. 2, pp. 237–238.
[63] I am not aware that Yeh Shih had brought up this point. For a brief statement
of the transmission of the Confucian schools, see *Po Hu T'ung*, pp. 82–89.
[64] HHCYHM 13:11.
[65] *Ibid.*, 49:11b. Legge, *Analects*, Bk. XVI, ch. 13.

The dates of Tzu-ssu, he alleged, that had been handed down by family tradition, were altogether untrustworthy.[66] It is thus foolish to presume upon the authenticity of doctrines merely because they were allegedly transmitted by the family of Confucius.

Another obnoxious aspect of the *tao-hsüeh* movement was the intellectual arrogance of its adherents. Claiming to be followers of the way of the sages, they looked down upon all other forms of learning as beneath their dignity.[67]

Implicit in this attitude was a hierarchical conception of the academic disciplines, namely, the conception that the sundry forms of learning were not of equal value, although they were all valid in that they corresponded to the different levels of intelligence or natural endowments of men who cultivated them. This hierarchical conception was probably influenced by the Buddhist example, which, in the form of T'ien-t'ai or Hua-yen, was able to harmonize the divergent teaching of different forms of Buddhism by assigning them to the different levels at which truth might be perceived. The most elaborate enumeration of the levels of learning in a non-Buddhist context that I have encountered is that by Li Chih-ts'ai, an alleged mentor of Shao Yung. According to Li:[68]

Beyond the learning of the civil service examination (*k'o-chü*), there is the learning of moral principles (*i-li*); beyond the learning of moral principles, there is the learning of physical principles (*wu-li*); beyond the learning of physical principles, there is the learning of human nature and human destiny (*hsing-ming*).

The numerological school that Li belonged to played only a minor role in the formulation of *tao-hsüeh* ideology. Consequently, some of the levels of learning that he enumerated were mere typological positions with little substantive basis, for example, that of "physical principles". Nevertheless, his contention that there was a whole world of learning beyond that geared to the civil service examination remained the basis and *raison d'etre* of the *tao-hsüeh* movement. *Tao-hsüeh* scholars did not deny the validity of the examination-oriented system of instruction. However, in their view, that system was intended only for the dull-witted and those of inferior natural endowments who were not fit for anything better. Chu Hsi, for instance, assigned his son to this category.[69]

The lack of esteem accorded to the examination-oriented learning was

---

[66] *Ibid.*, 17:11b.

[67] Huang Ch'en was also critical of this attitude. But he attributed it primarily to the school of Lu Chiu-yüan. See SYHA 58:24, "Hsiang-shan hsüeh-an".

[68] See Chu Hsi, *Wu-chao min-ch'en yen-hsing lu* 10, section on Ch'en T'uan.

[69] CWCKCC 33, "Letter to Lü Tsu-ch'ien".

due to the fact that it was tainted with self-seeking, being the road to office and emoluments. Thus, it was not an end in itself but a means to an end, consequently, not genuine learning. Learning that was worthy of the name ought to be disinterested, bringing no material reward but spiritual and moral edification.

The revulsion against examination-oriented learning also extended to its components. Success in the examination hall required more than "knowing the ropes" or techniques of the examination, but also considerable virtuosity in composing prose or poetry, responding to questions on the classics, histories, and contemporary affairs. The patrons of these forms of scholarship which had a bearing on the examination, viz., the man of letters, the commentator or exegete of classics, the historian, the commentator on contemporary affairs, shared somewhat the same odium as the examination candidate. In the absence of evidence to the contrary, the presumption was that they were motivated by fame-seeking.

The *tao-hsüeh* mentality thus precluded an all-round curriculum of education. The one important thing was moral cultivation in pursuit of the goal of becoming a sage. All other things were superfluous and even harmful. This single-minded, unitary approach to education may be seen in the pedagogical systems of the great *tao-hsüeh* teachers. Chu Hsi, for instance, for all his versatility, lectured only on a limited range of topics, viz., those of immediate concern to the task of moral cultivation. He kept the more profound of his thoughts on history, the classics, political institutions, and the physical universe to himself. The only person deemed worthy of sharing his lofty ideas was Ts'ai Yüan-ting (1135–1198), whom he treated more as a friend than as a disciple.[70]

This *tao-hsüeh* insistence on a single norm of learning was contrary to the traditional spirit of education. Previously, in spite of the predominance of the ideal of public service in Confucian education, scholars were nevertheless permitted considerable lattitude. The sundry types of learning patronized by scholar-officials did not all carry the same prestige. The more technical fields of study such as astronomy and mathematics had always limited appeal for the elite. The most highly prized learning, if it could be called learning at all, was that of the all-round man, who, as Shao Shuo-chih (1053–1110) described him:[71]

---

[70] SYHA 62.

[71] Shao Shuo-chih, *Sung-shan chi* 14, "Chiu-hsüeh lun" (A Discourse on the Nine Varieties of Learning). It may be interesting to note that among the nine varieties, Shao mentioned that of the classicist, the historian and the hermit. The last mentioned may be an indirect reference to the *tao-hsüeh* scholars.

When given employment, his blessings reached to the nine regions of the world; and, in retirement at home, his culture transformed the neighborhood.

However, for learning which could be actively cultivated, such as skill in composing poetry or prose essays, historical or classical scholarship, there was no overt hierarchy of values. Each field had its ardent devotees and it was not uncommon for some outstanding scholars to be proficient in more than one of these fields.

Yeh Shih's self-image as a teacher was no doubt derived from the great teachers of antiquity, who recognized that different students had different interests and aptitude, and who accordingly sought to tailor their instruction to the capacity of the student. Yeh Shih did not require his students to conform to a rigid norm. His broad conception of education brought him to collide head on with *tao-hsüeh* intransigence. Part of his critique of *tao-hsüeh*, therefore, involved the vindication of the traditional scheme of education.

The key element of his defense was the argument of Kao Yao. Kao Yao was the reputed minister of punishment for the sage-ruler Shun. The sagacity of Shun was such that the men he selected to assist him in the task of government were also generally credited with being sages themselves. Nevertheless, the ministers of Shun were seldom accorded the recognition that sages deserved. Their fame was over-shadowed by Shun and other first-line sages who were sovereign rulers.

In the chapter on the "Counsel of Kao Yao" in *Shu-ching* (Book of History), we have Kao Yao's views on government. An important part of his ideas on government was what he called the "nine virtues", an enumeration of the desirable qualities in men recruited for government service:[72]

Kao Yao said, "Affability combined with respectfulness; mildness combined with firmness; bluntness combined with reverence; docility combined with boldness; straightforwardness combined with gentleness; easiness combined with discrimination; vigor combined with sincerity; valor combined with righteousness. When these qualities are displayed, and that permanently, have we not the good officer?"

Searching for arguments to combat the intransigence of the *tao-hsüeh* position on education, Yeh Shih saw the significance of the chapter "Counsel of Kao Yao". Kao's "nine virtues" were a vindication of the common-sense view that no single norm valid for all men existed, and that there was a legitimate place in society for men of all descriptions and talents. The fullest exposition of his argument was to be found in

---

[72] James Legge, *The Chinese Classics*, vol. 3, "The Shoo King", Bk. III, pp. 68–75.

an essay commemorating the founding of the prefectural school of Liu-an, which tradition alleged to be the birthplace of Kao Yao:[73]

With the advent of Kao Yao, who used to nurture the talents of the empire in accordance with the nine categories of virtue, it is not the absence of sages that was a cause of concern, but the absence of men of solidity and talent. If men of solidity and talent were indeed available, they would be treated honorably with no attempt to change their nature by force. On the other hand, they would be afforded opportunities to nurture their talents so that from insignificant beginnings they would attain to substantial proportions. With men of talents properly employed, family and state would become well regulated and their myriad affairs suitably attended to. Therefore, it is said that the way of education started with Kao Yao.

Applying himself consistently to the discovery and employment of the manifold talents of the empire, he was able to set the empire in order without resorting to unusual methods of government. Subsequent rulers of China from the time of Yü and T'ang till the Chou dynasty followed his approach unwaveringly. There was indeed no viable alternative. If one was to depart from his approach, it was virtually impossible to adhere to an impartial [yardstick of selection] and much potential talent in the empire would go untapped.

In recent years, scholars seek to augment their virtue with a view to becoming sages. Solidity is crushed and talents ignored. The same mode of instruction is applied indiscriminately to both the superior men and the pettyminded men and no one is deemed worthy of employment until he has attained the *tao*. The whole approach to education nowadays is surely based on principles very different from those of Kao Yao. Does it mean that we have developed the art of education so much that Kao Yao is now outmoded?

We will conclude this chapter with some remarks on Yeh Shih's "A Summary Account of His Teaching". This consists of an enumeration of, and commentary on, the ancient sages. Beyond doubt, we may take it as a statement of his version of the *tao-t'ung* tradition.[74]

We will not be surprised to find that he had made some alterations in the list of sages. For instance, Kao Yao and I Yin were added to the list of ancient sages, whereas Tseng-tzu and Tzu-ssu were dropped. Mencius, however, despite Yeh Shih's reservations, remained on the list. To indicate his final break with the *tao-hsüeh* camp, he repudiated

---

[73] YSC 9:146, "Liu-an hsien hsin hsüeh chi" (An Account of the New School in Liu-an District).

[74] HHCYHM 49:9–13b. The Japanese scholar, Morahashi Tetsuji, in his pioneering study of Sung Confucianism, included Yeh Shih's "Tsung-lun chiang-hsüeh ta-chih" among his examples of Sung idea on the *tao-t'ung*. He does not seem to have pointed out the ideological basis of Yeh's version of *tao-t'ung*. See *Jugaku no mokuteki to Soju Keireki shi Keigen hyaku rokushi nenkan no katsudo* (The Goal of Confucianism and the Activities of Sung Confucianists in the Hundred and Sixty Years from Ching-li to Ching-yüan), Taishukan: 1929, p. 145.

the idea that the transmission of *tao* came to an abrupt end with the death of Mencius and resumed again with the masters of the Northern Sung period. If people during the intervening period lived in the dark, he contended, it was not because they had no access to the *tao*, but because they were not willing to learn.

Yeh Shih's argument was based on the contention that all that was essential to Chinese civilization had been made known by the ancient sages and transmitted to posterity through the conservation effort of Confucius. In line with his view on Confucius, he also refuted the customary view that Confucius wrote the *Ch'un-ch'iu* and edited the *Shih-ching* and *Shu-ching*. The only writings Confucius ever did, according to Yeh Shih, were some commentaries on the *I-ching*. With regard to the other classics, what Confucius did was simply preserve the existing texts for posterity.[75]

This narrow circumscription of Confucius's lifework was hardly in keeping with the exalted position he enjoyed in Chinese history. What indeed had Confucius done to merit the place of honor among the ancient sages? In line with his self-image as a transmitter, we may say that his achievement consisted of restoring the pure *li* and *yüeh* of the as yet uncorrupted past. Certainly, Confucius himself set much store on it. However, this task could not have lasting value. Even if Confucius had succeeded in restoring the rituals and institutions of the former kings, his achievement could not long survive him. Yeh Shih admitted that the turmoil that gripped Chinese society intensified after Confucius's death so that by the time of Mencius, few traces of the admirable institutions of the former kings were to be seen. The only part of Confucius' lifework that survived the ravages of time were the Five Classics; yet how much of the five classics can be really credited to him? Having denied Confucius' role in writing the *Ch'un-ch'iu* and editing *Shih-ching* and *Shu-ching*, Yeh Shih in fact made Confucius out as a "glorified archivist" — as his critic Mou Tsung-san charges.[76]

It cannot be said that Yeh Shih had established a viable alternative to *tao-hsüeh*. In parting company with the *tao-t'ung* tradition, he claimed to be going back beyond the legacies of Mencius, Tzu-ssu and Tseng-tzu to that of Confucius himself. But what did this *fu-ku* restorationism amount to? An emasculated form of Confucianism. Disavowing the legacies of Tseng-tzu, Tzu-ssu, Mencius and Hsun-tzu, he threw out all that made Confucianism a vibrant, relevant part of traditional Chinese culture. Confucianism without the legacies of these great

---

[75] Yeh Shih was emphatic in refuting the traditional notion that Confucius edited the *Classic of Poetry*. See HHCYHM 6:13b, 13:1b, 49:11.
[76] Mou Tsung-san, *op. cit.*, pp. 245–246.

scholars was inconceivable — little more than a way of life (pre-Ch'in feudalism) which the forward march of history had long since rendered obsolete. It could have no relevance to the needs of contemporary Sung society.

IV

I WILL conclude this chapter with an appraisal of Yeh Shih's position in Chinese intellectual history. It may be recalled that his assault against *tao-hsüeh* intensified after his retirement from government employment in 1208. Thus he represented a post-Chu Hsi phenomenon. Granted the validity of my interpretation of the role of Chu Hsi and Lu Chiu-yüan in the propagation of the *tao-hsüeh* movement, the *tao-hsüeh* that Yeh Shih fulminated against was not a moral-intellectual movement in its prime; not a dynamic, innovative force, but a revered legacy. Within the world of learning, this legacy found expression in certain persistent forms. Yeh Shih's attack on *tao-hsüeh* was in fact directed against the manifestation of this legacy in the restricted sphere of learning. It may also be surmised that Yeh Shih himself represented an alternate pattern for the manifestation of the same legacy.

With the passing of the great *tao-hsüeh* masters, when all that was essential to the implementation of their ideal was made known, there was little that anybody could do except to seek to live up to it. The *tao-hsüeh* ideal encompassed both the world of public affairs and that of private life. However, for the majority of men, the world of public affairs was only a remote concern; the only part of the ideal that was immediately relevant was that which pertained to private life. Within the scope of private life, *tao-hsüeh* insisted on the lofty standards of the former sages. However, in a stable society where customary laws ruled most facets of social and economic life, there were comparatively few opportunities for men's profession of lofty standards to be put to test. It is therefore necessary for people who prized the prestige and assurance of participation in the community of *tao-hsüeh* scholars to place emphasis on the external trappings of this learning, viz. penchant for metaphysical discourses, a self-conscious mannerism and an intellectual arrogance towards other forms of learning.

We may infer a close affinity between the state of mind behind these behavioral traits and the Lu-Yang approach to self-cultivation. Scholars who claimed to be followers of the sages had a strong psychological need to justify to themselves that they were indeed entitled to the respect and consideration due to their assumed status. They had to show "evidence" that they were making satisfactory progress in the direction expected of them. In this regard, the empirical emphasis of the Ch'eng-Chu formula for self-cultivation did not seem to satisfy their psychological need as much as the idealistic Lu-Yang tradition. The Ch'eng-Chu approach did not provide for a readily applicable criterion for measuring the progress of the student in self-cultivation. The long-range goal of attaining sagehood was beyond the reach of most mortals. The short-range goal of *pien-hua ch'i-chih* (transformation of the physical endowment of men) was vaguely defined and difficult to verify. In any case it did not have the psychological impact of the mystical experience that accompanied "enlightenment" (*wu*) in the Lu-Yang tradition. People who had the inner assurance of "enlightenment" were convinced that they belonged to the community of the elect. They did not need any other assurances; they had something akin to the baptism of the Holy Spirit.

This line of speculation is borne out by the course of Chinese intellectual history. There is no question that during the Yüan, Ming and Ch'ing period, the Ch'eng-Chu school represented the orthodox Neo-Confucian tradition. Being the orthodox tradition, however, does not guarantee it a preponderant role in shaping the conscious mind of the scholars. This is because what the Ch'eng-Chu school contributed to the Neo-Confucian tradition, viz. doctrines on government and ethics, had been mostly absorbed into the official ideology and as such became the axioms of thought in the conduct of private and public life, thus effectively removed from the sphere of conscious debate and dissent. It was only in the sphere of self-cultivation that Neo-Confucian ideas continued to excite controversy. In the latter sphere, the influence of the Ch'eng-Chu school was often overshadowed by that of Lu Chiu-yüan and Yang Chien. This Lu-Yang tradition found a worthy successor in the Ming idealist Wang Yang-ming (1472–1529). Wang's terminology was slightly different but his message was the same. Like the striving for enlightenment in the Lu-Yang tradition, Wang's doctrines centered around the necessity of introspective, intuitive learning, "striving for the innate goodness" as he called it.[77] Under his pervasive influence, the quest for the mystical experience of "attaining the innate goodness" became a prominent motif in Ming intellectual life. Not unexpectedly, this emphasis on introspective, intuitive learning gave rise to abuses such as an arrogance towards other forms of learning, and a nonchalent

[77] For the philosophy of Wang Yang-ming, see Frederick G. Henke, *The Philosophy of Wang Yang-ming* (London, Open House Publishing House: 1916); also Wing-tsit Chan, *Instructions for Practical Living and Other Neo-Confucian Writings* (Columbia University Press: 1963).

attitude towards the constraints of conventional morality (*li*) as the marked decline of classical scholarship and the phenomenon of the so-called "Wildcat Ch'an School" attested.[78]

Just as *tao-hsüeh* excesses during the Southern Sung period provoked the reaction that Yeh Shih exemplified, so the excesses of the self-styled followers of Wang Yang-ming provoked the reaction of the empiricists (Han Learning) during the early years of the Ch'ing period.[79] From the point of view of the early Ch'ing empiricist scholars such as Huang Tsung-hsi (1610–1695) and Ku Yen-wu (1613–1682), the obsession of Ming scholar-officials with metaphysical issues was responsible for the disarray in government affairs resulting in the collapse of the Ming dynasty and the Manchu conquest of China. To counteract the undesirable legacy of the Ming period, they sought to encourage empiricist learning, putting a premium on subjects that had an immediate bearing on the task of government (*ching-shih* learning). Later on when the original impetus of *ching-shih* learning was spent by the middle of the Ch'ing period, Han Learning gained a new accession of strength by espousing a new reason for scholarship—the quest of learning for the sake of learning. Inspired by this ideal, scholars of the empiricist research school (*k'ao-cheng hsüeh*) such as Hui Tung (1697–1758) and Tai Chen (1724–1777) achieved admirable results in philology, phonology, textual criticism, and epigraphy. Through their cumulative efforts, we are able to read the classics today with greater confidence in the fidelity of the text and accuracy of the annotations.

For both Yeh Shih and the early Ch'ing scholars, their commitment to utilitarian learning was prompted or accompanied by a clearly definable academic position — stout opposition to the hitherto prevalent idealism. It may be observed that despite the sound and fury of the early Ch'ing scholars against the excesses of Wang Yang-ming's school, (for example, the sarcastic remarks of Li Kung,) they seldom went as far as Yeh Shih in their critique of the Sung learning, of which *tao-hsüeh* was the most significant part. Most of the early Ch'ing scholars were indeed out of sympathy with the learning prevalent in the Ming period, and sought to go back to a more congenial past for inspiration. In this back-to-antiquity movement, a few halted at the Sung period, satisfied with the comprehensive scholarship of Chu Hsi. The majority went beyond the Sung period to the great masters of the Han period, hence the

[78] The phenomenon is well exemplified by Li Chih (1527–1602). See Kung-ch'üan Hsiao, "Li Chih: an Iconoclast of the Sixteenth Century", in *T'ien-hsia Monthly* 6 (1938), pp. 317–341.

[79] For a concise account of the development of Han Learning, see Liang Ch'i-ch'ao, *Intellectual Trends in the Ch'ing Period*, trans. by Emmanual C.Y. Hsu (Harvard University Press: 1959).

name Han Learning. Few, however, saw the necessity of carrying the doubting spirit beyond the authorities of the Han masters to the immediate disciples of Confucius, as Yeh Shih did.

Conclusion

IN THE introductory chapter of this book, I pointed out that China's relatively early headstart in attaining the basic features of modern society was not followed by sustained socio-economic development, as that which characterized early modern times in Western Europe. This observation set the stage for an inquiry into the nature of the forces that tended to resist societal change as well as those that tended to promote it.[1] Falling into the former category were China's bureaucratic tradition and the Confucian ideology; in the latter, the *hui-fu* ideology and the perception of the dynastic cycle.

China's bureaucratic tradition and the Confucian ideology were treated as independent variables in the introductory chapter. I dealt with them separately because I meant to pursue a line of investigation with regard to the potentialities of Confucianism as the ideological basis of Chinese culture. I put forth the hypothesis that at a time when Confucianism itself was in a state of flux, there was a distinct possibility that it could have evolved into an innovative force and provide the needed ideological sanction for the process of change in Chinese society. That possibility did not materialize. The intellectual ferment that characterized the Northern Sung Confucian revival was cut short by the authoritarian state under the control of partisan politics. A significant part of the Northern Sung heritage did survive the literary inquisition and blossom during the Southern Sung period, viz. *tao-hsüeh*. In its heyday, the teaching of *tao-hsüeh* masters doubtless had reinvigorating, challenging effects on Chinese culture and in its doctrine of *tao-t'ung* (legitimate succession of sagely teachers) provided a mechanism for legitimating the re-interpretation of traditional ideas to accommodate to a changing world. However, as I suggested in Chapter Eight, the

---

[1] In my explanation of the stability of traditional Chinese society, I follow a straightforward, non-technical approach, with emphasis on the absence of incentives for change. S.N. Eisenstadt, in his comparative study of bureaucratic empires, approaches the subject from the political scientist viewpoint, using a sophisticated conceptual framework. He asserts that traditional Chinese society persisted for almost two thousand years without major structural changes because most of the changes that occurred in Chinese society were of what he calls the "accommodable type". See S.N. Eisenstadt, *The Political System of Empires: The Rise and Fall of the Historical Bureaucratic Societies* (Free Press, Glencoe: 1963).

doctrine of *tao-t'ung* quietly faded into the background with the passing of the great *tao-hsüeh* masters of the Southern Sung, and with their passing away the principle of legitimation was permanently left in abeyance. The era of innovation and original thinking was over and *tao-hsüeh* henceforth no more than a conservative force.

Having ceased to have any leavening effect on Chinese culture, *tao-hsüeh* in fact became a powerful deterrent against change. To be sure, *tao-hsüeh* scholars were normally not satisfied with the drift of contemporay politics or the tenor of popular customs. However, their ideal world order was not in fundamental conflict with contemporary reality — it was little more than a rationalization or idealization of the latter. They had in mind a world order, in which the scholar-official class was the center of attention, the norm for all self-respecting men. In so far as the scholar-official class was the political and cultural elite of Chinese society in Sung and subsequent dynasties, *tao-hsüeh* may be said to have provided a strong sanction for the *status quo*.

Thanks to the operation of the civil service examination, the *tao-hsüeh* norm was diffused throughout Chinese society. Starting with T'ang times when examinations were held on a regular basis, the examination system was available to the population at large as a channel of upward mobility. By Ming and Ch'ing times with the introduction of the *sheng-yüan* and *chü-jen* degrees which rewarded success at the lower reaches of the examination system, more and more people were aware of the opportunities for self-advancement that the system provided.[2] Awareness of these opportunities diminished the psychological distance between social classes and made it easier for men in humble circumstances to identify, or have a sense of solidarity, with their social superiors. As the research of Professor Ping-ti Ho indicates,[3] there was no lack in real life of this kind of vicarious identification. For instance, a washerwoman or a wet-nurse secretly hoped that her own son would one day pass the examination and take his place among the gentlemen whom she currently served. To this end, she would instruct her son in the ways of gentlemen such as love of book-learning, and a patronizing attitude towards other professions. Thus the value-system of gentlemen percolated down to the masses. There was hardly any social class or occupational group who were not brought under the sway of the official ideology. As a consequence, the talents and energies of the entire people were channelled into the scholar-official norm of success.

[2] For a definitive description of the Ming and Ch'ing examination system and its impact on social mobility, see Ping-ti Ho, *The Ladder of Success in Imperial China* (Columbia University Press: 1962), particularly ch. 1.

[3] Ping-ti Ho, *op. cit.*, ch. 2.

The wide acceptance of the scholar-official norm was undoubtedly the strongest buttress for traditional Chinese society. It prevented the rise of rival classes with their own value-systems. The merchants of China did not develop into a Western-style bourgeoisie because, among other things, there were no effective barriers against their participation in the universal norm. Enterprising individuals from the mercantile communities were thus more likely to seek advancement for themselves or for their sons in a scholar-official career.[4] Having cast their lot with the universal norm, their talent was lost to the mercantile communities. A major reason why trade and industries did not outgrow their traditional limits in Chinese society was because of the absence of a definite social class who staked their sense of worth on mercantile activities. The traditional pattern of life, the mundane expression of the *tao-hsüeh* world order, was therefore unlikely to be challenged by the non-elite classes.

Nor were the scholar-official elite likely to threaten the permanence of the traditional pattern of life. Being the beneficiaries of the system, considered as a group, they could not be expected to do anything that would jeopardize their stake in the establishment. Regardless of their consciously proclaimed ideals, the guiding principle in their actions was obviously the preservation of their vested interests. In the Southern Sung context, this preoccupation de-fused the *hui-fu* ideology, rendering it inoperative; concern for national and territorial integrity had to give way to concern for self-preservation. The same preoccupation also warped their perception of the reality of dynastic decline, reducing their ability to cope with it. Neither the challenge of barbarian presence in the country nor the prospect of social and economic disaster was able to stir them to action.

Their inertia in the face of a strong challenge from both within and without Chinese society provides a clue to their pattern of behavior in subsequent dynasties. Prizing immediate security above all other considerations, they showed an unsusceptibility to the call of nationalism (or racism). Collaboration with the alien conquerors of China was the appropriate course of action if such collaboration was required to preserve their vested interests.[5] The same goes for their attitude towards regimes founded as a consequence of peasant rebellions. On their part,

[4] See a classic study of these mercantile communities by Ping-ti Ho, "The Salt Merchants of Yangchou: A Study of Commercial Capitalism in Eighteenth Century China", in *Harvard Journal of Asiatic Studies*, vol. 17 (1954), pp. 130–168.

[5] For the extent of Southern Sung collaboration with the Mongol conquerors, see Meng Ssu-ming, *op. cit.* For Ming officials' collaboration with the Manchu conquerors, see Franz Michael, *The Origin of Manchu Rule in China* (Johns Hopkins University Press: 1942).

the imperial masters of China, either of alien or indigenous origins, could not dispense with the service of the scholar-officials as administrators or moral leaders of the masses. In the absence of a viable alternative to the imperial bureaucratic system for organizing the political and social life of China, which the alien conquerors or successful leaders of peasant rebellions could not provide, the scholar-officials could not be knocked down from their pedestal in Chinese society. Like a statue on a pedestal, they survived best by not doing anything exceptional.

Apart from the class situation of the scholar-officials which has been seen to operate as a deterrent against change in Chinese society, it may be surmised that their conscious mind also operated to the same effect. Their thoughts were to a great extent shaped by the civil service examination. There is no question that examination candidates were quick to accommodate to the political or ideological prejudices of the faction in power. During the reign of Emperor Shen-tsung when Wang An-shih was in control, scholars held his "New Learning" in high esteem; however, when the Conservatives gained the upper hand during the succeeding reign, they hastened to parade their knowledge of Ssu-ma Kuang's writings.[6] It was customary for commercial firms to print and circulate widely the papers of the successful candidates of each triennial examinations.[7] A collection of these examination papers which differed markedly in tone or ideological emphasis from the papers of the preceding triennual examination was an unmistakable sign that a major power struggle in court had been resolved in favor of a new dominant faction.[8] Nevertheless, factional struggles accompanied by clearly identifiable ideological issues were rare in Chinese history. In any event, examination candidates were isolated from the real sancta of power where the decision-making process originated. Without access to up-to-date information on the exact ideological complexion of the court, they generally preferred to avoid making statements of contemporary import. Nor would high government officials want the examination candidates to poke closely into court politics. Prudence dictated for both candidates and the men who set examination papers that they

[6] The Northern Sung scholar, Pi Chung-yu specifically drew attention to this phenomenon in a memorial to Emperor Che-tsung, in Hsi-t'ai chi 1, "Ko-chang tsou-chuang".

[7] See Chu Ch'uan-yu, Sung-tai hsin-wen shih, ch. 5, section 5, "Ch'eng-wen" (Examination Essays).

[8] A case in point was Wang Shih-peng who headed the list of successful examination candidates in the palace examination of 1157, one year after the death of the powerful Prime Minister Ch'in Kuei. Vehemently denouncing the evils of power-usurpation by ambitious ministers, in his examination paper Wang called upon the emperor to reassert his authority. See Mei-ch'i Wang hsien-sheng wen-chi, hou chi 29, his own tomb inscription.

steered clear of controversial topics. The desire to dwell on politically innocuous themes explained the popularity of Wang An-shih's philological works during the ascendancy of the Reform Faction. By the same token, with the establishment of *tao-hsüeh* as the state orthodoxy since the waning days of the Southern Sung period, it was the politically innocuous part of *tao-hsüeh* learning, viz. classical exegesis and metaphysics that became the major concern of examination candidates. For the latter's convenience, the state in Ming times published a definitive version of *tao-hsüeh* metaphysics, *Hsing-li ta-ch'üan* (The Complete Compendium of Statements on Universal Principles and Human Nature).[9]

The philological-moral platitudes that scholars absorbed in preparing for examinations undoubtedly had some effect on their individual view of the world. It is not unreasonable to assume that many of them consciously reacted, in a manner not dissimilar to Yeh Shih, to the *tao-hsüeh* notion of history which viewed all imperial dynasties after the sagely Three Dynasties as corrupt. Like Yeh Shih they probably saw nothing worthy of emulation in the achievements of the greatest imperial dynasties, the T'ang and the Sung. If that was indeed the case there would be no incentive for change because no viable alternative to the *status quo* existed. The wide dissemination of this attitude was no doubt a strong reinforcement of the inertia to which the scholar-official class was naturally prone.

[9] According to *Ssu-k'u ch'üan-shu tsung-mu* 93, ju-chia 3, *Hsing-li ta-ch'üan* was comprised of seventy *chüan* and compiled in accordance with an imperial edict in 1415 by Hu Kuang *et al.*

Glossary

An Lu-shan　安祿山

Cha-tzu　箚子
Ch'ai　柴
Chang Chieh　章傑
Chang Chiu-ch'eng　張九成
Chang Chün　張浚
Chang Lai　張耒
Chang Liang　張良
Chang Shih　張栻
Chang Tsai　張載
Chang Tun　章惇
chao-ching-lang　朝請郎
Chao Hsiung　趙雄
Chao Ju-tang　趙汝譡
Chao Ju-yü　趙汝愚
Chao Kuan-chia　趙官家
Chao Ting　趙鼎
che-chung　折衷
Che-hsi　浙西
che-pi　折帛
Che-tsung　哲宗
Che-tung　浙東
Chekiang　浙江
chen　眞
chen　鎭
chen-fu-shih　鎭撫使
Chen Hsi-shan　眞西山
Chen Te-hsiu　眞德秀
Ch'en Chün-chü　陳君舉
Ch'en Fu-liang　陳傳良
Ch'en-kuan　貞觀
Ch'en Liang　陳亮
Ch'en Shih-tao　陳師道
Ch'en Ssu-ch'eng　陳思誠

Ching-ssu　景思
Ch'en Tung-fu　陳同甫
Cheng Ching-wang　鄭景望
Cheng-meng　正蒙
Cheng-ming　正名
Cheng Po-hsiung　鄭伯熊
ch'eng　誠
ch'eng-chieh-lang　承節郎
Ch'eng-Chu　程朱
Ch'eng Hao　程灝
　Ming-tao　明道
Ch'eng I　程頤
　I-ch'uan　伊川
ch'eng i-chia-yen　成一家言
ch'eng-wen　程文
chi　極
chi-chu　集注
chi-kang　紀綱
ch'i　氣
Ch'i (Mount)　岐(山)
ch'i-chih　氣質
ch'i-min　齊民
Chia Ssu-tao　賈似道
Chia-ting　嘉定
Chiang-Huai chih-chih shih　江淮
　制置使
Chiang-ling　江陵
Chiang-nan　江南
ch'iang-kan jo-chih　强幹弱枝
chiao-wang kuo-cheng　矯枉過正
chieh-tu-ssu　節度使
chien-chü　薦舉
Chien-ning　建寧
chien-ping　兼併
chien-ping chih chia　兼併之家

chien-ssu 監司
Ch'ien I 錢乙
Ch'ien-lü ts'e 千慮策
chih-chü 制舉
chih-tu 制度
ch'ih 治
Chin 晉
Chin 金
Chin-chou 蘄州
Chin-chüan 進卷
chin-chün 禁軍
Chin-hua 金華
Chin-ssu lu 近思錄
Chin-yang 晉陽
Ch'in 秦
ch'in-cheng 親征
Ch'in Kuei 秦檜
Ch'in Shih-huang-ti 秦始皇帝
Ching-k'ang 靖康
ching-shih 京師
ching-shih 經世
ching-shih 經史
Ching T'ang 京鏜
Ching-ti 景帝
ching-t'ien 井田
ching-tsung-chih ch'ien 經總制錢
Ch'ing 青
Ch'ing-chou 荊州
Ch'ing-hsiang 荊襄
ch'ing-miao ch'ien 青苗錢
Ch'ing-yüan 慶元
Ch'iu Chung 邱崇
ch'iung-li 窮理
Cho-ku lun 酌古論
Chou Hsing-chih 周行己
chou-hsüeh 州學
Chou-i 周易
Chou-li 周禮
Chou-li ting-i 周禮訂義
Chou Nan 周南
Chou Nan-chung 周南仲
Chou Pi-ta 周必大

Chou Tun-i 周敦頤
    Lien-hsi 濂溪
Chu Hsi 朱熹
chu-hu 主戶
Chu-ko Liang 諸葛亮
Ch'u 楚
Chü-chou 衢州
chü-jen 舉人
Ch'ü-li 曲禮
Ch'ü Yüan 屈原
chuan-men chih-hsüeh 專門之學
chuan-yün p'an-kuan 轉運判官
ch'uan-hsin 傳心
chüan 卷
ch'üan 權
Ch'üan-chou 泉州
Ch'üan-fu 泉府
ch'üan-hsüan 銓選
Ch'üan Tsu-wang 全祖望
Chuang-tzu 莊子
Ch'un-ch'iu 春秋
chün-hsien 郡縣
chün-tzu 君子
chung 忠
Chung-hsing wu-lun 中興五論
Chung-tu 中都
Chung-yu 沖佑
Chung-yung 中庸

en 雁

fa 法
fa-tu 法度
Fa-tu tsung-lun 法度總論
Fan Ch'eng-ta 范成大
Fan Chung-yen 范仲淹
Fan Yü 范育
feng-chien 封建
Feng Ch'uan-chih 馮傳之
Fu Hsi 伏羲
fu-ku 復古
fu-ping 府兵

fu-yu t'ien-hsia 富有天下
Fukien 福建

Hai-ling 海陵
Han 漢
Han Hu 韓滹
Han Shih-chung 韓世忠
Han T'o-chou 韓侂冑
Han Wu-ti 漢武帝
Han Yü 韓愈
Hangchow 杭州
hao 號
hao 蒿
Hao-chou 濠州
hao-jan chih-ch'i 浩然之氣
hao-min 豪民
Heng-shan 橫山
Ho 和
ho-mai 和買
Ho Tan 何澹
Hou-tsung 後總
Hsi 羲
Hsi Hsia 西夏
Hsi-hsüeh chi-yen hsü-mu 習學
　記言序目
hsiang 鄉
hsiang-chün 廂軍
hsiang-shuo 詳說
Hsiang Yü 項羽
Hsiao-tsung 孝宗
hsien-liang fang-cheng 賢良方正
Hsien-sheng 憲聖
Hsien-yün 獫狁
hsin 心
hsin-cheng 新政
Hsin Ch'i-chi 辛棄疾
hsin-ch'uan 心傳
hsin-hsüeh 新學
Hsin-shu 新書
hsin-tang 新黨
Hsin T'ang-shu 新唐書
hsing 性

hsing-chuang 行狀
Hsing-li ta-ch'üan 性理大全
hsing-ming 性命
hsiu-ch'i 修齊
Hsiung-nu 匈奴
Hsü 徐
hsü-fa 序發
Hsü I 徐誼
hsü-li 胥吏
Hsü Shen 許慎
Hsü Tzu-ch'ih t'ung-chien
　ch'ang-pien 續資治通鑑長編
Hsüan-jen 宣仁
Hsüeh Chi-hsüan 薛季宣
Hsüeh Ching-shih 薛景石
　Shan 山
　Jen-ching 仁靜
Hsün-tzu 荀子
Hsün-yü 獯鬻
Hu An-kuo 胡安國
Hu Chün-ming 胡浚明
Hu Hüng 胡紘
Hu I 胡沂
hu-jen 胡人
Hu shang-shu tsou-i hsü 胡尚書
　奏議序
Hu T'ai-ch'u 胡太初
Hu Yin 胡寅
Hu Yüan 胡瑗
hua-hsia 華夏
Hua-yen 華嚴
Huai 淮
Huai-hsi 淮西
Huai-tung 淮東
Huai-tung tsung-ling chün-ma
　ch'ien-liang 淮東總領軍馬錢糧
Huang-chi ching-shih shu 皇極
　經世書
Huang Kan 黃幹
Huang-ti 黃帝
Huang T'ing-chien 黃庭堅
　Shan-ku 山谷

Huang Tsung-hsi 黃宗羲
Huang Tu 黃度
hui-fu 恢復
hui-i 會意
Hui-tsung 徽宗
Hui Tung 惠棟
huo yu tse ts'ai-hsiang yüeh 或有
責宰相曰

i 意
i 義
I-ching 易經
i-fa 義法
i-li 義理
i-ti 夷狄
I Yin 伊尹

jen 人
Jen-tsung 仁宗
Jih-lu 日錄
ju-lin 儒林
Jürchen 女眞

K'ai-feng 開封
k'ai-ho 開闔
K'ai-hsi 開禧
K'ai-pao 開寶
kan-pan kung-shih 幹辦公事
Kao-tsung 高宗
Kao Ling-jen 高令人
Kao Yao 皐陶
k'ao-cheng hsüeh 考證學
ke-wu 格物
k'e-chi fu-li 克己復禮
Kiangnan 江南
k'o-chü 科舉
Kou Chien 勾踐
kuan-hu 官戶
ku-wen 古文
Ku-wen Shang-shu 古文尚書
Ku Yen-wu 顧炎武
kuan-chia 官家

Kuan-chung 關中
Kuang-tsung 光宗
Kuang-yao 光堯
Kung Mou-liang 龔茂良
Kung-shou 弓手
K'ung Li 孔鯉
kuo-shih 國史
Kuo-shih yüan 國史院
kuo-tzu ssu-yeh 國子司業
Kwangtung 廣東

lang-chung 郎中
Lao-tzu 老子
li 禮
Li-chi 禮記
li-ch'i 理氣
Li Chih-ts'ai 李之才
Li Chung-chü 李仲舉
Li Hsin-ch'üan 李心傳
Li Kuang 李光
Li Pi 李璧
li-pu 吏部
Li Shih-chen 李時珍
Li-tai chih-tu hsiang-shuo 歷代
制度詳說
Li Tao 李燾
Li-tse shu-yüan 麗澤書院
Li T'ung 李桐
Liang-Che 兩浙
Liang-Huai 兩淮
Liang-Kwang 兩廣
Lin Cheng-chung 林正仲
Lin Li 林栗
Lin Tse-hsü 林則徐
lien-san 歛散
Liu Chih-chi 劉知機
Liu Hou-ts'un 劉後村
Liu K'ai 柳開
Liu Pang 劉邦
Liu Pei 劉備
Liu Shu 劉恕
Liu Tsai 劉宰

Liu Ts'ai-shao 劉才邵
Liu Yü 劉愈
Lo 洛
Lo Ken-che 羅根澤
Lo Ts'ang-yen 羅宗彥
Lou Yüeh 樓鑰
Lu 虜
Lu Chiu-yüan 陸九淵
Lu Jih-hsin 盧日新
Lu Tien 陸佃
Lu Yu 陸游
Lü Chen-yü 呂振羽
Lü Tsu-ch'ien 呂祖謙
Lü Tsu-t'ai 呂祖泰
Lung-ch'uan chi 龍川集
Lung-ch'üan 龍泉

Ma Kuang-tsu 馬光祖
Mao Tun 冒頓
men-fa 門閥
Meng Ching-tzu 孟敬子
Meng-tzu 孟子
mi-shu lang 秘書郎
ming 名
ming 命
Ming ch'en yen-hsing lu 名臣
　言行錄
ming-ch'i 名器
mo-k'an 磨勘
mou 畝
mu-chih ming 墓誌銘

nei-tsang-k'u 內藏庫
Nieh Ch'ung-ch'i 聶崇岐
nien-p'u 年譜
Ning-tsung 寧宗

Ou-yang Hsiu 歐陽修

pa 霸
Pan Ku 班固
P'an Ching-yü 潘景愈

p'an-kuan 判官
pao-chia 保甲
Pen-ts'ao kang-mu 本草綱目
p'eng 蓬
pi-chi 筆記
pien 變
pien-hua ch'i-chih 變化氣質
pien-wen 駢文
Pin 豳
P'ing-yang 平陽
po 伯
po t'ung lun lei t'ung ku chin chih
　pien 博通倫類通古今之變
(Prince) Chia 嘉
P'u-san K'uei 僕散揆

San-ching hsin-i 三經新義
San-kuo chi 三國誌
San Tai 三代
Shan-yüan 澶淵
shang-shu tso-hsüan lang-kuan
　尚書左選郎宮
Shao-sheng 紹聖
Shao Shuo-chi 晁說之
Shao Yung 邵雍
she-ts'ang 社倉
Shen Pu-hai 申不害
Shen Tao 愼到
shen-tao pei 神道碑
Shen-tsung 神宗
Sheng-chiang (Gate) 生薑
sheng-hsüeh 聖學
sheng-yüan 生員
shih 石
shih 實
shih 師
shih 勢
shih 史
Shih-chi 史記
shih-fu 詩賦
Shih Hao 史浩
Shih-huo 食貨

shih-i 史議
Shih-i 十翼
shih-i 市易
Shih-lu yüan 實錄院
Shih Mi-yüan 史彌遠
shih-mou 實謀
shih-p'ing 史評
Shih-t'ung 史通
shou-i ts'ao-lang 授儀漕郎
shu 恕
Shu (King of) 舒
Shu-ching 書經
Shu-Han 蜀漢
shu-shu 術數
shu-yüan 書院
shuai hsing 率性
Shun 舜
Soochow 蘇州
ssu 似
Ssu-k'u ch'üan-shu 四庫全書
Ssu-k'u ch'üan-shu ti-yao 四庫
　全書提要
Ssu-ma Ch'ien 司馬遷
Ssu-ma I 司馬懿
Ssu-ma Kuang 司馬光
Ssu-ming 四明
ssu-nan 四難
ssu-pu 四部
ssu-tuan 四端
ssu-t'un chu ta-ping 四屯駐大兵
Su Che 蘇轍
Su chüeh 宿覺
Su Hsün 蘇洵
Su Shih (Tung-po) 蘇軾(東坡)
sui-pi 隨筆
Sun Chih-hung 孫之宏
Sun Ch'üan 孫權
Sun Fu 孫復
Sun I-yen 孫依言
Sung Chi 宋祁
Sung hui-yao chi-kao 宋會要輯稿
Sung wen-chien 宋文鑑

Szechwan 四川

Ta-hsüeh 大學
tai-shih 待時
Tai-yü chi 待遇集
T'ai-ch'ang 太常
T'ai-ch'ang ssu 太常寺
t'ai-chi 太極
t'ai-hsüeh 太學
t'ai-hsüeh cheng 太學正
T'ai-tsu 太祖
T'ai-yüan 太原
T'ang 湯
T'ang Keng 唐庚
T'ang shih i yü chih yü nung
　唐始一寓之於農
T'ang T'ai-tsung 唐太宗
tao 道
tao-hsüeh 道學
Tao Hung-ching 陶宏景
Tao-te ching 道德經
tao-t'i 道體
tao-t'ung 道統
tao wen hsüeh 道問學
T'ao Chu-kung 陶朱公
ti-kung lang 廸功郎
t'i-chü 提舉
T'ien-hsi 天禧
t'ien-hu 佃戶
t'ien-ming 天命
t'ien-ming chih wei hsing 天命
　之爲性
T'ien-t'ai 天台
ting-hai 丁亥
Ting Shao-chan 丁少詹
Tsa-shuo 雜說
Ts'ai Ching 蔡京
Ts'ai Pi-sheng 蔡必勝
Ts'ai Yüan-ting 蔡元定
ts'an-chih cheng-shih 參知政事
ts'an-i 參議
Ts'ao Hsün 曹勛

ts'ao-shih 漕試
Ts'ao Ts'ao 曹操
tse-chung 折衷
ts'e-lun 策論
Tseng Kung 曾鞏
Tseng-tzu 曾子
Tso-chuan 左傳
tsu-tsung 祖宗
tsun te hsing 尊德性
tsun Yao 尊堯
Tsung-i 總義
tsung-ling chün-ma ch'ien-liang
  總領軍馬錢糧
tsung-ling so 總領所
Tsung-lun chiang-hsüeh ta-chih
  總論講學大旨
Tu 杜
Tu-shih kuan-chien 讀史管見
tu-tieh 道牒
t'u-ping 土兵
t'ui-kuan 推官
Tung Cho 董卓
Tung-lai po-i 東萊博議
T'ung-shu 通書
T'ung-tien 通典
Tzu-ch'ih t'ung-chien 資治通鑑
Tzu-hsia 子夏
Tzu-shuo 字說
Tzu-ssu 子思

Wai-kao 外稿
wan-wu chieh pei yü wo 萬物皆
  備於我
Wan-yen shu 萬言書
wang 王
Wang An-shih 王安石
Wang Chih 王質
Wang Huai 王淮
Wang Po 汪勃
Wang Shih-p'ing 王十朋
Wang Tsao 汪藻
Wang Yang-ming 王陽明

Wang Yü-chih 王與之
Wei 濰
Wei 魏
Wei Cheng 魏徵
wei-hsüeh 偽學
Wei Liao-weng 魏了翁
Wen 文
Wen-chou 溫州
Wen-ti 文帝
Wu 吳
wu 物
wu 悟
Wuchang 武昌
wu-chi 無極
Wu Chü 吳琚
Wu-i 武夷
wu-li 物理
wu pu-k'o 五不可
Wu-shang 烏傷
Wu Ta-shou 吳大受
Wu Tzu-liang 吳子良
Wu Yung 吳泳

Yang Chien 楊堅
Yang Chien 楊簡
  Tz'u-hu 慈湖
Yang Shih 楊時
Yangtze 揚子
Yang Wan-li 楊萬里
Yao 堯
Yao Ying 姚穎
Yeh Kuang-tsu 葉光祖
Yeh Kung-ch'i 葉公濟
Yeh Shih 葉適
  Cheng-tse 正則
  Shui-hsin 水心
Yelü Chu-ts'ai 耶律楚材
Yen-ch'i 剡谿
yen-chiang chih-chi-shih 沿江
  制置使
yen-hai chih-chi-ssu 沿海制置司
Yen Hsü-hsin 顏虛心

Yen Yüan　顏淵
yin　蔭
Yu Chung-hung　游仲鴻
yu tse ts'ai-hsiang yüeh　有責宰
　相曰
Yu Tso　游酢
yü-lu　語錄
yü-ping yü-nung　寓兵於農
Yü Yün-wen　虞允文
Yüan Chi-kao　袁季皐
Yüan Tao-chien　袁道潔

Yüan-yu　元佑
Yüan-yu t'ang-jen　元佑黨人
Yü　禹
yüeh　樂
Yüeh　越
Yüeh-chou　越州
Yüeh Fei　岳飛
Yüeh K'o　岳柯
Yung-chia　永嘉
Yung-k'ang　永康

Bibliography

Primary Sources

Chang Lai 張耒, *K'o-shan chi* 柯山集, TSCC ed.

Chang Tsai 張載, *Chang-tzu ch'üan-shu* 張子全書, SPPY ed.

Chang Chih-tung 張之洞, *Chang Wen-hsiang kung ch'üan-chi* 張文襄公全集, Ch'u-hsüeh ching-lu 楚學精盧 ed.

Chen Te-hsiu 眞德秀, *Hsi-shan hsien-sheng wen-chi* 西山先生文集, SPTK ed.

Ch'en Fu-liang 陳傅良, *Chih-chai hsien-sheng wen-chi* 止齋先生文集, SPTK ed.

———, *Yung-chia hsien-sheng pa-mien feng* 永嘉先生八面鋒 (Eight Cutting Edges), ed. with the colophon of Yamaga Hironobu 山家博信, 1830.

Ch'en Liang 陳亮, *Ch'en Lung-ch'uan chi* 陳龍川集, SPPY ed.

Ch'en Shih-tao 陳師道, *Hou-shan hsien-sheng chi* 後山先生集, woodblock ed. of 1885.

Chiang Yu-ching 江畬經, comp., *Li-tai hsiao-shuo pi-chi hsüan* 歷代小說筆記選, Hong Kong, Commercial Press.

Chin-shih 金史, Po-na 百衲 ed.

Ch'ing-yüan t'iao-fa shih-lei 慶元條法事類, Yenching University Library ed.: 1948.

Chu Hsi 朱熹, *Chu Wen-chung kung wen-chi* 朱文忠公文集, SPTK ed.

———, *Wu-chao ming-ch'en yen-hsing lu* 五朝名臣言行錄, SPTK ed.

Chu I-tsun 朱彝尊, *Ching-i k'ao* 經義考, SPPY ed.

Ch'ü-wei chiu-wen 曲洧舊聞, TSCC ed.

Ch'eng I 頤程, *Erh-Ch'eng ch'üan-shu* 二程全書, SPPY ed.

Han Hu 韓淲, *Chien-ch'üan jih-chi* 澗泉日記, TSCC ed.

Ho-nan Shao-shih wen-chien hou-lu 河南邵氏聞見後錄, TSCC ed.

Han Yüan-chi 韓元吉, *Nan-chien chia-i kao* 南澗甲乙稿, TSCC ed.

Hsin Ch'i-chi 辛棄疾, *Chia-hsüan shih-wen ch'ao-ts'un* 稼軒詩文鈔存, ed. by Hsin Ch'i-t'ai 辛啓泰, revised by Teng Kuang-ming 鄧廣銘, Hong Kong, Hai-wai tu-shu fa-hsing kung-ssu 海外圖書發行公司: 1957.

Hsin T'ang-shu 新唐書, Po-na ed.

Hsüeh Chi-hsüan 薛季宣, *Lang-yü chi* 浪語集, Yung-chia ts'ung-shu ed.

Hu T'ai-chu 胡太初, *Tsou-lien hsü-lun* 晝簾緒論, TSCC ed.

Huang Kan 黃幹, *Huang Mien-chai hsien-sheng wen-chi* 黃勉齋先生文集, TSCC ed.

Huang Sung chung-hsing liang-chao sheng-cheng 皇宋中興兩朝聖政, Taiwan, Wen-hai ch'u-pan she 文海出版社 ed.

Huang Tsung-hsi 黃宗羲, *Sung-yüan hsüeh-an* (SYHA) 宋元學案, expanded version, Taipei, Chung-hua shu-chü ed.

Abbreviated version, ed. by Ch'en Shu-liang 陳叔諒 and Li Hsin-chuang 李心莊, Shanghai, Shih-chieh shu-chü, 1936.

Li Hsin-ch'üan 李心傳, *Chien-yen i-lai chao-yeh tsa-chih* 建炎以來朝野雜記, TSCC ed.

————, *Chien-yen i-lai hsi-nien yao-lu* 建炎以來繫年要錄 (Chronicles of Major Events since the Reign of Chien-yen), Taiwan, Wen-hai ch'u-pan she ed.

Li Kou 李覯, *Chih-chiang Li hsien-sheng wen-chi* 直講李先生文集, SPTK ed.

Li Kuang 李光, *Chuang-chien chi* 莊簡集, SKCSCP ed.

Li Tao 李燾, *Hsü Tzu-ch'ih t'ung-chien chang-pien* 續資治通鑑長編, Taipei, Shih-chieh shu-chü 世界書局 ed.

Liao Kang 廖剛, *Kao-feng wen-chi* 高峯文集, SKCSCP ed.

Liu Hou-ts'un 劉後村, *Hou-ts'un hsien-sheng ta-ch'üan chi* 後村先生大全集, SPTK ed.

Liu K'ai 柳開, *Ho-tung hsien-sheng chi* 河東先生集, SPTK ed.

Liu Tsai 劉宰, *Man-t'ang chi* 漫塘集, Chia-yeh t'ang ts'ung-shu ed.

Liu Ts'ai-shao 劉才邵, *Shan-ch'i chü-shih chi* 檆溪居士集, SKCSCP ed.

Lou Yüeh 樓鑰, *Kung-ku'ei chi* 攻媿集, SPTK ed.

Lu Tien 陸佃, *T'ao-shan chi* 陶山集, TSCC ed.

Lu Yu 陸游, *Fang-weng wen-chi* 放翁文集, Kuo-hsüeh chi-pen ts'ung-shu ed.

————, *Lao-hsüeh-an pi-chi* 老學庵筆記, TSCC ed.

Lü Tsu-ch'ien 呂祖謙, *Li-tai chih-tu hsiang-shuo* 歷代制度詳說, Hsü Chin-hua ts'ung-shu ed., 15 *chüan*.

————, *Tung-lai po-i* 東萊博議, Shanghai, Shih-chieh shu-chü revised ed.: 1947.

Pi Chung-yu 畢仲游, *Hsi-t'ai chi* 西臺集, TSCC ed.

Shao Shuo-chi 晁說之, *Sung-shan chi* 嵩山集, SPTK ed.

Shih Nai-an 施耐庵, *Shui-hu chuan* 水滸傳, Peking, Tso-chia ch'u-pan she ed.: 1960.

Ssu-k'u ch'üan-shu tsung-mu 四庫全書總目, Shanghai, Ta-tung shu-chü ed.

Ssu-ma Kuang 司馬光, *Wen-kuo Wen-cheng Ssu-ma kung chi* 溫國文正司馬公集, SPTK ed.

Su Che 蘇轍, *Luan-ch'eng ying-chao chi* 欒城應詔集, SPTK ed.

Su Chou 蘇籀, *Shuang-ch'i chi* 雙溪集, TSCC ed.

Su Hsün 蘇洵, *Chia-yu chi* 嘉祐集, SPTK ed.

Sun I-jang 孫詒讓, *Chou-kao shu-lin* 籀膏述林, Jui-an 瑞安: 1916 ed.

Sun I-yen 孫依言, comp., *Ou-hai i-wen* 甌海軼聞 (Anecdotes of the Ou-coast), Jui-an: 1886 ed.

Sung-hui-yao chi-kao 宋會要輯稿, Taipei, Shih-chieh shu-chü ed.

Sung Shih 宋史, Po-na ed.

SSCSPM *Sung-shih chi-shih pen-mo* 宋史紀事本末, Shanghai, Kuo-hsüeh chi-pen ts'ung-shu ed.

T'ang Keng 唐庚, *Mei-shan T'ang hsien-sheng wen-chi* 眉山唐先生文集, SPTK ed.

Ts'ao Hsün 曹勛, *Sung-yin chi* 松隱集, TSCC ed.

Tu Yu 杜佑, *T'ung-tien* 通典, Wan-yu wen-k'u ed.

Wang An-shih 王安石, *Chou-kuan hsin-i* 周官新義, TSCC ed.

————, *Lin-ch'uan chi* 臨川集, SPTK ed.

Wang Chih 王質, *Hsüeh-shan chi* 雪山集, TSCC ed.

Wang Shih-peng 王十朋, *Mei-ch'i Wang hsien-sheng wen-chi* 梅溪王先生文集, SPTK ed.

ang Tsao 汪藻, *Fou-ch'i chi* 浮溪集, SPTK ed.

Wang Ying-lin 王應麟, *K'un-hsüeh chi-wen* 困學紀聞, SPTK ed.
Wei Liao-weng 魏了翁, *Ho-shan hsien-sheng wen-chi* 鶴山先生文集, SPTK ed.
Wu Ching 吳儆, *Wu Wen-su-kung chi* 吳文肅公集, Ming woodblock ed.
Wu Yung 吳泳, *Ho-lin chi* 鶴林集, SKCSCP ed.
Yang Shih 楊時, *Yang Kuei-shan hsien-sheng chi* 楊龜山先生集, Kuang-hsü (1875–1907) woodblock ed.
Yeh Shih 葉適, *Hsi-hsüeh chi-yen hsü-mu* (HHCYHM) 習學記言序目, Ching-hsiang lou ts'ung-shu 敬鄉樓叢書.
————, *Yeh Shih chi* (YSC) 葉適集, ed. by Li Che-fu 李哲夫, Peking, Chung-hua shu-chü 中華書局: 1961.
————, *Yeh Shih chi pieh-chi* (YSC PC) 葉適集別集, ed. by Li Che-fu, Peking, Chung-hua shu-chü.
Yüeh K'o 岳柯, *T'ing-shih* 程史, SPTK ed.

Secondary Sources in Chinese and Japanese

Chao Tieh-han 趙鐵寒, "Sung-Chin hia-shang chih meng shih-mo chi" 宋金海上之盟始末記, *Ta-lu tsa-chih* 大陸雜誌 25:5–7 (1962).
Ch'en Yin-ko 陳寅恪, "Sui-T'ang chih-tu yüan-yüan lüeh-lun" 隋唐制度淵源略論, in *Ch'en Yin-ko hsien-sheng lun-chi* 陳寅恪先生論集, Taipei, Chung-yang yen-chiu yuan li-shih yü-yen yen-chiu so: 1971.
Chiang Fu-ts'ung 蔣復璁, "Sung-tai i-ko kuo-ts'e ti chien-t'ao" 宋代一個國策的檢討, *Ta-lu tsa-chih* 9:7 (1954), pp. 21–40
Chin Chung-shu 金中樞, "Pei-Sung k'o-chü chih-tu yen-chiu" 北宋科舉制度研究, *Hsin-ya hsüeh-pao* 新亞學報 6:1 (1964), pp. 165–242.
Chu Ch'uan-yü 朱傳譽, *Sung-tai hsin-wen shih* 宋代新聞史, Taipei, Chung-kuo hsüeh-shu chu-tso chiang-chu wei-yuan hui 中國學術著作獎助委員會: 1967.
Chung-kuo ts'ung-shu tsung-lu 中國叢書綜錄, 3 vols., ed. by Shanghai Tu-shu-kuan, published by Peking, Chung-hua shu-chü: 1959.
Fukuzawa Yokurō 福澤與九郎, "Sōdai chiho seiji ni kansuru ichi kanken" 宋代地方政治に關する一管見, *Tohōgaku* 東方學 19 (1959), pp. 63–76.
Higashi Kazuo 東一夫, *Ō Anseki shinpō no kenkyū* 王安石新法の研究, Kazama shobō 風間書房: 1971.
Hisatomi Ju 久富壽, "Nansō no zaisei to keisō seisen" 南宋の財政と經總制錢, *Hokudai shigaku* 北大史學 9 (1964), pp. 32–54.
Ho Yu-shen 何佑森, "Liang Sung hsüeh-feng ti ti-li fen-pu" 兩宋學風的地理分佈, *Hsin-ya hsüeh-pao* 1:1 (1955), pp. 331–379.
Ide Tatsurō 井手達郎, "Nansō jidai no hatsu'unshi oyobi ten'unshi in tsuite" 南宋時代の發運使及よび轉運使について, *Tōyō shigaku ronshū* 東洋史學論叢 3 (1954), pp. 50–72.
————, "Sōryō kō" 總領考, *Saitama daigaku kiyō* 琦玉大學紀要 5 (1956), pp. 22–32.
K'o Chang-i 柯昌頤, *Wang An-shih p'ing-chuan* 王安石評傳, Shanghai, Commercial Press: 1933.
Liang T'ien-hsi 梁天錫, "Sung-tai chih ssu-lu chih-tu" 宋代之寺祿制度, *Ta-lu tsa-chih* 29:2 (1964), pp. 14–26.
Lo Ch'iu-ch'ing 羅球慶, "Pei-Sung ping-chih yen-chiu" 北宋兵制研究, *Hsin-ya hsüeh-pao* 3:1 (1957), pp. 167–270.

Lo Ken-che 羅根澤, *Chung-kuo wen-hsüeh p'i-p'ing shih* 中國文學批評史, Shanghai, Ku-tien wen-hsüeh ch'u-pan she: 1961.

Masuda Tadao 增田忠雄, "Sōdai no chizu to minzoku undō" 宋代の地圖と民族運動, *Shirin* 史林 27 (1942), pp. 66–81.

Meng Ssu-ming 蒙思明, *Yüan-tai she-hui chieh-chi chih-tu* 元代社會階級制度, Peiping: 1938.

Mikami Tsugio 三上次, *Kindai seiji seido no kenkyū* 金代政治制度の研究, Chūō koron bijutsu shuppan: 1970.

Miyasaki Ichisada 宮崎市定, "Sōdai suken seido no yurai to sono tokusoku" 宋代州縣制度の由來とその特色, *Shirin* 36:2 (1953).

Morahashi Tetsuiji 諸橋轍次, *Jugaku no mokuteki to Soju Keireki shi Keigen hyaku rokushi nen kan no katsudo* 儒學の目的と宋儒慶曆至慶元百六十年間の活動, Taishukan 大修舘: 1929.

Mou Tsung-san 牟宗三, *Hsin-ti yü hsing-ti* 心體與性體, Taipei, Cheng-chung shu-chü 正中書局: 1968.

Nieh Ch'ung-ch'i 聶崇岐, "Sung-tai chih-chü k'ao-lüeh" 宋代制舉考略, *Shih-hsüeh nien-pao* 史學年報 2:5 (1938), pp. 17–37.

T'ao Hsi-sheng 陶希聖, "Pei-Sung chi-ko ta ssu-hsiang chia ti ching-t'ien lun" 北宋幾個大思想家的井田論, *Shih-huo* 食貨 2:6 (1935), pp. 35–38.

T'ao Jing-shen 陶晉生, *Chin Hai-ling Ti ti fa Sung yü Ts'ai-shih chan-i ti k'ao-shih* 金海陵帝的伐宋與采石戰役的考釋, Taipei, National Taiwan University: 1963.

Toyama Gunji 外山軍治, *Kindai shi kenkyū* 金代史研究, Kyōto, Tōyō shi kenkyū kai: 1964.

Umehara Kaoru 梅原郁, "Sōdai naisō to sasō" 宋代內藏と左藏, *Tōhō gakuhō* 東方學報 42 (1971), pp. 127–176.

Wang Chien-chiu 王建秋, *Sung-tai t'ai-hsüeh yü t'ai-hsüeh sheng* 宋代太學與太學生, Taipei: 1965.

Yamauchi Masahiro 山內正博, "Nansō chimbu shi kō" 南宋鎮撫使考, *Shien* 史淵 64 (1949), pp. 62–90.

———, "Nansō seiken no sui-i" 南宋政權の推移, Iwanami kōza *seikai rekishi* 岩波講座世界歷史, chūsei 中世 3, Iwanami shoten: 1970.

Yao Ts'ung-wu 姚從吾, "Nü-chen Han-hua ti fen-hsi" 女眞漢化的分析, *Ta-lu tsa-chih* 6:3 (1951).

Secondary Sources in Western Languages

Balazs, Etienne, *Chinese Civilization and Bureaucracy* (Yale University Press: 1964).

Bielenstein, Hans, "The Census of China during the Period 2–742 A.D.", in *Bulletin of the Museum of Far Eastern Antiquities*, vol. 19 (1947), pp. 125–163.

Catholic University of America, ed., *New Catholic Encyclopedia*, (McGraw Hill: 1967), 15 vols.

Chan, Wing-tsit, "Neo-Confucianism: New Idea in Old Terminologies", in *Philosophies East and West*, vol. 17, nos. 1–4.

Chang, Carson, *The Development of Neo-Confucian Thought*, vol. 1 (New Haven, United Printing Services: 1957).

Ch'i, Ch'ao-ting, *Key Economic Areas in Chinese History* (London, Allen & Unwin: 1936).

Chin-ssu lu, compiled by Chu Hsi and Lü Tsu-ch'ien, translated by Wing-tsit Chan as *Reflection on Things at Hand* (Columbia University Press: 1967).

Chow, Tse-chung, *May-fourth Movement* (Harvard University Press: 1960).

Creel, Herrlee G., *Confucius: The Man and the Myth* (John Day: 1949).

Crozier, Michel, *The Bureaucratic Phenomenon* (University of Chicago Press: 1964).

DeBary, William, "A Reappraisal of Neo-Confucianism", in Arthur F. Wright, ed., *Studies in Chinese Thought* (University of Chicago Press: 1953).

Eisenstadt, S.N., *The Political System of Empires: The Rise and Fall of Historical Bureaucratic Societies* (Glencoe, Free Press: 1963).

Franke, Herbert, "Chia Ssu-tao, Last Bad Prime Minister?" in *Confucian Personalities*.

———, "Treatise between Sung and Chin in Etudes Song", in Francoise Aubin, ed., *Melanges Offerts a la Memoire d'Etienne Balazs* (Paris, Ecole Pratique des Hautes Etudes: 1971).

Fromm, Eric, *Escape From Freedom* (Routledge and Kegan Paul: 1961).

Fung, Yu-lan, *History of Chinese Philosophy*, vol. 2, translated by Derk Bodde (Princeton University Press: 1953).

Gernet, Jacques, *Daily Life in China on the Eve of the Mongol Invasion*, translated by H.M. Wright (New York, Macmillan: 1962).

Graham, A.C., *Two Chinese Philosophers: Ch'eng Ming-tao and Ch'eng Yi-ch'üan* (Lund Humphries: 1958).

Hartwell, R., "Financial Expertise, Examination and the Formulation of Economic Policy in Northern Sung China", in *Journal of Asian Studies* 30:2 (1971).

———, "A Revolution in the Chinese Iron and Coal Industries during the Northern Sung, 960–1126 A.D.", in *Journal of Asian Studies* 21 (1962).

———, "Historical Analogism, Public Policy and Social Science in 11th and 12th Century China", in *American Historical Review* 76:3 (1971).

Ho, Ping-ti, *The Ladder of Success in Imperial China* (Columbia University Press: 1962).

Hsü, Cho-yun, *Ancient China in Transition* (Stanford University Press: 1965).

Huang, Siu-chi, *Lu Hsiang-shan, a Twelfth Century Chinese Idealist Philosopher* (New Haven, American Oriental Society: 1944).

Hughes, E.R., *The Great Learning and the Mean-in-action* (New York, Dutton: 1943).

———, *Two Poets: Vignettes of Han Life* (Princeton University Press: 1960).

Hughes, H.S., *Consciousness and Society* (New York, Knopf: 1958).

Kaplan, Edward H., *Yüeh Fei and the Founding of the Southern Sung*, University of Iowa, Ph.D. thesis, 1970.

Kierman, Frank Algerton, Jr., *Ssu-ma Ch'ien's Historiographical Attitudes as Reflected in Four Warring States Biographies* (Studies on Asia, Far Eastern and Russian Institute, University of Washington: 1962).

Kracke, Edward, Jr., *Civil Service in Early Sung China* (Harvard University Press: 1953).

———, *Translations of Sung Civil Service Titles* (Materiaux pour le Manual de l'Histoire des Song, Paris: 1957).

———, "Change Within Tradition", in *Far Eastern Quarterly* 14 (1954–55), pp. 479–488.

Legge, James, editor and translator, *The Chinese Classics: with Critical and*

Exegetical Notes, Prolegomena and Copious Indexes, reprint edition (University of Hong Kong Press: 1960).

Levenson, Joseph, *Confucian China and Its Modern Fate*, vol. 2 (University of California Press: 1964).

Li, Dun J., *The Essence of Chinese Civilization* (New Jersey, V. Nostrand: 1967).

Lin, Yutang, *The Gay Genius : the Life and Times of Su Tung-po* (John Day: 1947).

Liu, James T.C., *Change in Sung China*, edited together with Peter J. Golas (D.C. Heath: 1971).

———, "An Early Sung Reformer: Fan Chung-yen", in John K. Fairbank, ed., *Chinese Thought and Institutions* (Chicago University Press: 1957).

———, *Ou-yang Hsiu: an Eleventh Century Neo-Confucianist* (Stanford University Press: 1967).

———, *Reform in Sung China: Wang An-shih, 1021–1086* (Harvard University Press: 1959).

———, "The Sung Views on the Control of Government Clerks", in *Journal of Economic and Social History of the Orient* 10:2–3 (1967).

Martin, Henry Desmond, *The Rise of Chingis Khan and his Conquest of North China* (Johns Hopkins University Press: 1950).

McKnight, Brian E., *Village and Bureaucracy in Southern Sung China* (University of Chicago Press: 1971).

Meskill, John, *The Pattern of Chinese History* (D.C. Heath: 1965).

Michael, Franz, *The Origin of Manchu Rule in China* (Johns Hopkins University Press: 1942).

Schurmann, Franz, *Economic Structure of the Yüan Dynasty* (Harvard University Press: 1956).

———, *Ideology and Organization in Communist China* (University of California Press: 1966).

Shiba Yoshinobu, *Commerce and Society in Sung China*, translated by Mark Elvin (Center for Chinese Studies, University of Michigan: 1970).

Shirokauer, Conrad, "Chu Hsi as an Administrator", in *Etudes Offerts a la Memoire d'Etienne Balazs*.

Soothill, William Edward and Levis Houdous, *A Dictionary of Buddhist Terms* (London, Kegan Paul and Co.: 1943).

Tao Jing-shen, "Yü Ching and Sung Policies Towards Liao and Hsia (1042–44)", in *Journal of Asian History* 6:2 (1972), pp. 114–122.

T'eng, Ssu-yü and Knight Biggerstaff, *An Annotated Bibliography of Selected Chinese Reference Works* (Harvard University Press: 1950).

Tjan Tjoe Som, *Po Hu T'ung* (The Comprehensive Discussions in the White Tiger Hall) (Leiden, E.J. Brill: 1949).

Twitchett, Denis Crispin, *Financial Administration Under the T'ang Dynasty* (London, Cambridge University Press: 1963).

Waley, Arthur, *The Analects of Confucius* (London, Allen & Unwin: 1938).

Wang, Yu-chuan, "The Rise of Land Tax and the Fall of Dynasties", in *Pacific Affairs*, vol. 9 (1936), pp. 201–220.

Whitney, Joseph B.R., *China, Area, Administration and Nation-building* (University of Chicago, Geography Department Research Paper No. 123: 1970).

Wright, Arthur F., ed., *Confucianism in Action* (Stanford University Press: 1959).
Wright, Arthur F., and Denis Twitchett, eds., *Confucian Personalities* (Stanford University Press: 1962).
Yang, Lien-sheng, *Studies in Chinese Institutional History* (Harvard University Press: 1961).
Yinger, J. Milton, *Religion and the Individual* (New York, Macmillan: 1957).

Index

葉適